THE FUTURE OF CRIME AND PUNISHMENT

Praise for
The Future of Crime and Punishment

"In *The Future of Crime and Punishment*, William R. Kelly tells us where crime and justice policy has been and where it needs to go. Drawing on a wealth of scholarship, Kelly incisively diagnoses the misdirections and misspending that have left America holding the tab, with far too little to show for it. More important, he identifies critical lessons from mistakes of the past and presents compelling, research-based strategies for advancing public safety and justice." —**Daniel P. Mears**, PhD, Mark C. Stafford Professor of Criminology, Florida State University

"Consensus now exists that the punishment paradigm that guided American criminal justice policy for four decades is bankrupt. Kelly diagnoses why this is so, but he also instructs us on how, at this unique policy turning point, to be smart rather than tough on crime. Clearly written and compellingly argued, this volume is an invaluable resource for scholars and ideal for classroom use." —**Francis T. Cullen**, distinguished research professor emeritus, University of Cincinnati

"William Kelly offers a comprehensive, insightful look into the world of criminal justice. Kelly grabs the reader from the initial pages and maintains that level of engagement as he takes his audience on a historical journey through the U.S. criminal justice system—hitting on major political and policy elements that have contributed to mass over-incarceration. This book is a must-read for everyone who has ever considered our criminal justice system and asked 'how did we get here?' or 'how can we fix it?'" —**Maxine L. Bryant**, PhD, professor of criminal justice, Armstrong State University, Savannah, Georgia

"This book is a must-read for anyone interested in understanding why punishment alone will not work in changing criminal behavior. Kelly offers a thought-provoking analysis of the criminal justice system and provides a road map for changing how we do business." —**Edward Latessa**, University of Cincinnati

THE FUTURE OF CRIME AND PUNISHMENT

Smart Policies for Reducing Crime and Saving Money

William R. Kelly

ROWMAN & LITTLEFIELD
Lanham • Boulder • New York • London

Published by Rowman & Littlefield
A wholly owned subsidiary of The Rowman & Littlefield Publishing Group, Inc.
4501 Forbes Boulevard, Suite 200, Lanham, Maryland 20706
www.rowman.com

Unit A, Whitacre Mews, 26-34 Stannary Street, London SE11 4AB

British Library Cataloguing in Publication Information Available

Library of Congress Cataloging-in-Publication Data

Names: Kelly, W. R. (William Robert), 1950– author.
Title: The future of crime and punishment : smart policies for reducing crime and saving money /
    William R. Kelly.
Description: Lanham : Rowman & Littlefield, 2016. | Includes bibliographical references and index.
Identifiers: LCCN 2015048688 (print) | LCCN 2015049333 (ebook) | ISBN 9781442264816 (cloth :
    alk. paper) | ISBN 9781442264823 (electronic)
Subjects: LCSH: Criminal justice, Administration—United States. | Crime—United States. | Punish-
    ment—United States.
Classification: LCC HV9950 .K454 2016 (print) | LCC HV9950 (ebook) | DDC 364.40973—dc23
LC record available at http://lccn.loc.gov/2015048688

∞ ™ The paper used in this publication meets the minimum requirements of
American National Standard for Information Sciences Permanence of Paper for
Printed Library Materials, ANSI/NISO Z39.48-1992.

Printed in the United States of America

CONTENTS

ACKNOWLEDGMENTS

Many individuals have played very key roles in the writing of this book, and I would like to take this opportunity to acknowledge and thank them. First, and most important, my wife, Emily, has made all of this possible by believing in me, supporting and encouraging me, and giving me the time and space to go down this road. Emily, you are quite a gift. Thank you for being in my life.

The idea for this book originated in a conversation I had with my good friend Robert Pitman, who at the time was the U.S. attorney for the Western District of Texas. He now serves as a federal district court judge in the same judicial district. Just after I finished *Criminal Justice at the Crossroads*, a book aimed more at academics, researchers, lawyers, and practitioners, Robert said I should write a book on criminal justice reform that brought the issues to a broader audience of nonacademics and nonexperts in crime and justice matters. The intended audience for this book is individuals who are interested in a variety of issues, such as crime, punishment, public policy, recidivism, mental health, neuroscience, drug-control policy, public spending, politics, and probably a couple of dozen others. Thank you, Robert. I think it was a terrific idea!

I wish to thank my dear friends Sabrina and Bill Streusand for their enduring friendship, support, encouragement, and enthusiasm for this book, the prior one, and the one that is under way. Bill is a psychiatrist and provided very important advice and answered a variety of questions regarding psychiatric and neurodevelopmental matters as they relate to criminal offending. Sabrina and Bill also generously shared Casa de

Streusand de Durango, a beautiful piece of heaven that is an excellent venue for book writing. Bill, Robert Pitman, and I have launched a collaborative book on criminal intent or culpability. It looks at the legal, psychiatric and neurodevelopmental, and criminal justice policy aspects of criminal responsibility.

Sheldon Ekland-Olson, a longtime friend, colleague, and coauthor, willingly read drafts and provided excellent critiques, which have rendered the end product much improved. Thank you. My friend Dan Mears, a criminologist at Florida State University and a prior graduate student of mine, read drafts of chapters and raised a number of very important points. Both Sheldon and Dan encouraged me to keep going down this path of writing for a broader audience.

Patricia Sanchez provided valuable research assistance on chapter 7 when she was an undergraduate student of mine at the University of Texas at Austin. She just recently began doctoral studies at the John Jay College of Criminal Justice.

I also asked a handful of friends and relatives who I believe represent the audience I had in mind to read sample chapters. Jack Gray, Robert Pitman, Maydelle and Sam Fason, Frances and Oskar Cerbins, and Jerry Eyink all dutifully provided invaluable feedback that led to significant changes but also affirmed that they thought this book was a really good, timely idea. I thank them for their interest and support.

The editors at Rowman & Littlefield, particularly Kathryn Knigge, have been a delight. I thank you for making this process extraordinarily pleasant and efficient.

Finally, I wish to thank the several thousand students who, over the past five years or so, have had to unwittingly test drive many of the ideas that are offered here. Their reactions have been very helpful in the process of developing some of the central themes in this book.

INTRODUCTION

There were seven million violent crimes and twenty million property crimes in the United States in 2014.[1] The majority were committed by offenders who had already been through the justice system at least once before. Moreover, there were at least seven million victims of these violent crimes and at least twenty million victims of these property crimes. Much of this is avoidable, as is a significant portion of the $100 billion we spend annually on criminal justice.

U.S. criminal justice policy has evolved out of a political frenzy of "tough on crime" and resulted in a nearly unilateral emphasis on punishment and control. Today, the United States is home to 5 percent of the world's population; yet we have 25 percent of the incarcerated population in the world. "Tough on crime" sounds compelling, proactive, and solution focused. The problem is that despite common sense, logic, and even our own personal experience, punishing criminal offenders does not change their behavior.

Recidivism is the term that applies to the rate at which already convicted individuals reoffend. It usually refers to individuals who have been released from prison or jail or who are on some form of community supervision like probation. Seventy-seven percent of offenders recently released from prison were rearrested within five years, and 55 percent were reincarcerated. We have spent $1 trillion over the past forty years on criminal justice, not including the $1 trillion spent on the war on drugs. This has been an experiment that bet the farm on punishment. We lost the farm.

So why does punishment not reduce criminal offending? The short answer is because it does not change the circumstances related to much of criminal offending. What is it about being in prison that mitigates addiction, mental illness, neurocognitive disorders, the effects of poverty, educational deficits, chronic unemployment, and/or homelessness? I am not arguing that these are excuses for crime. Nor am I suggesting that they should evoke sympathy or entitle one to a get-out-of-jail-free card. Rather, these are reasons for crime; they are profoundly common, and identifying them and changing them should be the primary focus of American criminal justice. Much of this book is about how we do that.

I am not advocating shuttering America's prisons. We need prisons and jails to separate criminal offenders from the rest of us. But we need to be much more selective in who we decide needs to be separated from us. There are offenders who commit violent crimes and those who are particularly bad and dangerous, and they just need to be locked up. There are those for whom the probability for behavioral change is low, including many long-term career offenders. Then there is retribution, an entirely legitimate, acceptable, but expensive rationale for incarceration. For all of these offenders and more, prison or jail is an appropriate consequence. But we must not go about incarceration in the wholesale, freewheeling manner that has defined the past forty years of American criminal justice. We must more clearly differentiate between who we are just mad at and who we rightfully fear. Prison should be reserved mainly for those we rightfully fear.

It is important to realize that prison and jail are expensive and, in many respects, counterproductive. There is an old saying that offenders come out of prison worse than when they went in. As it turns out, that old saying is true. We need to be aware that the vast majority of prison inmates will be released at some point and that, when they are, we should assume that the majority will reoffend.

This is not a book about due process, equity, or judicial fairness per se. To be sure, these are profound issues in the American justice system. Racial disparities in arrests, convictions, and incarceration unfortunately define U.S. justice policy and practice. Michael Morton and all of the other exonerations that have resulted from the efforts of the Innocence Project are testaments to error, ineptitude, and bias in prosecution and the court system. To be clear, exonerations only shine a light on a fraction of the mistakes that are made in the arrest, prosecution, conviction, and punishment of individuals. Because prosecutors' caseloads and judges' dockets are so full, the primary focus of the American court system is to process as many people through the courts as quickly as possible. That is why over 90 percent of criminal indictments are plea negotiated and why many observers describe the court system as assembly-line justice. These are but a few of the very serious ethical, equity, and due process concerns that plague our justice system. They are very important, but they are not our primary concern here.

Rather, the goal here is to describe where American criminal justice policy has been in recent decades and where it needs to go in order to significantly reduce crime, recidivism, victimization, and public spending. I will show in these pages that the majority of crimes are preventable and the majority of victimizations are avoidable. In turn, by preventing large numbers of crimes, we stand to save tens of billions of dollars annually in criminal justice costs alone.

Critics may declare that criminal justice reform focusing on rehabilitation and behavioral change is just another example of liberal bias. Fair enough, but before we go down that road, I would suggest one take a look at Right on Crime, a conservative criminal justice policy organization with signatories including Jeb Bush, Newt Gingrich, William Bennett, Edwin Meese, Grover Norquist, J. C. Watts, Ralph Reed, and Gary Bauer, among many, many other conservative leaders. Right on Crime, for example, advocates for reducing the prison population, increasing probation and parole, eliminating mandatory sentences for nonviolent crime, and providing drug treatment for those offenders with substance abuse problems. They have gone a long way in establishing criminal justice reform as a bipartisan concern. On January 7, 2015, Charles Koch, chairman of the board and CEO of Koch Industries, and Mark Holden, general counsel and senior vice president of Koch Industries, published an op-ed piece on *Politico* titled "The Overcriminalization of America: How to Reduce Poverty and Improve Race Relations by Rethinking Our Justice System."[2] In this article, they recommend reducing incarceration, changing sentencing laws to eliminate harsh sentencing, and restoring the rights of those released from prison. Importantly, they state, "To bring about such a transformation, we must all set aside partisan politics and collaborate on solutions."[3]

Still, skeptics may suggest that the logic here is simply wrong. After all, the U.S. crime rate has declined as we have increased the number of criminals behind bars. Yes, and at the same time, there is a very strong correlation between U.S. spending on science, space, and technology, on the one hand, and the number of suicides by hanging, strangulation, and suffocation. Or there is an equally strong correlation between per capita consumption of cheese in the United States and the number of people who died by becoming entangled in their bedsheets. Just because two things may appear related does not mean one causes the other. Many factors influence crime rates, only one of which is punishment. The evidence shows that, at the most, U.S. incarceration has accounted for 10–15 percent of the decline in crime during the decades of the 1990s and 2000s.[4] Many governors, state legislators, and members of Congress, as well as the Obama administration, are questioning that return on investment.

Despite the evidence, there is powerful opposition to reform. For example, on March 10, 2015, Chuck Grassley, the chair of the Senate Judiciary Committee, went on the record in a floor speech opposing the federal Smarter Sentencing Act, which reduces the number of mandatory minimum sentences for some individuals convicted of possession of drugs and gives federal judges more discretion in sentencing. In particular, if they are nonviolent and have a limited criminal history, the court may avoid imposing a mandatory sentence. Grassley claims that reducing sentences for drug offenders will increase crime and cost $1 billion. He calls the movement to reduce mandatory federal sentences for low-level, nonviolent drug offenders the "leniency industrial complex."[5] While he has the facts wrong (it will actually reduce crime and result in a net $3 billion annually in cost savings), he nevertheless has a powerful podium from which to advance his opinions.

There is also a reluctance to envision a bigger picture of criminal justice reform. Essentially, everything that has surfaced in the 2016 election campaign involves only piecemeal change. Nearly every candidate for president in this election cycle has voiced support for reform but only in bits and pieces, such as rolling back some mandatory sentences or ending mass incarceration. Banning the box (the requirement to disclose past criminal justice involvement on employment applications) is common, as is reducing the use of solitary confinement, reforming indigent defense, treating more drug abuse, abolishing the death penalty, and using "best practices." These all may be ideas worth considering, but, at the end of the day, their individual effects will be quite limited.

October 2015 saw the unveiling of federal criminal justice reform bills from both chambers of Congress. The Senate Sentencing Reform and Corrections Act of 2015 and the House Sentencing Reform Act are purported to be "landmark" and "game-changing" legislation. In reality, neither addresses recidivism reduction to any significant extent. They are still promoting a punishment-focused federal criminal justice system. Federal initiatives are important for many reasons, including that the federal system is truly in need of reform and because while federal reforms do not directly apply to the states, they do set examples for what reform looks like from the federal perspective. What the feds do is quite visible in the media and can set the stage for state-level initiatives.

From my perspective, true criminal justice reform that can substantially reduce crime, recidivism, victimization, and cost must be comprehensive. There is no single initiative that will be the silver bullet. Ending mass incarceration is certainly one of the goals, but that is not an isolated strategy. What do we replace it with? What do we do with those we no longer incarcerate? It is that bigger picture that is lacking in discussions of reform and that guides much of what follows.

I write this book after nearly three decades teaching and researching crime, criminal justice, and public policy. I have also worked extensively in a large number of criminal justice settings, creating and evaluating a range of justice programs and policies. Thus, I have in-depth knowledge of the scientific literature on crime, punishment, and behavioral change, as well as the practical experience of designing, implementing, and assessing efforts to change offender behavior. The result of all of that is in the next nine chapters.

Chapter 1 describes how and why we created the world's largest prison system and became the world's leading imprisoner. The incarceration and corrections explosion was a matter of not only bricks and bars but also a penchant for retribution and punishment, a central role of partisan politics, fundamental changes to our sentencing laws and procedures, and a war on drugs, among others. In chapter 2, we look at what America's punishment binge accomplished in terms of recidivism, crime, victimization, and cost. We look at cost in a variety of ways, none of which cast a favorable light on how we do the business of crime and punishment.

Chapter 3 takes a hard look at why people commit crime, including the variety of crime-related or crime-producing factors, such as poverty, mental illness, substance abuse, neurocognitive impairment and deficits, chronic unemployment, and many others. These are not excuses for crime. They are identifiable and changeable conditions and circumstances, the mitigation of which can substantially reduce recidivism. Thus begins our discussion of where we go from here. How do we go about the business of changing criminal behavior within the institutions of the American criminal justice system?

Chapter 4 focuses on strategies for diverting offenders from traditional criminal prosecution, sentencing, and punishment. Drug courts are a common venue for diversion to treatment of offenders with substance abuse problems. These problem-solving or diversion courts can be quite effective in successfully treating offenders and substantially reducing recidivism. There are also some diversion programs and problem-solving courts for the mentally ill, a segment of the correctional population that has increased at an alarming rate over the past forty years.

Chapter 5 tackles how to change criminal prosecution and sentencing. Here I suggest that prosecutors are the most important decision makers in the American criminal justice system. Their power and influence are unmatched. They can be primary roadblocks to fundamental change. How we alter prosecution and prosecutors is an important topic in chapter 5, as is changing sentencing laws and procedures. We also go down a road that is not often traveled when discussing criminal justice reform, the matter of criminal responsibility. Under what conditions should we hold offenders accountable or responsible for their criminal actions? This is not an invitation to give these offenders a walk; rather, as we have learned more and more about mental illness and neurocognitive impairments and deficits, is it reasonable to hold offenders with such illnesses and impairments as culpable as any other offender? I suggest it is time to rethink this issue.

Chapter 6 considers how we should use punishment, including prisons, jails, probation, and parole, in the future. This includes the death penalty, a topic of considerable uneasiness in American society as more and more death row inmates are exonerated and eighteen states have abolished the death penalty, six since 2007. The crime trifecta of guns, drugs, and gangs is taken up in chapter 7. We discuss the war on drugs and strategies for mitigating the drug problem, organized crime, and the Second Amendment and proliferation of guns on our streets.

While this book is mainly about the adult criminal justice system, chapter 8 focuses on juvenile justice. Though much smaller in scale, the juvenile justice system is fundamentally important since it is a direct pipeline into the adult system. Our failures at the juvenile justice level result in an extraordinarily high probability of continued offending into the adult years. It need not be that way. Chapter 8 presents an overview of what is wrong with the juvenile justice system and how to fix it.

There is much wrong with how we go about the business of criminal justice in the United States. Changing it is fraught with many roadblocks and challenges. The concluding chapter takes on the big picture of reforming criminal justice, potential barriers to change, the momentum that is already under way, and what we need to consider and do in order to make fundamental changes to how we deal with those who break the law.

I

AMERICAN CRIMINAL JUSTICE

The Punishment Is the Crime

On October 2, 2009, Travis Bourda, a twenty-nine-year-old Louisiana oil rig worker, was sentenced to fourteen years in prison for possession of roughly a quarter of a pound of marijuana. Because Bourda had two prior convictions, he received the fourteen-year sentence required under Louisiana's three-strikes law. The tough-on-crime prosecutor was not satisfied. He appealed the sentence to the Louisiana appellate court, arguing that it was excessively lenient. The appellate court agreed and sentenced Bourda to life without parole.

Jack Marble was a twenty-two-year-old African American who was arrested and convicted of robbery. He was unarmed when he committed the robbery, and it was his first offense as an adult or juvenile. He was sentenced to four years in a Texas prison.

Brian Aitken, twenty-five, was recently divorced and moving from Colorado to New Jersey to be closer to his two-year-old son. After arriving at his parents' home in New Jersey, Aitken, under a good bit of stress, lost his temper and jumped in his car to go for a drive to cool off. His mother was concerned for his welfare when he did not return, so she called 911. The police greeted him when he returned to his parent's house and asked to search his car. Buried under clothing and other personal items was a bag containing two disassembled, cleaned, and wrapped handguns, which he had legally purchased in Colorado. Police also found large-capacity magazines and bullets, also legally purchased in Colorado.

The police arrested him because transporting the weapons and magazines without a special permit is illegal in New Jersey. The prosecutor indicted the case, and it went to trial. The judge did not allow the jury to consider an exemption in the law for individuals who are in transit or moving. Aitken was convicted and sentenced to seven years in prison.

These stories, all of which reflect lawful sentences, serve to illustrate the past four decades of American criminal justice.[1] For a variety of reasons, some good, some illogical and hard to fathom, we have been conducting an experiment of all-out punishment for those who break the law. We refer to it as *crime control*, also called *tough on crime* or *zero tolerance*, and we use catchy phrases like "lock 'em up and throw away the key" and "do the crime, do the time." Prosecutors say that by imposing this harsh punishment, they are sending a message to the community. Judges tell offenders that they are giving this tough sentence to teach them a lesson and to deter them from committing additional offenses. Legislators pass punitive three-strikes and mandatory minimum sentence laws to ostensibly get offenders off the streets and back up their tough-on-crime rhetoric. We have been angry at criminals, and that anger has seen expression in the extensive punishment we mete out to those who break the law.

AN AMERICAN PENCHANT FOR PUNISHMENT

The United States has been engaged in what some refer to as "waste management" incarceration, in which we round up large numbers of bad guys and warehouse them to make the streets safer. It sounds right— putting distance between the offenders and the public. Segregating criminals by placing them in secure prisons and jails to give them time to contemplate their wrongdoing and see the light certainly seems, on the surface, like a reasonable way to go. Simple, intuitive, proactive, and tough. How could it not work?

The evidence of America's punishment binge is compelling. In 1980, we imprisoned about 320,000 inmates in state and federal prison facilities. In 2014, we incarcerated 1,570,000 (roughly the population of Philadelphia). This is nearly a 400 percent increase (see figure 1.1).

The growth in federal incarceration has outpaced that of the states. Between 1980 and 2014, the number of federal prison inmates increased by 600 percent, compared to the state increase of 330 percent. Much of the federal increase has been driven by drug enforcement.

Figure 1.1 depicts the increase in prison inmates in state and federal facilities between 1936 and 2014.[2] This growth in the prison population is something unprecedented in U.S. history and, as best we know, unprecedented in the history of any other nation.

When we add those in jail, typically awaiting disposition of their cases or sentenced to confinement after conviction for a misdemeanor, the total number of incarcerated offenders is over 2.3 million. That amounts to the combined population of San Diego and San Jose, California, the eighth- and tenth-largest cities in the United States.

As stated in the introduction, the United States is presently home to 5 percent of the world's population; yet we have 25 percent of the world's incarcerated population. Consistent with that percentage, the United

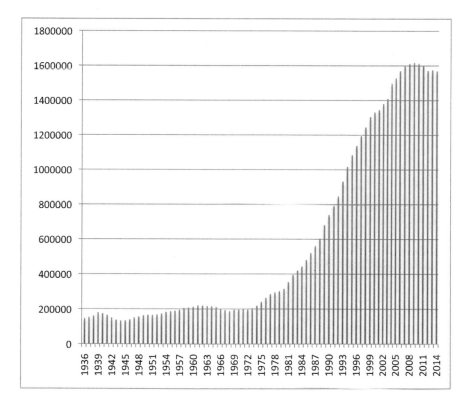

Figure 1.1. State and Federal Prisoners, 1936–2014

States has the highest incarceration rate (the number incarcerated per one hundred thousand population) in the world. Our imprisonment rate of 716 per 100,000 U.S. residents far exceeds that of all other nations, including many that we probably consider rather punitive, countries such as Russia, China, Rwanda, Kazakhstan, Iran, Saudi Arabia, Pakistan, Singapore, and South Africa. There are currently 10.1 million individuals incarcerated worldwide. If the rest of the world incarcerated citizens like the United States (that is, had the same incarceration rate), the world's incarcerated population would increase fivefold to over fifty-three million.[3]

In the late 1990s, I was working with some researchers at the Criminology Institute at Cambridge University in England. On a visit to Cambridge, I was given a tour of one of their maximum-security prisons. Part of this tour was observing something they called a dialogue group, where the inmates sit in a room and discuss their concerns, fears, and so forth about incarceration and eventual release. When I was introduced, they were told I was from the United States and, in particular, Texas. They spent about an hour asking me about the reputation of the American criminal justice system, whether what they had heard was true about it being so tough, so punitive. This is what the marketers call "living the brand"—the U.S. justice system has a tough-on-crime brand, but it is not just words. We fulfill that perception on a daily basis.

What do we know about the inmates in state and federal prisons? They are mainly men and largely minorities. The black imprisonment rate is a phenomenal 2,290, 5.5 times that for whites. Today, one out of every nine young (twenty to thirty-four) black males is incarcerated; one in three black men can expect to be incarcerated at some point in their lives. The odds for Hispanic men are one in six; for white men, they are one in seventeen. The majority of individuals admitted to U.S. prisons are admitted for a nonviolent offense. In 2013, approximately 70 percent of prison admissions were for conviction of a property crime, drug crime, or public order crime. Only about 30 percent of prison admissions are for violent crimes.[4]

While the media typically focus on the massive increase in incarceration, referred to as the incarceration explosion, the reach of the justice system goes well beyond that. Understanding the overall scope of our crime policies requires a look at correctional control more broadly. Correctional control includes prison, jail, probation, and parole. Prison is reserved for the incarceration of convicted felons who have been sentenced to confinement. A *felony*, which is the label we give to more serious crimes, is defined as an "imprisonable offense." Jail is used to detain individuals who are awaiting disposition of their cases and to confine individuals convicted of the less serious category of crimes referred to as misdemeanors. *Probation* is defined as conditional, supervised release to the community. Probation is diversion from incarceration, used in lieu of prison. While on probation, offenders are subject to revocation to prison or jail if they violate the conditions of their release. Parole is conditional supervised release to the community after someone has served a period of confinement in prison. Parole violators are also subject to revocation back to prison if they violate the conditions of parole and are caught.

In 1980, there were approximately 1.9 million individuals under correctional control in the United States (again, prison, jail, probation, or parole).[5] By 2013, that had grown to eight million (seven million officially counted and an estimated one million in forms of control/supervision not included in the official counts). This is an increase of over 375 percent. The eight million represent the entire population of New York City or the combined populations of Wyoming, Vermont, the District of Columbia, North Dakota, Alaska, South Dakota, Montana, and Rhode Island.

What do we know about the officially counted seven million individuals under correctional control in the United States? Today, the majority (56 percent) are on probation, one-quarter are in prison, 12 percent are on parole, and 11 percent are in jail. They are mainly men and minorities. There is wide variation across states in the odds of being under correctional control. Georgia leads the way (one in thirteen), followed by Idaho (one in eighteen), Texas (one in twenty-two), Ohio (one in twenty-five), and Indiana and Louisiana (one in twenty-six). Those with the lowest rates of correctional control include New Hampshire (one in eighty-eight), Maine (one in eighty-one), West Virginia (one in sixty-eight), and Utah (one in sixty-four).[6]

These statistics do not adequately describe the impact of correctional control on certain communities in the United States. For example, in the 53206 zip code in Milwaukee, 62 percent of the males ages thirty to thirty-four have been to prison. Approximately two-thirds of the thirty-five thousand prisoners who are released from Illinois prisons each year return to just seven zip codes in Chicago. Ten zip codes in Houston account for over one-third of Texas's annual spending on incarceration. Eleven of the zip codes in Philadelphia account for over one-half of Pennsylvania's spending for incarceration.[7] It was not uncommon to see newspaper headlines in recent years declaring something to the effect that "56% of Young Black Men in Baltimore Are in the Justice System" or "50% of Black Men 18 to 35 in DC Are Under Correctional Supervision."

The dramatic growth in the scale and reach of the American corrections system over the past four decades was new to us and new to the world. One obvious question is "Why?"

WHY WE GOT HERE

Crime control is a series of policies, laws, and procedures that aim at getting tough on criminal offenders. The goal was to reduce crime and recidivism; the means was increasing the severity of punishment. Understanding why we got here involves a look back, initially, at the events of the 1960s and then turning our attention to a series of factors that played

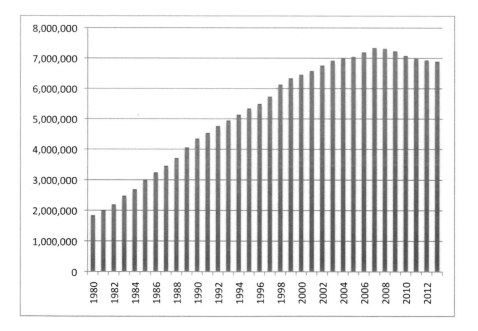

Figure 1.2.   U.S. Correctional Population, 1980–2013

very important roles in subsequent decades in sustaining what was launched in the late 1960s and early 1970s. The pivotal point in the birth of crime control was the 1968 presidential election, and the primary player was, ironically, Richard Nixon.

Crime and Chaos in the Streets

The 1960s was a period of profound domestic turmoil in the United States. Crime rates were at an all-time high and continuing to rise. In 1960, the violent crime rate was 160 per 100,000 inhabitants. By 1968, it was three hundred and rising.[8] These increases in crime were unheard of in the American experience.

Race riots swept across the nation, starting in 1965 in the Watts neighborhood of Los Angeles. That riot was followed by hundreds between 1965 and 1969. Essentially, every city of any size (roughly one hundred thousand and more) experienced substantial race-related violence. When it was over, the toll was sobering; approximately 750 separate riots, with 230 killed, 12,700 injured, nearly 70,000 arrested, and tens of billions of dollars in property damage.[9] Protests of the Vietnam War added to the disorder on America's streets and college campuses. The Robert Kennedy and Martin Luther King Jr. assassinations were high-profile events signaling the profound instability the United States was experiencing. Each night during the latter half of the 1960s, Walter Cronkite would report the events of the day, and the message was pretty clear—America was in the throes of chaos, lawlessness, and disorder.

As disorder unfolded in the streets, there were other events taking place in Washington that played a role in the shift in criminal justice policy. First, landmark federal legislation was passed as the Civil Rights Act of 1964 and the Voting Rights Act of 1965 became law. As Michelle Alexander tells us in her influential book *The New Jim Crow*:

> For more than a decade—from the mid-1950s to the late 1960s—conservatives systematically and strategically linked opposition to civil rights legislation to calls for law and order, arguing that Martin Luther King Jr.'s philosophy of civil disobedience was a leading cause of crime. Civil rights protests were frequently depicted as criminal rather than political in nature, and federal courts were accused of excessive "lenience" toward lawlessness, thereby contributing to the spread of crime. In the words of then–vice president [*sic*] Richard

Nixon, the increasing crime rate "can be traced directly to the spread of the corrosive doctrine that every citizen possesses an inherent right to decide for himself which laws to obey and when to disobey them."[10]

The Warren Court and Judicial Liberalism

In addition to civil rights and voting rights, the U.S. Supreme Court, under the leadership of Chief Justice Earl Warren, was handing down historic decisions regarding the protection of criminal defendants' constitutional rights. Cases included *Mapp v. Ohio* (1961), which applied the exclusionary rule to state prosecutions, stipulating that when law enforcement violates a suspect's Fourth Amendment protection against unreasonable searches and seizures, the evidence discovered in such a search shall be suppressed or excluded at trial. The Warren Court also gave us *Escobedo v. Illinois* (1964), which provides the right to counsel during custodial interrogation of criminal suspects, and *Miranda v. Arizona* (1966), which codified the now well-known Miranda warnings, which advise criminal suspects to remain silent and to seek legal counsel. *Gideon v. Wainwright* (1963) established that any individual arrested for a felony shall have counsel provided by the state if the individual is indigent. The series of cases that the Warren Court decided constituted the incorporation of a variety of due process protections in the Bill of Rights, requiring that state procedural standards be in line with federal requirements.

There were quite negative reactions to many of these decisions. *Mapp* was seen as a major impediment to proactive law enforcement and prosecution of criminals. Such was the reaction to *Escobedo* and *Miranda*, where objections predicted substantial declines in confessions and convictions and, in turn, increases in crime. On balance, efforts at enhancing due process, focusing on upholding the procedural protections that the Constitution affords suspects and defendants, are often seen in opposition to crime control. Heightened attention to due process issues, as well as the consequences of violating due process rights, are seen as hindering criminal investigation, prosecution, conviction, and punishment. This was the case when the major procedural decisions of the Warren Court were handed down. And it was no secret that the Nixon administration and many members of Congress had very strong, vocal objections to the Warren Court's due process decisions.

Richard Nixon avoided the more conservative "Impeach Earl Warren" initiative, but even his relatively controlled communications made clear his position on Chief Justice Warren. In his 1968 address "Toward Freedom from Fear," Nixon stated:

> Only one of eight major crimes committed now results in arrest, prosecution, conviction and punishment—and a twelve percent chance of punishment is not adequate to deter a man bent on a career in crime. Among the contributing factors to the small figure are the decisions of a majority of one of the United States Supreme Court . . . the cumulative impact of these decisions has been to set free patently guilty individuals on the basis of legal technicalities. . . . The barbed wire of legalisms that a majority of one of the Supreme Court has erected to protect a suspect from invasion of his rights has effectively shielded hundreds of criminals from punishment. [11]

Additionally, in a 1967 *Reader's Digest* article, Nixon stated, in reference to Lyndon Johnson's initiatives on poverty (which reflected Johnson's belief that a war on crime must be linked to a war on poverty in order to address the root causes of crime), "Far from being a great society, ours is becoming a lawless society." He placed blame on "judges who have gone too far in weakening the peace forces against the criminal forces," referring in particular to the Warren Court. [12]

The launch of crime control emerged from massive civil unrest, assassinations, and high crime rates, but the political upheavals were associated with the civil rights movement, the Civil Rights Act, and the Voting Rights Act, as well as the affront to public safety that many, including Nixon and many conservatives in Congress, perceived the Warren Court's due process decisions to be. All of these elements undeniably played a part, some more than others, but the fact that they all coincided in the 1960s set the stage for a sea change in American criminal justice policy.

The Conservative Agenda: Nixon through Bush 41

Political strategists and elected officials used the events of the day to begin linking crime, civil rights legislation, and the urban riots with racial insecurities among whites, especially whites in the South. What became known as the "southern strategy" was an effort to bring southern and northern working-class whites into the Republican Party by appealing to racial anxieties. These appeals linked crime and disorder to race, leveraging the fact that many whites felt threatened and marginalized by advances in the civil rights of blacks. Not only was this strategy successful in propelling crime control onto the national agenda, but it also fundamentally changed the landscape of electoral politics in the United States.

Part of the irony of the launch of crime control is the role played by Richard Nixon. Nixon came back on the national political scene in 1967 and won the Republican nomination for president in 1968. In speeches and TV ads during the 1967–1968 presidential campaign, Nixon, along with the Republican National Committee, articulated the chaos, disorder, and lawlessness the nation was experiencing. In his 1968 "Toward Freedom from Fear" address, Nixon hit a variety of points regarding crime and its solution:

> If we allow it [crime increase] to happen, then the city jungle will cease to be a metaphor. It will become a barbaric reality, and the brutal society that now flourishes in the core cities in America will annex the affluent suburbs. This nation will then be what it is in fact becoming— an armed camp of two hundred million Americans living in fear . . . it would be difficult to exaggerate the urgency of the need for greater police presence—of the danger to social order if we do not get it. . . . We can reduce crime by making it a more hazardous and less rewarding occupation.[13]

The message was concise—there is good reason for fear and anxiety, and the solution is more criminal convictions and more incarceration. Nixon stated during the campaign, "Doubling the conviction rate in this country would do more to cure crime in America than quadrupling the funds for Humphrey's war on poverty"[14] (Hubert Humphrey was Nixon's opponent in the 1968 presidential election campaign). Nixon and the Republican Party latched onto crime and disorder (and the resulting fear and insecurity) as the problem, and punishment as the solution. "Tough on crime" was the message, and it resonated. Needless to say, Nixon beat Humphrey in the 1968 presidential election, and the southern strategy played a significant role in Nixon's election—Nixon won five formerly Democratic states in the South.

Thus was born crime control and the profound political leverage it provided. After taking office, the Nixon administration primarily relied on tough rhetoric and leveraging fear (replacing the war on poverty with the war on crime), sponsorship of congressional funding for local law enforcement, a new initiative focused on drug control, and heightened investigation and prosecution of organized-crime activities.

After Nixon left office with his own legal problems in 1974, crime and crime control took a bit of a hiatus, with Gerald Ford completing Nixon's second term and then the Carter administration from 1977 to 1981. The Carter administration was distracted by a variety of other issues and was relatively silent on crime.

The crime-control momentum reemerged in 1980 with the Reagan administration, which repeatedly dismissed social and economic explanations of crime and drug use and rejected anti-poverty and public assistance remedies in favor of punishment and control. This Reagan quote sums up how the fortieth president thought about crime and punishment: "We must reject the idea that every time a law's broken, society is guilty rather than the lawbreaker. It is time to restore the American precept that each individual is accountable for his actions."[15]

The Reagan administration sought and found new ways for the federal government to be involved in crime control at the local level. The primary avenue for federal involvement was a renewed drug-control effort, which gave federal law enforcement an enhanced role in local crime since state and federal authorities share jurisdiction over drug cases.[16]

The Reagan administration also oversaw massive changes to federal sentencing laws, substantially ramped up drug-control enforcement as a consequence of the introduction of crack in the early 1980s, and continued the escalation of crime-control efforts through numerous get-tough changes to federal laws and policies. Among other results of these federal initiatives, the Reagan administration set examples for states to emulate. Most noteworthy is the 1984 Sentencing Reform Act, which ushered in the highly punitive federal sentencing guidelines, a sentencing scheme that was tough all around but particularly targeted drug offenders. The federal guidelines are known, among other things, for mandatory minimum drug sentences and for the crack/powder cocaine differential of one hundred, meaning possession of one gram of crack has the same punishment as one hundred grams of powder cocaine. Much of the hypersensitivity regarding crack was due to the violence that accompanied its introduction into urban drug markets and the demographics of those involved in dealing and using crack. That violence, thought at the time to be an effect of ingesting crack, was actually due to gangs "negotiating" markets for the new, popular, highly profitable drug.

The election of George H. W. Bush (Bush 41) in 1988 serves as one of the clearest examples of the political power of fear, anxiety, and race, on the one hand, and tough-on-crime rhetoric, on the other. The Bush campaign was relentless in its portrayal of his Democratic opponent Michael Dukakis as a liberal who was soft on crime. Perhaps the quintessential illustration of this is the Willie Horton TV ad that aired during the campaign. Willie Horton was an inmate in the Massachusetts prison system, and Dukakis was the governor of that state. The ads relay the story of Horton, a scary-looking black man, who was incarcerated for violent crime and allowed to leave prison on a weekend furlough (his term of incarceration was nearly over). While on furlough, Horton kidnapped a couple and raped the woman. The video shows, among other things, a line of tough-looking inmates walking down a corridor of fencing and razor wire through a revolving door. The message was clear—Dukakis and liberal Democrats were to blame for all of the Willie Hortons in the nation, as well as the revolving door of the criminal justice system. It was a masterful mix of fear, race, crime, and weakness in portraying Dukakis as the ineffectual liberal and Bush, by contrast, as the tough, proactive crime solver. Bush's solution was the familiar one: more convictions, more prisons, and a continuing, ramped up war on drugs.

The Nixon, Reagan, and Bush administrations masterfully leveraged fear and anxiety. They "managed" fear by coming to the rescue with tougher and tougher crime-control policies, much to the political detriment of Democrats. That was about to change.

Clinton and the Democrats Get Tough on Crime

By 1992, the national Democratic Party had learned the political lesson of being perceived as soft on crime. Bill Clinton campaigned as a different kind of Democrat. Among other things, Clinton effectively leveraged fear much as his Republican predecessors had—he campaigned for more police on the streets, boot camps for juvenile offenders, expansion of prisons, and tougher drug penalties. To reinforce the point, Clinton took time out of the 1992 campaign to return to Arkansas (the state where he served as governor) with media in tow to witness the execution of an individual convicted of capital murder. The message was clear—it's time for Clinton and Democrats to get their share of tough on crime. And they did.

The centerpiece of the Clinton crime-control effort was the Violent Crime Control and Law Enforcement Act of 1994. The act, which had substantial bipartisan support, provided $7 billion for crime prevention, $4 billion for local law enforcement, and $10 billion for state prison expansion. It did not take long for the Democrats to see the benefits of these efforts in public-opinion polls showing that Republicans no longer held the monopoly on tough on crime. At the same time, congressional Republicans were calling for more punitive approaches. The 1994 Republican "Contract with America" called for even tougher treatment of criminals through changes to sentencing laws, $10 billion to states to expand prisons, elimination of funding for crime prevention, and a legislative package called the Taking Back Our Streets Act, which in the end accomplished little but sounded tough.

September 11, Fear, and the War on Terror

The terrorist attacks on the World Trade Center and the Pentagon helped define the George W. Bush presidency and substantially impacted crime policy for the first decade and a half of the 2000s. The 9/11 attacks and the subsequent anthrax scare changed the landscape of criminal justice policy in important ways, including the enhancement of the federal role in local criminal matters and drawing connections between everyday crime and terrorism. As then President Bush stated in a speech given at the signing of the Drug Free Communities Reauthorization Bill, December 14, 2001, "It is so important for Americans to know that the trafficking in drugs finances the work of terror, sustaining terrorists. Terrorists use drug profits to fund their cells to commit acts of murder. If you quit drugs, you join the fight against terror in America." The 9/11 attacks thus served to instill even more insecurity and fear where fear and anxiety were well entrenched. The aftermath of 9/11 was, among other things, the reinforcement of the standard of tough, but now tough on crime *and* terrorism.

One of the most far-reaching anticrime bills ever passed was the USA Patriot Act (an acronym for Uniting and Strengthening America by Providing Appropriate Tools Required to Intercept and Obstruct Terrorism). Passed with little debate or opposition, the Patriot Act dramatically expanded the investigative abilities of law enforcement through bypassing provisions of the Fourth Amendment's protection against unreasonable search and seizure and expanding opportunities for warrantless searches. While the intentions of the framers of the Patriot Act may have been to facilitate investigation of terrorist activity, there is considerable opportunity for spillover into the investigation of traditional, predatory street crime.

On balance, it seems that in the 1960s there was good reason to launch a radical new path for reducing crime and enhancing public safety. While there was no compelling scientific evidence at the time supporting the idea that harsher punishment would reduce crime and recidivism (and there still is none today), it did not seem to matter. Punishment is intuitive and logical. It is something that we all routinely experience. It is what, in part, shapes our behavior. Thus, the message that we are going to go down a different road, one defined by increasing the severity of punishment, made sense at the time. It seemed clear that what we had been doing in order to control crime was not working. High crime rates and massive disorder certainly reinforced that conclusion. Common sense and the profound political power of tough on crime set in motion and sustained an elaborate shift in priorities, policies, laws, politics, and spending that all led to the United States as the world leader in mass punishment.

Obama and the 2008 Recession: The Beginning of Something Different?

The first term of the Obama administration pretty much stayed the course in terms of crime policy. At the same time, the recession that began in 2008 required states to take a hard look at how much they spend, including how much they spend on incarceration and crime control. The impact of the recession triggered the front end of modest reductions in prison populations. It has also provided the opportunity to begin discussing alternatives to mass incarceration. In August 2013, U.S. attorney general Eric Holder launched a new Smart on Crime Initiative, which, among other things, focused on lessening the punishment of low-level, nonviolent offenders and bolstering prison reentry efforts to reduce recidivism. The Justice Department has also recently been pressing for the release of lower-level drug offenders incarcerated in federal prison on lengthy mandatory sentences. In July 2015, President Obama commuted the prison sentences of forty-six nonviolent federal drug offenders. Perhaps a step in the right direction, but forty-six does not register on any radar.

The Obama administration is approaching its twilight, and Attorney General Holder resigned in the fall of 2014. Loretta Lynch took his place in February 2015. Lynch's position on Smart on Crime is unclear, and where Obama's criminal justice policy goes from here is anyone's guess.

The Politics of Crime: Leveraging Tough

It is undeniable that the political impact of tough on crime is profound. One outcome of crime control becoming a bipartisan issue in the early 1990s was that each side of the aisle began trying to out tough the other. This bipartisan support goes a long way in explaining the sustainability of crime control long after the triggering events of the 1960s and 1970s disappeared and as crime rates began to decline significantly, especially in the 1990s, and drug use dropped beginning in the 1980s.

The National Democratic Party, in an effort to position Democrats as tough on crime, formally adopted a variety of crime-control initiatives and policies. The 1996 platform states:

> Today's Democratic party believes the first responsibility of government is law and order. . . . We believe that people who break the law should be punished and people who commit violent crimes should be punished severely. President Clinton made three-strikes-you're-out the law of the land, to ensure that the most dangerous criminals go to jail for life, with no chance for parole. . . . We provided almost $8 billion in new funding to states for new prison cells. . . . We call on states to meet the President's challenge and guarantee that violent offenders serve at least 85% of their sentence.[17]

The 2000 Democratic platform states:

> Bill Clinton and Al Gore took office determined to turn the tide in the battle against crime, drugs and disorder in our communities. They put in place a tougher more comprehensive strategy than anything tried before, a strategy to fight crime on every single front . . . more police on the streets . . . tougher punishments. . . . We will not go back to the old approach which was tough on the causes of crime, but not tough enough on crime itself.[18]

The 2004 Democratic platform promises "to keep our streets safe for our families, we support tough punishment for violent crime. . . . We will crack down on the gang violence and drug crime."[19]

These policies are largely out of the historical Republican playbook—rejection of the focus on the social and economic origins of crime in favor of a largely punitive approach, which included expansion of prison capacity; increasing time served in prison; mandatory sentencing, including three-strikes and mandatory minimums; more law enforcement presence; and continuing the war on drugs. Among other things, this added substantial momentum to America's punitive, crime-control path. And it ramped up the political rhetoric and kept considerable attention focused on crime and crime control. Consider the following recent examples from political campaign communications.

Phil Bryant, a Republican running for lieutenant governor in Mississippi in 2007, pledged in a campaign TV ad to require second-time crack and meth offenders to be sentenced to life in prison. Bryant was subsequently elected governor of Mississippi.

It is hard to comprehend the relevance of an ultra-tough-on-crime stance when running for the Alabama agriculture commissioner, but that is exactly what Dale Peterson, the Republican candidate, did in TV ads during the 2010 race. Peterson states in the ad that the agriculture commissioner is responsible for $5 billion, and then he says, "Bet you didn't know that. You know why? Thugs and criminals. If they can keep you in the dark, they can do whatever they want with all that money. And they don't give a rip about Alabama."[20]

The Republican Governor's Association has recently attacked South Carolina Democratic state senator Vincent Sheheen, who is running for governor. Their reason for the attack ad is because Sheheen is a lawyer who has defended accused criminals in court proceedings. The ad states that "Sheheen defended violent criminals who abused women and went to work setting them free." It ends with "Vincent Sheheen protects criminals, not South Carolina."[21] The South Carolina Republican Party joined the fray by issuing a press release detailing that Sheheen defended sex offenders, child molesters, and spouse abusers for pay.

Republicans have also been attacking their own. In Texas, Jerry Madden, the conservative Republican chair of the House Corrections Committee, was opposed for reelection in 2008 by a twenty-three-year-old

Republican who accused Madden of being soft on crime because Madden opposed the construction of more prisons in Texas.

In 2013, Joe Lhota, a Republican candidate for mayor of New York, ran an ad portraying his Democratic opponent Bill de Blasio as soft on crime. New York has been at the center of considerable attention over the years because of the turnaround in serious and petty crime in the 1990s and 2000s supervised by Mayor Rudolph Giuliani and Police Commissioner William Bratton. Today, New York City has the lowest crime rates (both violent and nonviolent) in decades. A recent *New York Post* headline proclaims that New York is on track to be the safest city in the nation. Those facts did not stop the Lhota campaign from running a classic fear-based, soft-on-crime attack ad. The claim is that, as a councilman, de Blasio voted in support of a Mayor Michael Bloomberg budget that reduced the New York Police Department's workforce. Because of that, a vote for de Blasio will take New York back to the days of rampant crime. The narrator states, "Bill de Blasio's recklessly dangerous agenda on crime will take us back to this," and then there are images of homicide victims, riots, bikers attacking citizens, a black man aiming a gun at someone, and graffiti-covered subway cars.

There are many, many more examples of candidates' positions on crime serving as a central, divisive element in political campaigns. Whether true or not, being perceived as soft on crime is a substantial political liability. Since the mid-1990s, both sides of the political aisle have been free to accuse opponents of being weak on crime, which has provided added exposure to crime and punishment in the political process. In turn, the political value of tough on crime has provided substantial momentum to crime-control policies and funding and played a significant role in carrying our punitive approach to where it is today.

The Media and Tough on Crime

There is an old adage in television news: "if it bleeds, it leads." When it comes to crime, the evidence indicates that this is more than just a clever rhyme. In fact, how local media, especially local TV news, cover crime influences public perception of crime, fear of crime, and support for punitive policies such as mandatory minimum sentences and longer time served in prison.

It is probably no surprise that economic forces have fundamentally changed news media. Financial considerations often drive content of the news, especially crime and criminal justice coverage. Local coverage of more sensational crime, especially violent crime, has increased substantially since 1990, precisely during the period when violent crime was dropping to the lowest levels in recent memory. Research shows that coverage of crime drives levels of fear of crime and the public's perceptions of the prevalence of crime.[22] Media coverage goes a long way toward explaining the disconnection between public perceptions of crime today and actual crime rates—the public believes crime is increasing when in reality crime rates have been declining. It also helps explain why fear of crime has remained relatively high even though crime rates have been dropping.

Crime is the number-one topic on local TV news. Coverage of crime, typically violent crime, ranges from roughly 20 percent to 45 percent of the content. How much of local TV news content is crime is unrelated to how much crime is occurring in that area.[23] Rather, it is determined by who is watching the programming (the demographics of viewers). Moreover, coverage of crime stories by what are called "high-crime stations" is treated more as entertainment—dramatic video, fast paced, little explanation, and teasers throughout about more crime stories to come.

The primary role the media have played regarding crime policy is in terms of helping to sustain the punitive focus of crime control. The media's influence in this is largely indirect but essential in driving public support for tough-on-crime initiatives. The narrow, sensational, graphic snapshot of crime that readers and viewers see influences their perceptions of the nature and frequency of violent crime, in turn promoting often-distorted beliefs that crime is more common and closer to home than is the reality. Such concerns have played into support for tough-on-crime policies.

We now turn to the question of how crime control was achieved. In the next chapter, we'll address what it did and didn't accomplish and what it cost.

HOW WE GOT HERE

Overcriminalization

It is the responsibility of state legislatures and Congress to determine which behaviors are crimes and incorporate those into what is usually called the criminal code. As more behaviors are identified as criminal, the reach of the justice system expands. Overcriminalization is the broad expansion of criminal law at both the state and the federal levels. As the net is cast more widely, more individuals end up in the justice system. Consider these examples.

Abner Schoenwetter spent six years in federal prison for legally importing lobsters from Honduras to the United States. The problem was that an obscure Honduran regulation required that lobsters be shipped in paper bags. Unfortunately for Mr. Schoenwetter, he was unaware of the regulation and shipped the lobsters in plastic bags. Even more unfortunate for Mr. Schoenwetter was the Lacey Act, which makes it a felony to violate any foreign law while importing plants or animals into the United States.

Skylar Capo, an eleven-year-old girl, saw a woodpecker about to be killed by a cat. She rescued the bird with the intention of nursing it back to health. She put it in a box and, because she did not want to leave it alone, she took it with her when her mother took her on an errand to a local home improvement store. A U.S. Fish and Wildlife agent who was in the store stopped Skylar and told her that under the Migratory Bird Treaty Act, transporting a woodpecker is a violation of federal law. The agent gave Skylar and her mom a ticket with a fine of $535.

Seventeen-year-old Cody Chitwood committed a felony by bringing a fishing knife to school. The knife was in the trunk of his car in a tackle box. Georgia law stipulates that possessing a knife with a blade of two inches or more in a school zone is a felony. There is no requirement in this law that there be any criminal intent. All that is required is that the knife is in a school zone.[24]

Today there are over forty-five hundred federal criminal laws and three hundred thousand federal regulations with criminal consequences.[25] This is a product of a zealous Congress, which enacts, on average, fifty new federal criminal laws each year, as well as zealous bureaucrats who are responsible for developing administrative regulations. This expansion of the criminal law sometimes comes at the expense of *mens rea*, or criminal intent. A joint 2010 report by the Heritage Foundation and the National Association of Criminal Defense Lawyers notes this concern: "The recent proliferation of federal criminal laws has produced scores of criminal offenses that lack adequate *mens rea* requirements and are vague in defining the conduct that they criminalize."[26] As the late Bill Stuntz recently noted in his book *The Collapse of American Criminal Justice*, "criminal intent has become a modest requirement at best, meaningless at worst."[27]

States are far from immune to these trends. Whether a product of selective lobbying, media reports of particular crimes, or simply tough-on-crime legislators, the states have held their own when it comes to overcriminalizing. For example, Texas has eleven felony laws related to harvesting and handling oysters, in addition to the other seventeen hundred criminal laws on the books. Illinois has identified special offenses of theft of delivery containers, damaging library materials or an animal facility, defacing delivery containers, and damaging anhydrous ammonia equipment.[28] Illinois also has forty-eight separate assault crimes and ten kidnapping crimes. Virginia law identified twelve distinct kinds of arson and attempted arson and seventeen trespass crimes. Massachusetts law has 170 different crimes against property.

Expanding the scope and reach of criminal law is illustrated, for example, by laws that cover possession of drug paraphernalia. Simply being in possession of certain devices (blenders, bowels, spoons) that can be used to compound or consume drugs is a crime, whether drugs are present or not. There are also laws making it a crime to be in possession of burglary tools, which could include simply having a screwdriver or crowbar. There are also many enhancements in the criminal law, such as certain acts that occur in a school zone or a drug-free zone. It is estimated that roughly 70 percent of American adults have, often unwittingly, committed a crime for which they could be incarcerated.[29]

Much of overcriminalization involves overlapping offenses, such that the same behavior is covered under different laws. This can be in the form of lesser-included offenses, such as aggravated assault and assault or aggravated robbery and robbery. This can also be in the form of different crimes sharing common criminal elements. For example, an offender stealing a car when the driver is present could be charged with robbery, motor vehicle theft, assault, and perhaps kidnapping if the owner is in the car when the offender drives off. That could also involve an enhancement to carjacking under federal law. One consequence is that criminal prosecution is easier since there is more leverage on the government's part by bringing multiple charges. This is a practice called *charge stacking*, and it usually results in easier plea negotiation for the government. Another consequence is that enhanced punishment is more easily obtained because of conviction on multiple charges.

The combination of the expansion of criminal law and the relaxing of the criminal intent requirement results in more individuals more easily entering the justice system and being successfully prosecuted and more severely punished.

Building Prisons and Jails and Increasing Supervision Capacity

As correctional populations have exploded, one obviously necessary component to accommodate this is increased capacity. Over the course of our crime-control policies, from the mid-1970s onward, prison capacity in the United States increased by 430 percent, requiring a massive capital outlay for construction and a subsequent massive outlay for operations and maintenance.[30] While the responsibility for funding the expansion and operation of state prisons is that of the states, the federal government played a significant role in capacity expansion by providing funding to the states for prison construction.

One perhaps unwitting player in the expansion of prison capacity was litigation over prisoner's rights, especially overcrowding. Between 1969 and 1996, there were eighty federal lawsuits filed in forty-one states over allegations of prison overcrowding creating violations of the Eighth Amendment protection against cruel and unusual punishment. All in all, the courts found for the plaintiffs in seventy out of the eighty cases in forty of the forty-one states. While the likely intention in the litigation and the courts' decisions was to divert offenders from incarceration and therefore reduce prison populations, the effect appears to have been to increase capacity.[31]

At the same time, jail populations and jail capacity skyrocketed. Jails are used for pre-trial detention—detaining offenders prior to the disposition of their cases—as well as for individuals convicted on a misdemeanor and sentenced to incarceration. Beginning in the early 1980s, jail capacity began to expand dramatically, increasing fourfold over the following three decades.

When we speak of the revolving door of the justice system, it is appropriate to envision the door of a local jail, as jails are the gateway into the justice system. Not everyone with justice-system involvement goes to prison, but essentially all spend at least some time in jail.

On any given day, there are over 730,000 individuals in America's 3,000 jails. But these figures seriously understate the reach of America's jails. This year, nearly twelve million individuals will be booked into jail, a rate twenty times the admission rate to state and federal prisons. Not only has the admission rate to jail doubled over the past thirty years, but the average length of stay has likewise increased, from fourteen days in the 1980s to twenty-three days today. [32]

What these statistics don't tell is how we use jails and the consequences of that use. First, the vast majority of individuals in jail have not been convicted of a crime. Roughly two-thirds of local jail populations consist of individuals too poor to post bond or, less commonly, those who have been denied release. The majority are in jail for relatively minor crimes such as nonviolent traffic, property, drug, and public order offenses.

Community supervision (probation and parole) also increased dramatically in recent decades (probation by 390 percent and parole by 475 percent). However, the expansion of the capacity for probation and parole is much quicker and less expensive than for prisons and jails. In effect, all that is required to expand community supervision is to increase caseloads. The recommended caseload for a typical probation officer is fifty probationers. However, today the average probation caseload is 150–200. The typical caseload for parole officers is seventy to eighty, but this is across the board a higher-risk population since these individuals have been incarcerated and in all likelihood have much more extensive criminal histories than probationers. At seventy to eighty, these parole caseloads exceed recommended standards and make risk management of these offenders very difficult. [33]

Increasing capacity is not enough. "If you build it, they will come" did not always work in the world of criminal justice. There was a fundamental change that was required to get more offenders in prison for longer periods of time, to extend the reach of correctional control/supervision, and to bring crime control up to scale. That change is known as sentencing reform.

Sentencing Reform: More Offenders Serving Longer Sentences

Before the late 1970s, judges were the true gatekeepers of the American justice system. Yes, police investigate and arrest and prosecutors make key decisions such as who to prosecute and what to charge. But when crime control began, judges had nearly unfettered influence over the sentence.

Before sentencing reform, every convicted criminal defendant, state and federal, was sentenced under what are called *indeterminate sentencing laws*. Indeterminate sentencing is a system whereby the judge has considerable discretion in determining the sentence. This is because indeterminate sentencing typically provides for wide ranges of punishment, and the judge is to select something within that range. For example, Texas is generally an indeterminate sentencing state. Upon conviction of a first-degree felony (the most serious level of felony except for a capital felony), the punishment range is probation to five to ninety-nine years of incarceration to incarceration for life. Conviction of a second-degree felony involves the court selecting between probation and two to twenty years in prison. Third degree is probation to two to ten years in prison. Because the punishment ranges under indeterminate sentencing are typically so broad, judges are generally permitted under law to hear and assess a wide range of evidence at the sentencing hearing. The process is one where the prosecutor presents what is known as *aggravating evidence*, information designed to lead to a more severe sentence. The defendant presents *mitigating evidence*, designed to reduce the punishment. Judges then somehow consider the totality of the evidence, weigh it as they see fit, and determine an appropriate punishment. In addition to having free rein over their consideration of the evidence presented, judges are free to consider any of a number of sentencing goals: retribution, deterrence, incapacitation (getting the offender off the street), rehabilitation, and any combination of those. One of the primary benefits of indeterminate sentencing is that it allows tailored sentencing, where the judge can sentence not only the offense but also the offender.

And therein lie two of the perceived problems. First, there is a concern that although we hold judges to a standard of impartiality, they nevertheless are human—they have biases. The fact that judges have wide discretion under indeterminate sentencing and are subject to a variety of influences raises the concern of what is called *sentencing disparity*, a situation where similar offenders, convicted of similar crimes, receive different sentences. In its extreme version, sentencing disparity becomes discrimination (willful, intentional, illegal). As the argument goes, the law should not give judges such wide latitude or discretion when there is such potential for unfair outcomes. The sentence should not be the luck of the draw; the sentence should not depend on which judge gets the case or what mood the judge is in the day someone is sentenced.

It is not hard to make a case for sentencing disparity. It is undeniable that historically some judges have exhibited overt racism in American courtrooms. And it is not a huge stretch to think that some judges could consider characteristics and circumstances that someone else might think improper. Furthermore, there is simple disagreement about what should or should not be considered, as well as how it should be considered. For example, is substance abuse an aggravating factor or a mitigating factor? Should the fact that a female defendant has a nine-month-old child matter in sentencing? What about intellectual ability? An emerging area of the law considers legal responsibility and culpability for individuals with brain damage or other neurocognitive defects. Should that matter? It depends on who you ask and how you ask it. If it is couched in terms of equality or disparity, the answer is probably no, such things should not matter because the goal is that similar offenders convicted of similar crimes should receive essentially the same sentence. Most "extenuating" factors should not matter in the eyes of those behind sentencing reform.

The second perceived problem with indeterminate sentencing is the belief that when judges have so much discretion, they tend toward leniency in their sentences. Real or perceived, it can have important consequences. The Center for American Progress tracks partisan judicial election trends and reported the following recent examples of attack ads portraying judges as soft on crime:

> A 2012 candidate for the Ohio Supreme Court, for example, was attacked by the state Republican Party, which alleged in an ad that the judge—Democrat Bill O'Neill—had "expressed sympathy for rapists" in one of his opinions. During the 2004 West Virginia Supreme Court election, a group funded by coal mogul Don Blankenship warned that an incumbent justice "voted to release" a "child rapist" and then

"agreed to let this convicted child rapist work as a janitor in a West Virginia school." Another campaign ad, this one in the 2012 Louisiana Supreme Court race, claimed that one of the candidates had "suspended the sentence of a cocaine dealer, of a man who killed a state trooper, two more drug dealers, and over half the sentence of a child rapist."[34]

There is more evidence in support of the disparity argument than the leniency one, although in one-on-one judicial election campaign ads, attacks on leniency run rampant. And just because there is no systematic evidence that judges as a group lean in the direction of leniency, that did not hamper efforts at fundamentally changing sentencing in American courtrooms.

The fairness/equity issue, expressed mainly by liberals, and the leniency one, expressed mainly by conservatives, had the same solution—eliminate or reduce judicial discretion. Politically, sentencing reform was a bipartisan masterpiece. The momentum for sentencing reform was, therefore, substantial. And it played an absolutely fundamental role in accomplishing crime control.

The changes to sentencing did not result in a uniform set of sentencing laws in the United States. Rather, the outcome is a patchwork of sentencing statutes that all aim roughly in the same direction (reduced judicial discretion, increases in mandatory sentences, longer sentences, and greater time served) but do so in different ways and to different extents. One of the outcomes of this reform is what is called *determinate sentencing*, which, as the name implies, reduces the uncertainty of sentences by determining or specifying in the statute what the appropriate punishment is for each offense. For example, under determinate sentencing, the penal code may state that upon conviction of aggravated armed robbery, the punishment is fifteen years in prison. This is quite a contrast to five to ninety-nine years under Texas's indeterminate sentencing laws. When sentences are clearly prescribed, where the punishment range is narrowed considerably, and when the aggravating and mitigating evidence the court may lawfully consider is highly restricted, the discretion of the judge is substantially reduced, largely because there are not that many decisions for the judge to make.

Sentencing reform shifted much of the discretion from judges to legislators, on the one hand, and prosecutors, on the other. The legislative role is enhanced in states with determinate sentencing since legislators determine in the statute what the punishment is for a particular crime. They also have greater influence when they write mandatory sentencing laws. Prosecutors have enhanced discretion since the decisions they make, such as what to charge and what to plea negotiate, have the primary impact on the sentence.

The federal government implemented one of the more extreme versions of sentencing reform in the federal sentencing guidelines. The federal guidelines gutted indeterminate sentencing in federal cases, specified the particular punishment for each federal crime, and, in turn, reduced the judge's role dramatically. Some states followed suit and implemented guidelines, some shifted their statutes to determinate sentencing but without guidelines, and others maintained indeterminate sentencing but have incorporated mandatory sentences and mandatory minimum sentences. Whether states implemented guidelines, determinate sentencing without guidelines, or the hybrid indeterminate sentencing with mandatory sentences, the end result was a substantial shift in the responsibility for sentencing. It also resulted in stiffer punishment across the board. The goal of crime control is to get more individuals in prison, on longer sentences, and serving longer proportions of those sentences. Sentencing reform accomplished that by removing what was thought to be the weak link in the process (judges), by rewriting laws to increase the number of offenses and offenders that are subject to incarceration, and by increasing the sentences imposed.

There is one more piece to this sentencing reform effort—increasing time served for those sentenced to prison. Indeterminate sentencing is also called *indeterminate* because how much of the sentence imposed the offender actually serves is not up to the judge or prosecutor; it is up to the parole authorities, those individuals who assess when someone shall be released early from prison on parole. So until sentencing reform took place, the portion of the sentence imposed that the offender actually served was up to the discretion of the parole board, once a required statutory minimum of the sentence was served. Sentencing reform also included addressing concerns about what was labeled "truth in sentencing." Truth in sentencing refers to the gap between the sentence imposed (say, ten years) and the fact that the offender actually only serves four years because he or she is released early on parole. So we have a fairness/ equity issue, a leniency issue, and now an honesty issue. Truth in sentencing gained considerable traction as a fix to a broken piece of the justice system. The solutions varied from elimination of parole or early release altogether (that is, what the federal system and a handful of states did) to modifying parole eligibility laws across the board to persuading parole commissions to restrict release among those eligible for parole to implementing so-called truth in sentencing laws that target particular offenders, most typically violent offenders, to serve much longer percentages of their sentences before becoming eligible for parole consideration. A common truth in sentencing provision is 85 percent, meaning targeted offenders must serve 85 percent of the sentence imposed.

Prosecutorial Charging Decisions

As I have stated elsewhere and will suggest in later chapters, prosecutors are the most important decision makers in the American criminal justice system.[35] Recent evidence[36] demonstrates that among the mix of factors that have contributed to the growth of punishment and incarceration are changes in prosecutorial charging decisions. In effect, the likelihood that local prosecutors charge someone with a felony (as opposed to a misdemeanor) has increased significantly over time, resulting in increases in prison sentences. Specifically, in 1994 the odds that a prosecutor filed a felony charge per individual arrested was one in three. In 2008, those odds had increased to two in three. This change is not accounted for by increases in the seriousness of arrests. Rather, this is a reflection of local prosecutors becoming much more aggressive in how they file charges against individuals who are arrested. (It is important to point out that the office of the local district attorney is elective.)

Plea Negotiation: Expediting Case Processing

Plea negotiation or plea bargaining is a method of expediting the prosecution of offenders, making it not just easier but also possible to process the vast number of offenders that enter the justice system, many of them through the revolving door of recidivism. Today, 95 percent of all felony indictments are disposed of through a negotiated plea. This is the case in state and federal courts.

Plea bargaining played a primary role in facilitating the corrections boom. The 400 percent increase in the prison population and the 375 percent increase in the overall correctional population were accomplished with a modest 60 percent increase in the number of prosecutors.[37] That speaks to the efficiency of plea negotiation.

In addition, sentencing reform played a key role in plea negotiation and case disposition, further accelerating the flow of individuals into the correctional system. As punishments became more severe as a consequence of determinate sentencing and mandatory sentences, the leverage for plea negotiation was greatly enhanced.

One common way for prosecutors to get to where they want in terms of sentencing severity is to charge a defendant with multiple overlapping offenses (called *charge stacking*). Charge bargaining, a common plea negotiation strategy, involves reduction in the severity of the pled charge and/or dismissal of other, related, overlapping charges. The result is expedited guilty pleas and generally harsher punishment. For example, someone could be charged with possession of a controlled substance, as well as with intent to distribute, criminal conspiracy, and engaging in organized crime. The prosecutor generally has discretion to pursue all of the charges, none of them, or some subset. Part of the plea deal could be the prosecutor's promise to dismiss some of the charges in exchange for a plea and what the prosecutor sees as appropriate punishment. Or a defendant could be subject to a mandatory sentence. The prosecutor could agree to charge the defendant so he is not subject to the mandatory sentence. The leverage of facing much more severe punishment consummates the plea deal and results in generally harsher punishment.

A substantial priority in America's criminal courtrooms is the quick, efficient processing of people and cases. The pressure to dispose of larger and larger numbers of cases as quickly as possible has led to significant questions about due process. Stuntz points out in his 2011 book, *The Collapse of American Criminal Justice*,[38] that over the past thirty years or so, there was significant broadening of the laws that define criminal conduct, the overcriminalization discussed above. This broadening of criminal liability had important consequences for plea bargaining and the processing of large numbers of criminal defendants. At the same time, it created some compromises to criminal procedure. As Stuntz concludes:

> All these doctrines make guilty pleas easier to extract by eliminating issues that might otherwise lead to jury trials. The broader criminal liability is, the less likely the defendant can raise any colorable defense to the charges against him, and the more likely a defendant will agree to plead guilty. . . . The combination of these two related trends—

expanding criminal liability and a rising number of guilty pleas—
meant that, as the quantity of criminal punishments grew, its quality
declined. . . . Not only have Americans chosen, at least tacitly, to
punish millions more criminal defendants than in past generations, we
have also chosen to do the punishing with less justification and with
sloppier procedures. [39]

Drug Crime and the Scale of Correctional Control

The sheer size and scale of the corrections boom was significantly aided
by the influx of large numbers of drug offenders into prison, jail, probation, and parole. While admissions to prison increased for all felony
offenses, the admissions for drug offenders increased at a rate many times
that of other felonies, including murder, robbery, assault, burglary, and
sex offenses. Between 1980 and 2013, the overall state and federal prison
and jail populations increased by 345 percent. The number of offenders
incarcerated in state and federal prison and jail for drug offenses increased by over 1,100 percent. [40] Clearly, drug incarcerations far outpaced
any other offender type over the course of the incarceration boom. Today,
drug offenders are the largest single offense type among individuals incarcerated, averaging about 18–20 percent of state prison inmates and 50
percent of federal prison inmates. [41]

I am not suggesting a conspiracy, but the war on drugs provided a
robust supply of drug offenders, which dramatically expanded the size of
the incarcerated population over the course of the past forty years. In
terms of scale, the incarceration explosion would not have been nearly as
dramatic without the 3.8-million-plus drug offenders admitted to state
and federal prisons since 1980.

Dismantling Public Mental Health Treatment:
Prisons and Jails Became Default Asylums

A July 14, 2014, Associated Press story is titled "The Big Story—U.S.
Jails Struggle with Role as Makeshift Asylums." The good news is that
this is newsworthy. The bad news is that this is newsworthy. It is good to
bring attention to the issue, but it is not the new big story to those who
have had much involvement with mental health and criminal justice over

the past couple of decades. The stories and the statistics are becoming all too familiar.

Melissa C., twenty-two years old, has been sitting in the Cook County (Chicago) jail for a year. She was most recently arrested for felony robbery after she fought a security guard who caught her stealing food from a Whole Foods Market. Like so many mentally ill individuals, Melissa often refused to take her psychotropic medication in favor of street drugs. The former cheerleader has been homeless and addicted to heroin and has cycled in and out of jail and rehab facilities for much of her teen years and early twenties. [42]

Janet, a forty-five-year-old Latina, hears voices when she is not taking her medication. She has served six sentences in prison for drug possession and drug dealing and one stretch in jail for selling drugs to support her addiction. Her revolving door is often a product of lack of access to medication. "When I got out of jail this time I still didn't have no medication," she said. "I [couldn't] see a psych doctor until a month later. I don't think that shouldn't be like that." [43]

The largest mental institution in California is a wing of the Los Angeles County Jail known as the Twin Towers. It incarcerates fourteen hundred mentally ill offenders. The largest mental health facility in Illinois is the Cook County (Chicago) jail, housing between twenty-five hundred and twenty-eight hundred mentally ill inmates, or about 25–30 percent of the jail population. A recent report by the Board of Corrections documented that 40 percent of the 12,200 inmates in the Rikers Island Jail in New York City are mentally ill. [44] In forty-four states and the District of Columbia, there are more seriously mentally ill individuals in prisons and jails than in any state psychiatric in-patient facilities or hospitals. In fact, there are ten times more mentally ill individuals in prisons and jails than are in state mental hospitals. As was the case with drug offenders, the scale of the correctional boom was significantly supported by the influx of the mentally ill into the American criminal justice system. How did we get to this point?

In 1955, the United States had 340 public, in-patient mental health treatment beds per 100,000 population. By 2005, that had radically declined to seventeen beds per one hundred thousand. The decline has continued; in 2013, the ratio was fourteen per one hundred thousand. Today, public, in-patient treatment capacity is 4 percent of what it was in 1955. Or, put differently, 96 percent of the beds available in 1955 are no longer available today.[45] The in-patient psychiatric-bed capacity today is at the same relative level as it was in 1850, the era when the United States began to treat mental illness in an in-patient setting. Mental health experts have indicated that the consensus target for minimal in-patient capacity is fifty per one hundred thousand. There are eleven states that have fewer than twelve beds per one hundred thousand, and twenty-two with between twelve and twenty. One state, Mississippi, meets the minimal standard of fifty. By way of comparison, the ratio for England is sixty-three per one hundred thousand.[46]

This situation—the profound lack of public mental health treatment resources and the flood of mentally ill individuals into the American criminal justice system—is a consequence of what is called deinstitutionalization of public mental health treatment. Deinstitutionalization consisted of the release of individuals from long-term in-patient hospitals, the diversion of new admissions to alternative treatment, and the development of local, community-based facilities that make greater use of outpatient care and local resources. The first two components of this process (the release of existing patients and diversion of potential new patients) have proceeded very quickly. The third, the development of alternative, community-based treatment facilities, has lagged far behind and has not come close to meeting the need or demand.

The logic or motivation for these changes was therapeutic, on the one hand, and fiscal/pragmatic, on the other. The creation of local, alternative-treatment resources was seen from a clinical perspective as preferable to the long-term psychiatric hospital model. In theory, community-based treatment is more flexible, offering a wider array of services to meet the varying needs of patients. Research investigating treatment outcomes in those limited areas where community-based facilities have been adequately implemented indicates that the quality of care has improved, patient satisfaction is higher, and treatment outcomes are enhanced.[47] On the fiscal/pragmatic side, it was seen as more cost-effective. As it turns out, it has been "cheaper" but not more cost-effective since it has not been properly and adequately implemented. As one expert observer put it:

> Deinstitutionalization of people with psychiatric disabilities was by and large successful in opening the back doors of large state institutions so residents could leave—and in closing the front doors so that new residents could not come in. But it was less successful in promoting investments in the kind of community service infrastructure that

enables people with psychiatric disabilities to thrive in the community. [48]

Reductions in federal assistance for housing and Social Security Income (SSI) starting in the 1980s have conspired with deinstitutionalization to create a growing homeless population, significant proportions of
which suffer from mental illness. The evidence regarding the coincidence
of homelessness and mental illness is compelling: between one-third and
one-half of the homeless in the United States have a major mental illness
and roughly 75 percent suffer from a major mental illness, a substance
abuse disorder, or both. Whether the shuttering of the psychiatric hospitals was the primary culprit in the increase in the homeless mentally ill
population does not matter today. What does matter is that the community-based resources, services, and supports required to address the needs
of this population are largely absent.

For a variety of reasons that will be discussed later in this book, the
American criminal justice system has become the de facto asylum for
many of the individuals who have been released and diverted from mental
hospitals through the process of deinstitutionalization. The failure to provide an adequate community-based capacity to replace the loss of treatment beds has resulted in the criminal justice system becoming the system that just can't say no. A 2006 Department of Justice study revealed
that 56 percent of state prison inmates, 44 percent of federal prisoners,
and 65 percent of jail inmates had a mental health problem. Obviously,
the severity of those illnesses varies, but the bottom line is that the mentally ill are substantially overrepresented in prison, jail, probation, and
parole by a factor of two to four times the incidence in the general,
noncorrectional population. [49]

The fact that prisons and jails have become de facto mental institutions is not a positive thing. Managing criminal offenders is difficult
enough. Adding in large proportions of inmates who are mentally ill adds
dramatically to the complexity of operating prisons and has profound
consequences for public safety when mentally ill offenders are released.
Moreover, the evidence is clear that prison is not an environment that is
conducive to the effective treatment of the mentally ill.

The Public Broadcasting System's *Frontline* gained unique access to
the Ohio prison system a few years ago and produced a program on the
mentally ill in prison called "The New Asylums." While they profiled

many of the mentally ill inmates in the prison, Keith Williams is a metaphor for much of what's wrong. Williams was preparing to be released from prison after serving the full two years of his sentence. When asked where he would go, he said he would go to a homeless shelter to be with his people. When asked who "his people are" he replied, "my mommies, angels, and cats."[50] He was released with a two-week supply of psychotropic medication. The chief of the Bureau of Mental Health for the prison system informs us that it takes at least three months for released inmates to get an appointment to get their prescriptions renewed. Keith Williams was rearrested and reincarcerated less than a month after release when he assaulted a worker at the homeless shelter where he was staying. He had run out of his medication when the assault occurred.

John James was incarcerated in the Utah state prison system. His behavior in prison is in large part influenced by his psychiatric diagnosis of psychosis (paranoid states, delusional disorders). On one occasion, he was ordered to remove a cup and his hands from the port in the door where prison staff place food. Because he did not remove the cup and his hands quickly enough from the port, he was written up for refusing to fully and immediately obey an order. His punishment for this violation was twenty days in solitary confinement, an environment that promotes further decompensation among mentally ill offenders.

In 2002, I was visiting one of Texas's supermax prisons, a new type of facility for administrative segregation, and the realities of incarcerating the mentally ill became glaringly evident. Administrative segregation (ad seg) is a type of prison custody where individuals are single celled, with very limited access outside of the cell. They are fed through a slot in the door and are allowed out between one hour and three hours per week, depending on what type of restrictions they are assigned. Ad seg is designed for inmates who cannot behave in the general population, often due to assaultive behavior on inmates and/or staff. The cells have solid steel doors with a narrow vertical window and a slot for food trays. As I walked the range, looking into the cells, it was immediately obvious that most of the inmates were engaging in what most would consider bizarre behavior masturbating in the window, screaming, walking in circles in the cell, and so on. I asked the warden who was giving the tour how many of these individuals he thought were mentally ill. He replied, "None. If they were, they wouldn't be here. They would be in the mental health unit." I am not a psychiatrist, but it probably does not require clinical training to recognize that someone is mentally unstable, the conclusion I reached about most of the men I saw in that unit. It is a fact of life in most of the prisons across the country that ad seg is one of the few methods prison officials have for dealing with mentally ill inmates who do not (or cannot) follow the rules. It is also probably the worst thing that can happen to someone who is mentally ill.

The Prison-Industrial Complex

The label *prison-industrial complex* refers to substantial private-sector financial interests in corrections. Those interests include the construction of secure facilities as well as the management and staffing of correctional facilities. The major correctional facilities construction companies include Gilbane, Hensel Phelps, and Turner. These are all major capital construction companies. Hensel Phelps is number 218 on *Forbes*' list; Gilbane is number 137, and Turner is number 117. These corporations, and many of their smaller counterparts, have profited well from the expansion of prison and jail capacity over the past forty years. And they have a clear interest in maintaining that path. The major management and operations corporations include Corrections Corporation of America (CCA), the GEO Group, and the Management and Training Corporation (MTC). All three are publicly traded, and all three are financially robust. Over the past five years, CCA's stock price increased by over 200 percent. In February 2014, the GEO Group reported $1.52 billion in revenue. MTC employs nearly fifty-six hundred people in its corrections division and reported gross revenues of $704 million for 2012.

Today, for-profit corrections management companies operate about 10 percent of the correctional facilities in the United States. These companies make substantial revenues, thus they have a clear interest in maintaining prison populations and expanding their market share. In fact, many contracts that these companies have with state corrections agencies stipulate occupancy minimums, requiring 80–90 percent occupancy, and even if populations go below those limits, states are nevertheless required to pay them.

CCA, MTC, and the GEO Group all engage in aggressive lobbying of Congress and state legislatures, as well as making extensive contributions to political campaigns. Their lobbying budgets and campaign contributions are in the millions. Over the past few years, CCA has employed nearly 180 lobbyists in thirty-two states, and GEO Group has employed nearly 70 lobbyists across sixteen states.[51]

Financial interest in corrections also includes small, rural communities lobbying for prisons to be located nearby. In quite a contrast to forty years ago, when the prevailing attitude was "not in my backyard," small communities seek correctional facilities since the employment and tax revenue they bring are economic drivers.

For-profit corrections companies are expanding their reach beyond incarceration to probation, treatment, and community reentry programs such as halfway houses. One of the problems is that offenders are required to foot much of the cost of privatization. For example, for-profit probation companies collect not only probation and court fees but also their own fees, which the offenders are required to pay. The result is that it is cheaper for the local jurisdiction and the courts because more of the cost is shifted to probationers. The mounting financial burden on offenders, who often have significant problems finding legitimate employment, creates a pathway back into incarceration, as they are often revoked from probation for failure to pay the fees.

THE REVOLVING DOOR OF FAILURE CONTINUES

We tend to assume that when someone has finished a criminal sentence, the government has finished punishing and controlling them. In some respects, this is true. But the bigger picture is that substantial constraints are placed on ex-offenders, constraints that significantly limit where they work and live, as well as whether they are able to access community resources and assistance. When offenders finish lengthy periods in prison or are discharged from probation, they typically encounter considerable roadblocks to accessing things like housing, health care, employment, education, and mental health and substance abuse treatment, among others. Whether intentional or coincidental, we continue to punish offenders well after they have "paid their debt to society." In most states, legislatures have passed laws restricting ex-offenders from being employed in a wide variety of occupations that typically require state approval through licensing or certification. When we step back and take a good, hard look, it is no wonder that recidivism rates are as high as they are and that we have a true revolving-door justice system. What do we expect when we do little to change those crime-related factors that play a substantial, fundamental role in criminal offending? What do we expect when ex-offenders cannot find employment or cannot get access to psychotropic medications or drug treatment or cannot find suitable housing?

When the record is complete, we shall see that the past forty years of crime control have been substantially fueled by the failures of a variety of public institutions. It is impossible to quantify how many individuals have entered the justice system or are endlessly caught in its revolving door as a result of these failures, but the numbers would likely take our breath away. Consider what the American criminal justice system would look like if we had adequate capacity for publicly funded, evidence-based drug and alcohol treatment. After all, 80 percent of individuals in the justice system have alcohol and/or drug problems. Imagine a justice system in an era when those with mental illness can obtain appropriate, evidence-based treatment in the community. What would it look like if public education was fulfilling its promise? Again, these are not excuses for bad behavior. But we all have a role in this scenario. Conscious decisions have led to the current state of public drug/alcohol treatment, public mental health treatment, and public education, to name just three factors that share some responsibility for the current status of the justice system. Those decisions, made by either commission or omission, have led to the use of the American criminal justice system as the repository for many of these failures.

American criminal justice policy, culture, politics, laws, and funding have coincided in a very concerted effort to enhance public safety, reduce crime and recidivism, and make the public feel safer through the nearly exclusive reliance on punishment. With much rhetoric and posturing, with fear-inducing political campaign ads and very simple, tough messages, sometimes with accompanying swagger and occasional chest thumping and fist pounding, we launched and have sustained an all-out assault on crime, an offensive that has resulted in the largest prison system in the world, record-breaking incarceration rates and corrections populations, and massive expenditures of public funds. To what end? We address this question in the next chapter.

2

THE HIGH COST OF FAILURE

Ricky Minor was a meth addict who struggled with depression and drug addiction as he worked and tried to support his family. He had several relatively minor prior convictions (possession of drugs, simple assault), none of which resulted in incarceration. Based on a confidential informant's statement, local police found 1.2 grams of meth in Minor's home. They also found an over-the-counter decongestant, acetone, matches, and lighter fluid. Although they did not find a meth lab, these items were estimated to render nearly two hundred grams of meth. Minor stated he never sold meth and just made enough to support his and his wife's drug addiction. He was charged under state law in Florida but refused to cooperate with prosecutors, who wanted him to snitch on others. His case was transferred for federal prosecution, where he pled guilty and was sentenced to life without parole in 2001.[1]

Ricky Minor's case is a metaphor for tough on crime. While a relatively small number, the ten thousand individuals serving life or life without parole sentences in state and federal prisons for nonviolent crimes serve as just one example of our policy of intolerance. The vast majority of these life-without-parole sentences are mandatory, meaning the judges had no choice in the sentence. As we have become more punitive, getting more and more individuals into prison for much longer sentences and time served, the obvious question is: What is the result? We have been witness to one of the largest and costliest policy experiments in U.S. history. What are the consequences of this massive investment in punishment? Has it reduced crime, and, if so, how much? What about the effects of punishment on recidivism? Do we feel safer? Are there, perhaps, unanticipated or unintended consequences or outcomes? What are the financial and collateral costs of American crime policy?

WHAT HAVE WE ACCOMPLISHED?

> Tough punishment and no parole works. Our communities continue to get safer. Our violent crime rate is now lower than any time since the early 1960's, the lowest in the South and the 5th lowest in the nation. Our property crime rate is the lowest in the South and the 8th lowest nationally. Tough punishment and no parole works.
> —Bob McDonnell, Republican governor of Virginia, January 2013

Figure 2.1 displays trends in the prison population and crime rates between 1960 and 2013.[2] A quick glance would suggest that punishment has been pretty successful, as Governor McDonnell asserted in his address to the Virginia legislature in 2013.[3] As prison populations increased during the 1980s and 1990s, we saw both property crime and violent crime begin a precipitous decline, beginning in the early 1990s. That decline in violent and property crime has essentially persisted to today, as has the incarceration rate, with only minor reductions in the prison population in the past five years.

The decline in crime in the past two decades is often referenced as evidence of the effectiveness of punitive policies. Untold numbers of public officials and policy makers have enthusiastically passed stiffer sentencing laws and continued expanding prison capacity based on evidence like what is presented in the graph.

While logical, intuitive, and reasonable, the conclusion that crime control is responsible for the crime decline of the 1990s is routinely and substantially exaggerated. Consider the following claim made by the National Rifle Association on the relationship between legal gun ownership and crime rates:

> Gun control supporters believe that RTC laws cause crime. However, since 1991, when violent crime hit an all-time high, 25 states have adopted RTC laws, the number of people with carry permits has risen to over 12 million, and the nation's violent crime rate has decreased 51 percent, to a 43-year low.[4]

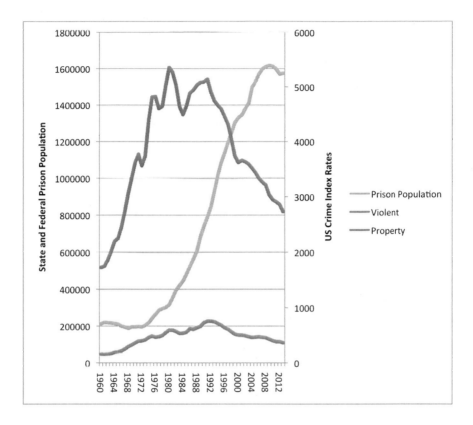

Figure 2.1.   Crime Rates and Prison Population, 1960–2013

The assertions of both the tough-on-crime advocates and the gun rights advocates appear to be based on something other than the criteria for establishing cause and effect. While the logic may seem convincing on the surface, a little scrutiny uncovers the flaw in the reasoning. First, nothing is as simple as *x* causes *y*. Crime is complex. There are many factors that influence crime rates, some far more important than others.

The drop in crime across the United States was comparable in terms of timing and scale. Crime began declining relatively uniformly across states and cities, regardless of how extensively those states and cities adopted tough-on-crime policies. States differed dramatically in terms of sentencing laws and prison capacity. Cities implemented a wide variety of law enforcement initiatives, some tougher than others. The point is that while the decline in crime was essentially uniform across states and cities, what they did in terms of crime policies differed considerably. Thus, other factors were influencing crime rates, factors that were independent of the presence and extent of crime-control policies.

The Crime Decline of the 1990s

Importantly, the crime decline of the 1990s, which has served many as evidence of the success of U.S. crime policy, was not a uniquely American experience. Other nations that had comparable reductions in both violent and property crime on roughly the same time line and scale as the United States include Canada, Australia, New Zealand, Belgium, England, Wales, Estonia, Finland, France, the Netherlands, Hungary, Russia, South Africa, Spain, Northern Ireland, Poland, Scotland, Switzerland, and Sweden, among others.[5]

On balance, between 1995 and 2004, twenty-six nations experienced substantial declines in crime, including a 77 percent decline in theft from cars, a 60 percent drop in theft from persons, a 26 percent reduction in burglary, a 21 percent decline in assault, and a 17 percent reduction in car theft. In the United States, crime dropped 29 percent during this period; violent crime fell by 31 percent, and property crime fell by 29 percent. None of these twenty-six countries that experienced the crime decline of the 1990s implemented tough-on-crime initiatives like the United States. A particular comparison of the U.S. and Canadian experiences is telling. The crime declines in both nations occurred at the same time and had the same defining characteristics in terms of scale and breadth. The punishment policies in the United States and Canada were radically different, with U.S. incarceration rates two to four times those of Canada. The evidence is clear. At best, American's correctional growth, and in particular the incarceration explosion, accounted for roughly 10–15 percent of the crime decline.[6] While counterintuitive, the evidence indicates that punishment policies had a quite modest impact on crime in the United States.[7]

Recidivism

A more direct indicator of crime control's effectiveness is recidivism. It is a more direct measure since it is specific to those who have been punished and assesses the outcome of that punishment in terms of reoffending. Recidivism is measured in various ways—typically rearrest, reconviction, and reincarceration. There are two primary ways in which individuals released from prison can recidivate: committing a new offense and/or violating the conditions of parole (this can lead to revocation of parole and reincarceration).

There have been two major U.S. recidivism studies released relatively recently, one in April 2014 by the Bureau of Justice Statistics in the U.S. Department of Justice[8] and another in 2011 by the Pew Center on the States.[9] To be clear, recidivism statistics are based on individuals who are caught. Substantial numbers of crimes are unreported, and many of those that are reported do not lead to an arrest. Moreover, many parole violations go undetected. Thus, official recidivism statistics are undercounts of actual reoffending and supervision violations.

What do we know about the recidivism of offenders released from prison during the period of time when more individuals were entering prison on longer sentences and serving longer proportions of those sentences? The Pew study tracked the reincarceration of inmates released from prison in 1999 and 2004. The study found that over 45 percent of those released in 1999 were reincarcerated within three years of their release. The reincarceration rate for those released in 2004 was 43 percent. The Pew researchers compared their results with those of earlier studies and concluded that reincarceration rates have been relatively constant since the early 1990s, suggesting that the ramp up in punitiveness in American corrections has *not* had an appreciable impact on recidivism over time.

The Justice Department recidivism study tracked offenders released in 2005 in thirty states. It uses rearrest and reincarceration outcomes as well as tracking prison releasees for five years. They found that two-thirds of those released from prison were rearrested for a new offense within three years of release and over three-quarters were rearrested within five years. Property offenders had the highest rearrest rate (82 percent) and violent offenders the lowest (71 percent). Fifty percent of offenders released in 2005 were reincarcerated after three years; 55 percent were reincarcerated within five years. A 2012 California study shows that two-thirds of inmates released from the California prison system between 2002 and 2008 were reincarcerated within three years.[10] The Justice Department researchers also conducted a special comparison of recidivism in twelve states among offenders released in 1994 and those released in 2005. The results indicate that the overall recidivism rates increased from 67 percent in 1994 to 72 percent in 2005, a pattern opposite of that one would expect if harsher punishment was deterring reoffending and parole violations.

It is difficult to know what an acceptable recidivism rate is. The architects of crime control never went on the record and said what they expected in terms of recidivism outcomes. However, it is probably safe to assume that a rearrest rate of 77 percent and a reincarceration rate of 55 percent are not the outcomes expected and probably do not represent a reasonable return on investment. Moreover, the fact that recidivism rates did not decline over the course of harsher and harsher crime-control policies, and in fact increased in many instances, raises very serious doubts about the effectiveness of the American punishment experiment.

Federal, state, and local governments have spent nearly $1 trillion on tough on crime over the past forty-plus years, not counting the war on drugs, which is another $1 trillion. This has been an experiment that bet the farm on punishment. We lost the farm.

Public Perceptions about Crime and Safety

Crime rates and recidivism aside, has crime control influenced how we feel about crime? Do we feel safer? Has fear of crime changed over the course of America's punishment binge? There are various ways of measuring fear of crime and perceptions of safety. Gallup, the national public opinion polling organization, has been tracking fear of crime and feelings of safety for many years. Fear typically has been assessed by asking respondents, "Is there any area near where you live—that is, within a mile—where you would be afraid to walk alone at night?" In 1964, 34 percent responded yes. During the latter 1960s and 1970s, the percentage increased and then peaked in 1982 at 48 percent. It then declined during the 1990s to a low of 30 percent in 2002. In 2012, it was back up to 38 percent. Today, the United States is experiencing the lowest crime rates in decades; yet fear is at the levels we saw in 1970, 1980, and 1990.[11]

We know that public opinion about crime is influenced by many factors, crime rates being only one of them. If the goal of crime control was to reduce crime and recidivism, thus helping us feel safer, the evidence regarding our feeling safer indicates otherwise. We are still relatively fearful despite decades of some of the most punitive policies in the world. A significant contributor to feelings of insecurity is the media treatment of crime. As we discussed in chapter 1, the media tend to sensationalize crime, especially violent crime, to the point where our fears of crime and crime risk are artificially inflated.

Best we can tell, crime control has not had a detectible impact on recidivism (except for the mounting evidence that incarceration actually increases recidivism), has only had a minimal impact on crime rates, and apparently has not made us feel much safer. We now turn to the question of how we make sense of this.

WHY PUNISHMENT DOESN'T WORK

Eric Hutchings is the chair of the Utah legislature's Criminal Justice Appropriations Committee. This is his take in an op-ed piece in the *Salt Lake Tribune* on March 10, 2015:

> Treating a drug addict or someone with mental illness the same as a hard core criminal has proven over time to do nothing to break the cycle. Our own data proves that when you put an addict and a real criminal in the same prison space together, all you get is a criminally-minded addict. We can no longer afford to run the system this way. It does not work.

Crime control is premised on the assumption that punishment will reduce crime and recidivism through two primary mechanisms: deterrence (where the punishment or its threat prevents engaging in crime) and incapacitation (physically preventing crime through incarceration). [12] While on the surface deterrence and incapacitation are reasonable, logical ways to reduce crime and recidivism, the evidence indicates otherwise. We begin with deterrence.

Deterrence

The deterrence argument proposes two different types of deterrence—specific and general. Specific deterrence refers to the effect of punishment on the particular individual being punished, suggesting that punishment lowers the likelihood that the offender will reoffend. General deterrence refers to the threat of punishment that keeps all of the rest of us from engaging in crime in the first place. Embedded in our crime-control policies is the explicit belief that the harsher the punishment, the greater the threat. I begin with the evidence for general deterrence.

We often hear or read about what is presumably general deterrence in action—a judge or prosecutor stating that a harsh sentence is intended to send a message to the community. Somewhere in the reasoning of crime control is the assumed need for this threat of severe consequences in order to keep crime in check. At some level, this makes intuitive sense. That is, after all, why we have laws and norms and rules and regulations that serve as the guidelines for proper behavior and social interaction. So in one sense, the threat of harsh punishment is simply an extension of all of these other mechanisms and processes that keep most of us on the straight and narrow.

Despite common sense and logic, the evidence is clear that there is no scientific support for a general deterrent effect from harsh punishment. While prosecutors and judges often articulate general deterrence in sentencing decisions, the research indicates that it just does not matter. The scientific community has weighed in on this issue:

> Can we conclude that variation in the severity of sentences would have differential general deterrent effects? The reply is a resounding no. . . . Given the significant body of literature from which this conclusion is based, the consistency of findings over time and space, and the multiple measures and methods employed in the research conducted, we would suggest that a stronger conclusion is warranted. . . . The severity of sentence does not matter. [13]

There are at least three reasons why sentence severity does not translate into a crime-reducing general deterrent effect: First, there is the requirement that the community hears the message that judges and prosecutors are sending. There is no compelling evidence indicating that the messages are being communicated in any systematic way or that the community is listening. A second reason is that the community may not need to hear the message in order to remain crime free. Most of us are law-abiding citizens, absent the occasional speeding ticket, petty misdemeanor, or creative tax accounting. We do not see the need to engage in crime (we have other options or alternatives) and/or we have too much to lose by going down that road (shame, loss of a job or family, the wrath of the IRS). We will remain crime free regardless of the consequences of breaking the law; thus, even if we hear the message, it is not going to alter our behavior. The third reason is that for those who should hear the message, those already involved in crime, the threat of harsh punishment is not sufficient to alter their behavior. (More on why this is the case below.)

Specific deterrence is based on the idea that as punishment severity increases, the experience becomes more negative, in turn, increasing the cost of committing crime. As the logic plays out, the harsher the punishment, and, in turn, the higher the cost, the lower the probability of reoffending. Again, this resonates with common sense. That would work for me, so why not for others? Common sense may very well have been the justification for the focus on punishment severity, because there was essentially no scientific evidence indicating that enhanced punishment would deter those we punish.

The evidence contrary to the harsh punishment–reduced recidivism argument is compelling. First, as we saw earlier, recidivism data indicate very high rates of reoffending and very little change in reoffending over the course of harsher and harsher punishment. Moreover, a wide variety of other research confirms what the recidivism rates reflect—a remarkable lack of evidence supporting the assertion that harsher punishment deters.[14] Research shows that, compared to noncustodial sentences (like probation), those who have been incarcerated either are no different in terms of subsequent offending or actually reoffend at higher rates, indicating that incarceration increases reoffending.

So what is the disconnect between common sense and logic, on the one hand, and reality, on the other? Perhaps the punishment is not harsh enough. Maybe we need to get to some tipping point where the punishment is sufficiently noxious to outweigh the rewards of crime. That is a road we probably don't want to go down for a variety of good reasons, including the fact that there is no evidence that it would be effective (after all, there is very little research supporting the assumption that the death penalty deters homicide),[15] in addition to the constitutional provisions against cruel and unusual punishment and concerns with due process and equal protection, to name but a few.

Another reason why punishment as we have done it does not deter is because policy makers rarely have considered all of the elements of the deterrence argument, which suggests that in order to deter, punishment needs to be severe, swift, and certain. We have nearly universally focused on severity to the exclusion of swiftness and certainty. It is not hard to see how these other two conditions are largely nonstarters in the American justice system. Consider the series of predicate events that are required before an offender can be punished. A felony crime needs to occur and then come to the attention of law enforcement. Law enforcement must then make an arrest; the prosecutor needs to indict, prosecute, and plea negotiate; and then the court needs to impose a harsh punishment. This may come as troubling news, but the odds are heavily in the offender's favor. First, across the board, approximately only one-half of violent crimes and 40 percent of property crimes are even reported to the police. Of those reported, half of violent crimes and one in five property crimes lead to an arrest. This is in part a function of offense severity. The greater the severity, the higher the likelihood of reporting. All else being equal, the greater the offense severity, the higher the likelihood that a reported crime results in an arrest. Overall, the odds of even coming in the front door of the justice system are relatively low, and many offenders probably know that. So certainty of punishment is problematic. Swiftness is also highly questionable. The due process requirements for a proper disposition of a case involve considerable time, something that runs counter to the swiftness element of deterrence. Severity was the one element of deterrence that could realistically be altered in the American criminal justice system, assuming that the architects of crime control even knew of deterrence theory.

Perhaps the greatest fallacy in the logic is how we generalize our experiences to those of criminal offenders. Punishment is a part of the socialization process, part of growing up. It is what shapes our behavior and helps us learn to engage in appropriate social interaction. Punishment is something that *we* understand and that *we* believe will work because it works for *us*. The problem is that criminal offenders are not "us." They differ in important ways from the rest of us, who are law abiding. A typical criminal offender comes from substantial disadvantage, has a substance abuse problem, and has a significant likelihood of having some form of mental illness or cognitive problems. It is also typical that those who cycle in and out of the justice system have limited education and infrequent opportunities for legitimate employment. Once they enter the justice system, their odds of turning their lives around drop dramatically. We make it that much more difficult for offenders to find housing, employment, and education, and the list goes on and on. For many criminal offenders, crime is seen as the norm—an understandable or "rational" response to their perceived situation.

This is not an apology for crime. It is not a pass or a get-out-of-jail-free card for criminal offenders. Rather, it is an explanation for why the principles that seem reasonable to us do not work for others. If we appreciate the circumstances of many criminal offenders, we can begin to understand why punishment does not deter. Punishment likely does not outweigh the lack of opportunity and the barriers many offenders face. What kind of a threat is potential punishment to someone addicted to drugs? Or someone who realistically has no opportunity for legitimate work? Or someone who is unable to resist antisocial impulses because of a brain disorder?

Moreover, deterrence generally assumes a decision-making process in which an offender weighs the likelihood of getting caught and punished against the immediate rewards of a criminal act. Researchers have conducted extensive interviews with prison inmates. In those interviews, offenders describe the decision-making process as one of just not thinking about the consequences, since their immediate needs prevail.

> I didn't think about nuthin but what I was going to do when I got that money, how I was going to spend it, what I was going to do with it.

> See, you're not thinking about those things [arrest]. You're thinking about that big paycheck at the end of 30 to 45 minutes.

> At the time, you throw all your instincts out the window. . . . Cause you're just thinking about money, and money only. That's all that's on your mind, because you want that money.

Toss in drug or alcohol problems, something that characterizes the vast majority of criminal offenders, and the decision-making process is predictable and understandable.

> It gets to the point that you get into such desperation. You're not working, you can't work. You're drunk as hell, been that way two or three weeks. You're no good to your self, you're no good to anybody else . . . you're spiritually, physically, financially bankrupt. You ain't got nuthin to lose.

[You didn't think about going to prison?] Never did. I guess it was all that alcohol and stuff and drugs. . . . The day I pulled that robbery. No. I was so high, I didn't think about nuthin.

Often the decision to commit a crime is impulsive.

I see somebody leave their car runnin or something with the keys in it . . . I might just hop in and drive off. . . . .That's how easy it is. Just hop in the car and leave.

Dude was at the gas station in a Monte Carlo. . . . He's putting gas in there and I just jumped in the shit and drive off. . . . I just needed a ride home. . . . With a young dude in a Monte Carlo, easiest thing in the world.

Oh yeah, you know . . . We stole and shit like that, you know. I didn't give it no thought, no plan, don't know how much money's in it. You know what I mean? Just go in there and say "We're gonna do it, we're gonna do it." That was it. [16]

When we consider that roughly 35–40 percent of offenders are mentally ill and many have substantial neurodevelopmental impairments or deficits, what sense does it make to presume a process of deliberation about cost and benefit, an assessment of reward and punishment? [17]

Punishment Does Little to Change Circumstance and Behavior

Importantly, punishment does essentially nothing to change behavior. How does incarceration make one employable? How does prison treat substance abuse or mental illness? How does solitary confinement overcome a neurocognitive impairment? Moreover, we continue to punish criminal offenders well after they have "paid their debt to society." We restrict access to housing, health care, employment, mental health care, substance abuse treatment, and education, to name a few. Thus, when we appreciate that many offenders experience limited opportunities, as well as significant deficits and impairments, when we realize that nothing that happens in prison changes any of that and that we make it even more difficult once released, it then makes sense to ask: What should we expect? Not hope or wish, but what should we realistically expect? The answer is precisely what we see—high recidivism rates.

We have gone about the business of sentencing assuming that punishment deters. Even if deterrence did work and severity reduced recidivism, we have no way of knowing how severe is severe enough. We make no effort to determine how much punishment is enough except for the tendency to maximize severity. And we put lawyers (and judges and prosecutors) in charge of making those decisions. As Judge Michael Marcus, Multnomah County district court judge, Portland, Oregon, put it in 2003:

> Sentencing has been a ceremony of punishment for a very long time. We wear robes and conduct what is in large part a morality play—maintaining a secular equivalent of a state church. . . . If our job is to deliver an appropriate sermon, we need only work on our delivery and steer towards severity. [18]

Incapacitation

The other function of punishment is incapacitation, physically removing the offender from the street and eliminating access to targets or victims. Unlike deterrence, which focuses on reducing motivation for offending, incapacitation focuses on interrupting criminal opportunity.

While "lock 'em up and throw away the key" may sound good in principle, the reality, as we have already seen, is that any effect incapacitation has on crime in the United States is quite modest. Moreover, the marginal return from incapacitation diminishes as incarceration increases. The logic is that as incarceration expands, as it has done dramatically in the United States, we eventually start incarcerating larger numbers of lower-risk offenders. As the risk of those being admitted to prison declines, the effectiveness of incapacitation and thus its marginal utility decline. Most experts conclude that we have long passed the point of significant marginal returns from incapacitation.

Even if the marginal utility of incapacitation was significant, one of the primary barriers to its effective implementation is knowing who specifically should be incapacitated. Who should be targeted for the greatest crime-reduction effect? We currently lack the means to accurately determine that.

Much of the attention in recent decades has been on habitual or career offenders, those who have been punished repeatedly and still keep reoffending. We have seen many attempts at incorporating incapacitation into sentencing, such as the creation of mandatory three-strikes laws, which target repeat offenders. These statutory approaches at identifying habitual offenders are fraught with error. When it comes to identifying a chronic offender, what is magical about the number 3 other than that it works with the baseball metaphor? When prosecutors or judges try to identify habitual offenders to incapacitate, they typically rely on prior criminal history and little else. While prior behavior is a predictor of future behavior, it is a rather imperfect predictor. The point is that while the argument sounds logical—lock up the career offenders and prevent their future offending—we just do not have accurate ways of knowing who these career offenders are. While incapacitation requires the precision of a rifle, we have used a shotgun. Our tendency over the past forty years has been overkill—locking up many more individuals for much longer periods of time. That has been ineffective, and from a cost-efficiency and marginal-utility perspective, it is wasteful.

There is another version of overkill when it comes to incapacitation. Just as age is related to the onset of criminal offending, age is also related to desistance from crime. Once offenders get to a certain point in the life cycle, beginning around age eighteen and continuing consistently as one ages, there are dramatic reductions in offending. By age forty, the likelihood of engaging in crime is one-seventh of what it was at age seventeen. By age fifty, it is nearly zero. That seems to be lost on legislators who write laws implementing mandatory long-term sentences and truth in sentencing laws requiring that very high percentages of sentences are served before parole eligibility. It also seems to be lost on prosecutors who make lengthy sentence recommendations, judges who sentence offenders to long terms in prison, and parole boards that keep offenders well past the age at which there is any risk of reoffending. Evidence of this is that the inmate population is aging at a rate that is many times that of the general population. Over the past seven years, the percentage of inmates age sixty-five and older has doubled.[19] The incapacitation effect from incarcerating someone who has aged out of crime is zero. The marginal utility is at least zero and perhaps negative.

Finally, the assumption that when we lock up the criminal, we lock up the crime is often incorrect. In many instances of criminal offending, there is a substitution or replacement effect. Take, for example, the case of drug dealing. If the police arrest a drug dealer and he or she is prosecuted and incarcerated (as we have done for hundreds of thousands of drug offenders over the years), we are not eliminating that drug dealing. The likely scenario is that someone will take his or her place. The same thing probably occurs when criminal offending is part of an organization such as a gang. Just because a member of the gang is caught does not mean that the crime goes with him or her to prison.

The Big Picture on Punishment

So where does this leave us in terms of punishment, deterrence, and incapacitation? Is this to say that no one is effectively deterred and no one is effectively incapacitated? No, it does not. But in terms of sentencing and corrections policy, the numbers of offenders who are effectively deterred and the numbers of crimes that are averted because the perpetrator is incapacitated are small indeed. Moreover, focusing on punishment severity has been counterproductive since the evidence indicates that severity tends to increase recidivism.

Ironically, the idea that punishment does not change criminal behavior is embedded in federal law. In 18 U.S. Code § 3582—Imposition of a Sentence of Imprisonment—the federal code states,

> The court, in determining whether to impose a term of imprisonment, and, if a term of imprisonment is to be imposed, in determining the length of the term, shall consider the factors set forth in section 3553 (a) to the extent that they are applicable, recognizing that imprisonment is not an appropriate means of promoting correction and rehabilitation.

As we have incarcerated more and more individuals for longer periods of time, we have also reduced or eliminated many of the traditional incentives for good behavior while incarcerated. For example, substantial changes to release laws and reductions in good-conduct credit have significantly increased time served and limited early release from prison. As the incentives disappear, behavior worsens. One of the few methods for dealing with bad behavior while incarcerated is administrative segregation or solitary confinement. On any given day, America's prisons incarcerate eighty thousand to one hundred thousand inmates in solitary confinement.[20] Solitary is isolation and sensory deprivation. Inmates are essentially kept in their cells twenty-four hours per day, fed in their cells, and have very limited human contact. The goal is separation of offenders from other inmates and prison staff. Deprivation and isolation often take a tremendous toll on mental health. Far too often inmates end up serving their entire sentence in segregation since their behavior never improves to the point that they can go back to the general population. Every year, America's prisons discharge thousands and thousands of offenders who go from isolation directly to the community. Because they have served their entire sentence, they are not released under parole supervision. We have no legal ability to supervise or monitor them. So we cut loose thousands of offenders each year who are too dangerous to be in the general prison population, and we have no ability to monitor or supervise them in order to mitigate the risk they pose to the public. How smart is that? How is that in the interest of public safety?

As Judge Marcus puts it:

> The single most daunting impediment to meaningful sentencing improvement: our wholesale surrender to undifferentiated just deserts [punishment severity] as mainstream sentencing's only responsibility. That surrender is a demonstrably dysfunctional, cruel, and wasteful allocation of the bulk of corrections resources—jail and prison included. Our use of jail and prison under the resulting paradigm frequently does more harm than good. The harm consists of accelerated recidivism by offenders whose criminality would be better addressed with wiser sentencing choices, by victimizations that smarter sentencing would have avoided, the excessive punishments that serve neither society nor the offender, of an enormous waste of public resources, and a continuing erosion of public trust and confidence. [21]

THE COSTS OF PUNISHMENT

There are a number of ways to think about the costs of tough on crime. One is the financial cost associated with administering criminal justice (law enforcement, the courts, and corrections). Another is the cost of crime (victim costs, social costs). Yet another is the cost of the failure of the American justice system to effectively reduce recidivism—that is, the costs associated with repeat offenders' multiple entries into the justice system. There are also the costs of avoidable victimizations, also due to failures to reduce crime and recidivism. We will look at all of these in the following pages.

The administration of the American criminal justice system requires spending approximately $260 billion per year on law enforcement, prosecution, the court system, and corrections.[22] The United States spends more on criminal justice in one year than the total annual gross domestic product of 80 percent of the nations in the world. But this is only a portion of the total-cost picture.

Crime itself takes a tremendous toll on victims, on communities, on our sense of well-being, safety, and security. And this toll has economic consequences. Estimates of the financial costs of crime more broadly have been developed by monetizing various effects or impacts of crime.[23] These estimates are based on a limited number of offenses (just thirteen).[24] The broader costs associated with these thirteen crimes are estimated to be $200 billion annually. It is important to realize that this estimate is a fraction of the true cost of crime. First of all, these thirteen offenses represent just one-fifth of all arrests. Second, because these estimates are based on arrests, they include only reported crimes that, in turn, lead to an arrest. As discussed earlier, only about 50 percent of violent crimes and 40 percent of nonviolent crimes are even reported to law enforcement, and for those offenses reported, the arrest rate for violent crimes is just under 50 percent, and roughly 20 percent for reported property crimes.

Another estimate that includes unreported major crimes (murder, assault, rape, robbery, burglary, theft, arson, motor vehicle theft) puts the cost at $310 billion per year. Still another analysis, which includes all crimes, as well as direct and indirect justice system, victim, and society costs, places the net annual cost at over $1 trillion annually.[25] The $1 trillion annual estimate is based on the most comprehensive set of assumptions because it includes all crimes, not just major crimes, and does not rely solely on reported crimes.

All of these cost figures are estimates based on a variety of limitations and assumptions. The one thing they all share is that they highlight the extraordinary cost of the justice system and our failure to effectively address crime and recidivism. Moreover, since most of the costs of crime are public costs, we as taxpayers foot most of the bill.

The Pew recidivism study discussed above estimated the savings to corrections agencies due to the reduction in recidivism. They determined that the forty-one states in the study would save $635 million in the first year alone by reducing recidivism by 10 percent. California would save

$233 million, New York would save $42 million, and Texas would save $33.6 million, all in the first year. A separate study by the Pennsylvania Department of Corrections estimates a $44 million annual cost savings due to a 10 percent reduction in recidivism.[26] But these estimates are just the corrections cost savings. Each time an offender returns to the justice system, all of the costs are incurred again, including police resources to investigate, arrest, and book into jail; jail costs for post-arrest detention and subsequent pre-trial detention if the defendant is not bonded out prior to adjudication; costs of the prosecutor's office for reviewing and then indicting and prosecuting the case, including pre-trial hearings, grand jury hearings, and plea negotiations, arraignment, a plea negotiation hearing, and a sentencing hearing; costs of the court for many of the same proceedings listed above; and costs of corrections, including jail, probation, or prison and parole. So the estimated cost savings that are typically available, like the Pew figure of $635 million, are only a fraction of the total savings from reducing recidivism. And it is important to appreciate the cumulative cost savings over the longer term due to interrupting the cycle of recidivism of typical habitual or career offenders.

In 2014, there were twenty-six million criminal victimizations, roughly seven million violent victimizations, and nineteen million property victimizations.[27] Because the American justice system has failed to effectively reduce recidivism, the risk of criminal victimization is higher, resulting in hundreds of thousands of avoidable victimizations each year. The effective reduction of recidivism, which in turn leads to reductions in victimizations, has ripple effects in terms of reducing the costs to the justice system and victim costs, as well as effects on quality of life, among others.

Criminal offenders bring a variety of crime-related problems into the justice system (more on this in chapter 3), and the justice system does little to redress them. In fact, the evidence seems pretty clear that our justice policies often aggravate many of these problems, compromising public safety and aggravating other problems. Once an offender is released from incarceration, we end up passing on the problems to other agencies and institutions in the community. Justice policy has in effect created hundreds of thousands of dependents for public assistance, public housing, public health and mental health care, remedial education, and so on, as the typical individuals we turn out of the justice system are in need of more programs and services than when they went in. That seems to be the nature of what the American justice system churns out on a daily basis. These costs are rarely discussed in the big picture of the failures of the justice system.

Moreover, our failure to appropriately address crime and its causes has profound impacts on families and communities, impacts that increase crime and recidivism. As Professor Todd Clear recently stated in a PBS interview:

> One of the things we know is that going to prison reduces your lifetime earnings by 30 to 40 percent. So if you have a neighborhood where every male has been in prison, you have a neighborhood where the men as a group are earning 40 percent less income. . . . Having a parent going to prison increases the chances of a child ending up in the criminal justice system by about 25 percent. So if you have a neighborhood where all the adult males are going to prison, you have a neighborhood where the children's risk of going to prison . . . is about a quarter higher.[28]

On top of all this, there is a profound lack of accountability and responsibility in the American justice system. Jurisdiction is divided into multiple layers, including city, county, state, and federal governments. State legislatures write the laws and provide some funding (typically for prisons and parole), but almost everything else is funded locally. In operation, the American justice system is essentially a set of silos—law enforcement, prosecution and the courts, and corrections. And these various agencies act as silos, which has significant implications for oversight, responsibility, and accountability. Who is in charge of the criminal justice system? Who is accountable for recidivism? Who is responsible for overall performance and the return on investment? One would be hard pressed to find someone or some agency that will step forward and say, in Harry Truman's inimitable fashion, "the buck stops here."

Consider a corporation with gross revenue of $300 billion annually (which is a ballpark annual cost estimate for the operation of the U.S. justice system). This amount exceeds every company on the Fortune 500 list with the exceptions of Wal-Mart ($469.2 billion annual revenue) and ExxonMobil ($449.9 billion annual revenue). Then consider that this company had long-term performance ("long term" meaning twenty years or so) like that of the American criminal justice system. Granted, this is a silly analogy, since there is no single American justice system and because we are comparing for-profit corporations with government and comparing recidivism with profits or share price. But go with it for another minute. How long would this Fortune 500 corporation stay in business or avoid a major shake-up with performance like that of the American justice system? How long could a manufacturing company remain in business with a failure rate of 77 percent? How long could one of these companies remain viable with the lack of accountability and responsibility exhibited by the justice system? I'm no financial expert, but I would guess that Wall Street would have little tolerance of that kind of long-term performance. So why should we tolerate such ineffectiveness and financial waste from our justice system? Why should we remain silent about the hundreds of thousands of needless, avoidable victimizations every year due to the failure of criminal justice policies? Why does it seem that the high cost of failure is acceptable?

NEXT STEPS

The inability of the justice system to effectively reduce recidivism has direct and indirect costs on a variety things, including the administration of criminal justice, victims, families, and communities. While we lament the fact that most of the individuals who enter the justice system either have been there multiple times before or will return on a fairly regular basis, we do not always appreciate the financial impact of that failure, the financial cost of the revolving door. Newt Gingrich, former Republican Speaker of the House, said it well in a May 2014 interview with CNN:

> When a typical bureaucracy does its job this badly, it wastes money, time and paper. The corrections bureaucracy, in failing to correct the large majority of inmates in its charge, not only wastes money but also wastes lives, families and entire cities. The current system is broken beyond repair. It's a human, social and financial disaster. We need a radical strategy of replacement of these huge bureaucracies that lack any meaningful oversight. [29]

It seems that one way we can begin to gain some traction on changing criminal justice policy is not to focus on the emotional side of things, what is morally or ethically right or fair. Rather, what brought us to the point of beginning to question tough on crime and mass incarceration today has everything to do with the economic recession that began in 2008. Thus, it may be productive initially to forge the path to justice reform with a focus on the extraordinary financial waste of current policies.

The good news in all of this is that the rest of this book is devoted to where we can go from here to enhance public safety, reduce crime and recidivism, and reduce victimizations and to do all of this by dramatically reducing expenditures on the justice system. This path forward is evidence based, demonstrably effective at reducing crime and recidivism, and cost-efficient.

3

WHY PEOPLE COMMIT CRIME
AND WHAT WE CAN DO ABOUT IT

India, a 42-year-old woman, suffers from manic depression and post-traumatic stress disorder. She said she tried at various times to get psychiatric care but found it almost impossible, so she self-medicates when on the outside with heroin—and has spent almost all of her adult life in jails and prisons on a succession of nonviolent offenses relating to drugs and shoplifting.[1]

The stories are often disturbing but unfortunately all too common. We don't incarcerate folks for diabetes, but we do for drug addiction. We don't punish multiple sclerosis patients, but we certainly do punish the mentally ill. How did we get here?

We have tended to believe or assume that criminal offending is unrelated to circumstance; rather, it is simply a matter of bad decisions, poor choices, and hanging around with the wrong people. President Nixon made that clear, as did President Reagan and countless elected officials since then. And more recently, Mark Kleiman, a professor of public policy at UCLA, put it thus:

Why do some people keep committing crimes, to their own evident disadvantage? Because they're present-oriented and impulsive, with deficient capacities for shaping their current behavior in light of their future goals, and with poor judgment about their actual odds of getting caught. . . . If you're looking for a single "root cause" of crime, look no further: The cause is bad decision-making by offenders.[2]

Unfortunately, this way of thinking that crime is simply a matter of bad decision making has pervaded criminal justice policy for decades and has fit well with an approach that focuses primarily on punishment. Writing crime off as poor choices or bad friends dramatically misunderstands the situation. Where we stand today, it is clear that committing crime is a much more complex process, influenced by a substantial number of situations, conditions, influences, deficits, and impairments. Some are causal; others just facilitate crime. Many can be easily recognized and/or diagnosed. Others require more in-depth investigation and specialized expertise. Several of these crime-related conditions, disorders, and impairments can be mitigated, treated, managed, or repaired.

The point is to understand as much as possible about the underlying factors and conditions that are related to criminality. That is the first important step in developing alternatives to simply punishing offenders. The end game here is implementing behavior change interventions, which in turn can reduce crime, recidivism, victimization, and cost. Absent that, we have little choice but to continue with the revolving door of the justice system and the resulting compromise to public safety, excessive victimization, and extraordinary cost.

THE CAUSES OF CRIME AND THEIR ORIGINS

Substance Abuse

The United States leads most of the world in the use of illicit drugs. The United Nations Office on Drugs and Crime produces estimates of prevalence rates of the use of illegal drugs for many nations of the world. For nearly every drug category (opiates, cocaine, marijuana, amphetamines, and ecstasy), the United States prevalence rates are the highest in the world. In those instances when the U.S. rate is not the highest, it is in the top five.[3]

In 2012, twenty-four million Americans twelve years of age and older were current users of illicit drugs. This is nearly 10 percent of the U.S. population over the age of twelve and represents the combined populations of New York City, Los Angeles, Chicago, Houston, Philadelphia, Phoenix, San Antonio, San Diego, Dallas, and San Jose. One-half of Americans are current alcohol drinkers. Of those, 24 percent, or sixty million, are binge drinkers, and 7 percent, or seventeen million, are heavy drinkers. Problem drinking is especially acute among young adults (ages eighteen to twenty-five), with 40 percent reporting binge drinking and 13 percent heavy drinking.[4]

We have a serious drug and alcohol problem in this country, and it should come as no surprise that the criminal justice system is where much of this problem ends up. The relationship between substance abuse and crime is well established. Whether addiction, abuse, or dependence on alcohol, illicit drugs, and/or prescription drugs, substance abuse is one of the most prevalent elements in criminal offending. And the statistics confirm that the prevalence rates of substance abuse among those in the justice system are six to eight times the prevalence in the general population.

Referred to by academics and practitioners as a criminogenic (crime-producing) condition or problem, substance abuse is extraordinarily common among criminal offenders. The vast majority (80 percent) of criminal offenders in the justice system abuse drugs and/or alcohol. About two-thirds of jail and prison inmates are clinically addicted or are chronically dependent on drugs/alcohol. Roughly 60 percent of individuals arrested test positive for drugs at the time of arrest. Nearly 40 percent of individuals arrested report that they were drinking alcohol at the time of their arrest. Over one-quarter of individuals on parole release use illicit drugs while on parole; one-third of individuals on probation use drugs while on probation. It is estimated that about three-quarters of prison inmates need some form of substance abuse treatment. Incarceration itself has no effect since nearly all drug and alcohol abusers return to abuse after release from prison and jail.[5]

Below are the words of four incarcerated armed robbers explaining the role of drugs in their criminal activity:

> By me being involved with drugs, I keep a financial strain on myself. Unfortunate, but I do spend the majority of my money on drugs. . . . If it wasn't for drugs, I would just be doing what a normal person would do [rather than committing armed robberies].

> When you get it in your head to do [a robbery] and you get high, you ain't gonna care no more [about getting caught]. You go under the influence and you don't really trip off of it [worry about getting caught].

That's why we get high so much. . . . We get high and get stupid, then we don't trip off [worry about getting caught]. Whatever happens, happens. You just don't care at the time.

I think, when you're doing drugs like I was doing, I don't think you tend to rationalize much at all. I think it's just a decision you make. You don't weigh the consequences, the pros and cons. You just do it.[6]

Whether drug and alcohol abuse causes crime or facilitates crime or individuals commit crime to support their use is not all that important for our purposes here. The point is that drugs and alcohol are clearly implicated in the vast majority of crime. How the justice system does or doesn't address this has profound implications for crime, recidivism, victimization, and expenditure of tax dollars. Here are some illustrations of how the U.S. justice system deals with drug problems.[7]

Michaelene Sexton was a cocaine addict who sold cocaine to support her habit. Two of Michaelene's friends who had been arrested and then became confidential informants in order to reduce their punishment told police that she was selling drugs. Police arrested her for possession and sale of cocaine. She was sentenced to ten years in a Massachusetts prison. She had no prior convictions and was the single mother of three small children. She will receive no drug treatment while incarcerated.

Michelle Collette of Hanover, Massachusetts, was in an unhappy relationship with the father of her child, but she feared leaving him. To help numb the pain of that relationship, she started taking and then became addicted to Percocet, a prescription painkiller. She then began to sell Percocet to help support her addiction, which involved twenty to thirty pills per day. She was arrested for possession of several hundred Percocet pills. She pled guilty and was sentenced to seven years in prison under a Massachusetts mandatory sentence. "I don't think this is fair," said the judge. "I don't think this is what our laws are meant to do. It's going to cost upwards of $50,000 a year to have you in state prison. Had I the authority, I would send you to jail for no more than one year . . . and a treatment program after that."

Eric Marsh was a habitual cocaine abuser. He happened to be with two friends who were arrested for selling two ounces of cocaine to an undercover cop. Eric, in effect, had nothing to do with the transaction except for being there. Nevertheless, the two friends implicated Eric in order to reduce their sentences. Eric received a fifteen-year sentence to a New York prison. He had no prior convictions.

So how did we get to this point where so many substance-addicted, dependent, and abusing individuals are in the justice system? In 2012, slightly over twenty-two million individuals aged twelve and over were classified as having a substance abuse or dependence disorder based on standard diagnostic criteria established by the American Psychiatric Association (the *Diagnostic and Statistical Manual of Mental Disorders*, fourth edition, *DSM-IV*). About 3 million were abusing or dependent on alcohol and drugs, 4.5 million on drugs but not alcohol, and 15 million on alcohol but not drugs. Of those in need of treatment, only 2.5 million, or 11 percent, received any treatment.[8] The most common reason for not receiving treatment for those who wanted it was lack of insurance coverage or lack of money to pay for it. The bottom line is that there are a substantial number of people in the United States who need treatment for substance disorders but do not receive it. When their substance use becomes problematic and results in behaviors that are illegal, the justice system is ready and willing to accept them. The primary problem is that when the justice system is finished with them, they typically are no better off than when they entered. After all, what is it about punishment—incarceration in prison or jail or supervision on probation or parole—that treats substance abuse? One fallacy is thinking that abstinence is treatment. It is not. We have known for some time that if the answer was "Just Say No," as Nancy Reagan advised, we would not have the problem that we have today. Substance abuse is a chronic disorder that requires appropriate treatment and ongoing maintenance in order to effectively address and manage it. We just don't do much of that in the justice system. That is the primary reason we have the revolving door of substance-abusing offenders who are rearrested and reincarcerated at a significantly higher rate than offenders without substance abuse problems.

Mental Illness

Approximately 25 percent of the U.S. population, or sixty-two million individuals, has a diagnosable mental disorder; 6 percent of the U.S. population suffers from a serious mental illness, including schizophrenia, bipolar disorder, and major depression. Nearly one-half of individuals with any mental health disorder have at least one co-occurring mental disorder.[9]

Mental illness is disturbingly common in the criminal justice system, typically running 2 to 2.5 times the prevalence in the general population. While the estimates vary depending on how mental illness is defined and which segment of the justice population is being studied, experts agree that the majority of individuals in the justice system suffer from a mental disorder. Recent credible estimates indicate that about 50 percent of federal prison inmates, 55 percent of state prison inmates, and 50 percent of jail inmates have a mental health problem. Further, 15 percent of the prison and jail populations in the United States have severe mental illness, a rate that is 2.5 times that in the general population. Research indicates that mental illness both predates incarceration and is a result of incarceration. Many of the most common mental disorders identified among prison inmates originate in childhood and adolescence. At the same time, the experience of incarceration and the failure to treat mental health disorders lead to and aggravate a variety of mental illnesses. This is evident in estimated recidivism rates of 80 percent for mentally ill inmates released from prison. Moreover, mentally ill inmates return to prison approximately one year sooner than similar, non–mentally ill inmates.[10] The mental health of individuals on probation (supervised diversion from prison or jail) has not been very extensively studied. The best-guess estimate for the prevalence of mental disorders among this segment of the justice population is probably in the 35–50 percent range.

The exploding numbers of the mentally ill behind bars and on community release have caught the attention of the media in recent years, resulting in story after story about the "new asylums" or the "asylums of last resort" or "a mental hospital called jail." The headlines also relay the unfortunate reality of how there are ten times more mentally ill in prisons and jails than in the remaining psychiatric hospitals in the United States. All true. Below are illustrations of how the justice system deals with the mentally ill.

The story of Adam Hall is all too typical. Adam began exhibiting erratic behavior at age five. He tried to burn down the family home in what may have been an early suicide attempt. His mother knew something was wrong but had no money for treating him. Throughout his adolescence, Adam was in and out of psychiatric group homes, having been diagnosed with a variety of conditions, including bipolar disorder.

By the time Adam was twenty-two, he had been convicted of assault after he stole a car and resisted arrest. He was sentenced to three years in prison. As is the case with many, many mentally ill individuals in the justice system, particularly those in prison and jail, Adam had difficulty following prison rules. He was placed in solitary confinement as punishment. He eventually set fire to items in his cell. While prison officials could have considered his behavior a product of his mental illness and disciplined him internally, they chose to have him prosecuted for arson, which resulted in an additional three to six years in prison. In a letter Adam wrote in 2012, he said:

> It's hard in here for me. I feel like killing myself most of the time like I said but end up cutting myself to relieve the pain or just do things that help me relieve pain. Cutting myself seems the best way but one day I'm going to really cut myself and not tell no one so I can bleed out. That's how I am feeling nowadays. My life's gone down the drain.[11]

Trina N. first experienced psychotic episodes as a teenager in the form of tactile hallucinations, during which she would believe that she was being sexually violated. She was prescribed antipsychotic medication, which she resisted taking. By age eighteen, the former honors student had left home and was living in her car. She was no stranger to law enforcement, as her behavior routinely got her involved with the justice system. Trina then developed auditory hallucinations. She felt that the voice of God was telling her what to do. Her most recent run-in with the law was when the voices told her to pick up the salesman's keys at the Toyota dealer and drive off in a new Camry. Trina's parents expressed relief just knowing that she was in jail and not out on the streets.[12]

Jessica Roger was diagnosed with obsessive-compulsive disorder. At one point, she attacked her father. She also attacked her sister. She was charged with assault at the age of sixteen and sentenced to prison. Because of her psychiatric disorder, she had trouble complying in prison and was therefore placed in solitary confinement. While in segregation, she attempted suicide. She was transferred to the prison's psychiatric hospital for stabilization. When she returned to the prison unit, she was placed back in solitary, where eventually she did commit suicide.

The story of how we got here has already been discussed in chapter 1. Shuttering of many of the in-patient psychiatric facilities and subsequent inadequate capacity for community-based treatment resulted in the flood of the mentally ill into the justice system. Should the justice system be the first-choice, frontline institution for the mentally ill? Should criminal justice systems be the largest mental health facilities in in the United States?

Neurocognitive Development, Deficits, and Impairments

In June 2014, two twelve-year-old Wisconsin girls stabbed a female friend nineteen times because of some Internet character called Slenderman. Apparently, the girls thought Slenderman was real, and they wanted to please him. The point is that they stabbed their friend based on some childish, obsessive fantasy. These two girls have been transferred to adult court, and a judge has certified them to be tried as adults for attempted homicide. If convicted, they will be punished as adults and face up to sixty-five years in prison. Nearly one-half of the states have provisions for prosecuting and sentencing kids as young as ten as adults when they commit serious crimes.

There appears to be a profound disconnect between the law and the criminal justice system, on the one hand, and what is known about neurocognitive development and neurocognitive deficits and impairments, on the other. These two Wisconsin girls appear to be confusing fantasy and reality. A key question is whether they really understood what they were doing. Did they understand the consequences of their actions? It is, in part, a question of criminal responsibility and culpability for crimes committed by individuals whose neurocognitive functioning is significantly underdeveloped and/or impaired.

There are plenty of examples of offenders committing crimes without any regard for the victim (it often seems to be "me" focused) or the consequences of committing a crime. They simply do not consider such things. These inmates' first-person descriptions of their experiences illustrate the neurocognitive implications of engaging in crime, including not considering the potential consequences and the absence of any guilt:

> I never think about no chances [of getting caught], I just do [the stick-up] and get it over with.

> I don't think about nothing. I just do it.

I have never felt no pain for nobody. . . . That's how I was raised up. . . . So, I don't feel no pity for nobody.

I don't have no remorse. They got money. I got to get mine, so I'll take yours.

I don't feel sorry for [my victims] because I ain't got no money and they do.

Why feel sorry? [The victims] might try to do you the same way. I got to get some money. [13]

Neurodevelopmental and neurocognitive problems highlight critical crime-related conditions that can and do play a key role in criminal offending. Unfortunately, this is an area that has received less attention in the study of crime and even less in the intervention and treatment of criminal behavior. Here is what we know.

Recent developments in imaging technology have allowed scientists, in unprecedented fashion, to study the architecture of the brain, as well as the functioning of the brain and its components, under a wide variety of different conditions. Scientists are able to study how variation in the development of different parts of the brain influence behavior. It has also allowed for the study of how environmental experiences influence brain development and neurocognitive functioning.

Neurobiology focuses on the cells of the brain (neurons) and the communications among neurons through what are called *neurotransmitters*. Our experiences, observations, interactions, thoughts, attitudes, beliefs, and feelings are established in the brain by connections among neurons. These various interconnections are established and shaped by the combination of our environmental experiences and genetic tendencies. It is no longer nature versus nurture or genes versus the environment; it is now nature and nurture and how they interact. Congenital features of the brain interact with a variety of experiences in the environment, such as poverty, violence, abandonment, homelessness, neglect, abuse, and toxic substances, among others. Those interactions, registered in the brain as neural connections, determine how we think, react, feel, interpret, and perceive. These neural connections shape who we are, our thoughts, our identity, and our emotions and feelings. And they are experience dependent, meaning that they are influenced and shaped by what we are exposed to in the social and physical environment. As the brain registers our experiences, some of which are negative, traumatic, and toxic, there are neurological consequences, including intellectual and cognitive impairment, lack of empathy and self-control, addiction, and aggression, among others. The point is that there are very important implications for behavior, including criminal conduct.

The most important parts of the brain for understanding criminal behavior are the frontal lobes, especially the prefrontal cortex. It is the part that plays the primary integrative and supervisory role in the brain. It is also the part of the brain that develops last. The prefrontal cortex is responsible for regulating and guiding emotion, moral judgment, social cognition, affect, and executive functioning, which includes goal setting, impulse control, planning, analyzing, complex cognition, understanding consequences, goal-directed activity, attention, and self-monitoring. Executive functioning is the set of cognitive processes that allows individuals to be self-reliant and self-sustaining and is necessary for normal, prosocial adult conduct. There is undeniable evidence linking executive dysfunction, antisocial behavior, criminal conduct (including violent crime), and recidivism. Post-traumatic stress disorder (PTSD) is clearly implicated in executive dysfunction, as are schizophrenia, attention deficit/hyperactivity disorder (ADHD), autism spectrum disorder, and bipolar disorder, among others.

There are a variety of environmental origins of neurodevelopmental impairments and deficits. Poverty is directly implicated in neurodevelopment and neurocognitive functioning. *Poverty* is a broad term that is related to a variety of collateral effects on executive and behavioral functioning. Children raised in poverty score significantly lower on assessments of memory, impulse control, achievement, IQ, language skills, and attention. Poverty is also associated with child neglect and abuse, which in turn impact a variety of developmental and neurocognitive functions, such as executive functioning, IQ, memory, ADHD, conduct disorders, anxiety, PTSD, personality disorders, learning disabilities, risk taking, lack of remorse and empathy, impulsiveness, lack of self-control, and behavioral disorders.[14] Attachment disorder, also a correlate of poverty, has been clearly shown to have substantial negative neurodevelopmental consequences. Attachment disorder is the failure of the primary parent to establish a consistent, secure emotional bond with an infant. It can result in a number of negative consequences—impulsivity, aggression, lack of empathy, lack of conscience, oppositional behavior, and anger. Proper attachment can mitigate these consequences.

Exposure to violence is another significant environmental influence on neurodevelopment. Research on violence demonstrates clear neurological and physiological implications. One of the more pronounced physiological impacts is dysregulation of the hypothalamic-pituitary-adrenal axis, leading to chronic hyperarousal and hypervigilance or reduced responsiveness to the environment. Neurological impacts lead to a range of behavioral consequences, including PTSD, anxiety disorders, impaired academic functioning, low IQ, depression, and dissociative disorders.

Trauma is also a common condition in the environment, especially in areas of poverty and disadvantage. Trauma can lead to a variety of neuro-cognitive disorders, such as impaired executive functioning, impulse control, and violence. It is very telling that 60 percent of prison inmates in the United States have had at least one traumatic brain injury! [15]

Where does this leave us? First, it means that the idea of crime-related and crime-producing conditions, impairments, and deficits is a good bit broader and deeper than previously thought. As I concluded in a recent book:

> Many chronic, persistent, habitual offenders have neurocognitive and psychosocial impairments, including spatial and verbal impairments, impairments of memory and non-memory cognitive function, intellectual impairments, executive dysfunction, etc. . . . Longer-term habitual offenders . . . have pronounced and profound neurocognitive and psychosocial impairments that distinguish them from others. Brain scans comparing antisocial individuals with controls reveal significant reductions in the frontal lobe of the brain (between 9% and 18% reduction), that part of the brain responsible for executive functioning. Comparisons of the brains of psychopaths with controls showed deformations in the amygdala and up to an 18% reduction in the volume of the amygdala, which is a part of the limbic system responsible for memory and emotional regulation. . . . Neuroimaging studies of aggressive, violent and antisocial individuals . . . show consistent patterns of brain dysfunction and criminal activity, involving the prefrontal lobe . . . and the neural circuitry regulating emotion in aggressive and violent behavior. . . . "There is a significant neurological basis of aggression and/or violent behavior over and above contributions from the psychosocial environment." [16]

Identifying these neurological impairments, deficits, and developmental delays is fundamental to our understanding of the big picture of recidivism and how to reduce it. Unfortunately, we have no reliable data on the frequency or prevalence of such disorders among those in the justice system. These problems have not really been on the radar screens of those who are responsible for assessing and measuring them. Absent good data on frequency, we can still address the key question of what do we do about such neurodevelopmental and neurocognitive problems. How do we mitigate the impact of growing up in a violent neighborhood or with a disinterested or absent mother? Short of reducing poverty, which does not seem terribly realistic, how can we impact the neurodevelopmental effects of, for example, growing up poor or experiencing violence and other trauma?

The answer is *neuroplasticity*, the term that describes the fact that the brain is malleable, changeable. Plasticity is a key feature of the human nervous system, the idea that the brain can be "rewired," that neural pathways can be altered or eliminated and new ones created. Just as the brain can be altered by trauma, lack of attachment, poverty, and violence, it can be trained to forge new neural connections that support prosocial behavior. It is described in the following way by some leading neurodevelopmental researchers:

> Behavior will lead to changes in brain circuitry, just as changes in brain circuitry will lead to behavioral modifications. . . . Plasticity is the mechanism for development and learning, as much as a cause of pathology and the cause of clinical disorders. Our challenge is to modulate neural plasticity for optimal behavioral gain, which is possible, for example, through behavioral modification and through invasive and non-invasive cortical stimulation. [17]

Again, the point is not to excuse criminal behavior. Rather, it is important that we understand the implications of neurodevelopmental impairments among criminal offenders, how they impact crime, and what we can do about it.

Poverty and Disadvantage

Poverty is an overarching condition that can lead to a number of crime-related problems. In addition to the neurodevelopmental consequences associated with poverty and violence, disadvantage often results in poorer educational outcomes, income and employment problems, and marital/relationship instability, among others. In effect, poverty limits options, alternatives, and opportunities to such an extent that we celebrate those seemingly rare success stories of someone overcoming the barriers to achievement and success by climbing out of poverty or turning their life around after growing up in poverty, going to prison, and then becoming a productive citizen. We celebrate these because they are the exception. Given the potential real or perceived lack of options and alternatives due to poverty, it is one of the conditions that may make crime seem like a rational response to one's circumstances.

Short of reducing poverty, something we as a nation have not been able to accomplish despite occasional efforts, justice policy should identify the various ways in which poverty and its effects are implicated in crime and recidivism. In turn, a critical first step is prioritizing the mitigation of these crime-related impacts of poverty for those individuals who end up in the justice system. This is essential in order to accomplish the near-term goal of reducing recidivism. Broader concerns with eradicating poverty are another matter, which is beyond the scope of this book and which I do not discuss here.

Education

Limited educational achievement is strongly linked to crime and recidivism. The numbers tell the story. Today, over 80 percent of U.S. secondary students graduate from high school; however, the majority of inmates in America's prisons and jails did not complete high school. Two-thirds of state prison inmates, 70 percent of local jail inmates, and over one-half of federal prison inmates dropped out before completion of high school. School dropouts are between four and six times more likely than high school graduates to be arrested. Poor education seems to be a consistent pipeline to the justice system. On the other hand, more total years of education, higher high school grade point average, regular school attendance, and graduating from high school all reduce the likelihood of engaging in criminal activity. And education is fundamentally related to returning to the justice system. Research indicates a significant reduction in reoffending linked to participating in correctional education programs, such as obtaining a general equivalency diploma (GED). Inmates who participate in prison-based education programs reduce the likelihood of returning to prison by 43 percent and increase the probability of post-release employment by 13 percent. Unfortunately, the data also show that a very small percent of prison inmates participate in such programs (under one in five participate in GED/high school programs, and, of course, this says nothing about completion of these programs).

How does academic achievement translate into a reduced probability of criminal involvement? In microeconomic terms, education increases the opportunity costs of committing crime, in effect putting more at risk or having more to lose, including the investment in education and the opportunities and options education provides. Individuals with a high school degree and beyond have higher incomes through legitimate/legal work, reducing the perceived need to engage in crime. Moreover, the stigma and shame associated with arrest and conviction likely serve as a disincentive to crime for better-educated professional workers (again, having more to lose).

The current state of public education in the United States contributes to the undereducation problem. Standardized tests show that at best, one-third of eighth graders are proficient in math, science, and reading. The United States ranks forty-eighth in math and science proficiency out of 133 developed and developing nations. The Program for International Student Assessment tests high school kids in a variety of countries.[18] Recent results indicate that U.S. kids are behind sixteen other nations in the ability to read and integrate material. Student proficiency in math is even lower. The Center on Education Policy determined that students in 48 percent of public schools (amounting to forty-four thousand schools) failed to make adequate progress last year. Florida led the way, with 91 percent of its schools on the failing list, followed by the District of Columbia (87 percent), New Mexico (86 percent), and Massachusetts (82 percent).

The problems with U.S. public education are not uniformly distributed across cities and schools. Experts note the presence of two different public school systems: those in the wealthier, suburban neighborhoods and those in the poorer, minority-dominated inner-city areas. While the experts generally concur that the schools in the wealthier, suburban areas are mediocre and require improvement, those in the inner-city, poorer minority areas are in a full-blown crisis. While 83 percent of white students graduate from high school, only 55 percent of African American students and 57 percent of Hispanic students do so. In urban schools, the graduation rate is just over one-half; in particularly troubled urban districts like Detroit and Indianapolis, the graduation rates are 25 percent and 31 percent, respectively. [19] So there are clear disparities in graduation outcomes. There are also performance-based concerns. Among African American students who do graduate, 11 percent are proficient in math and 13 percent are proficient in reading. Hispanic students do not perform any better; one in six Hispanic graduates are proficient in math and only 4 percent are proficient in reading. [20] On top of all of these troubling numbers is the fact that this is not news. These problems have been well known for decades.

There is plenty of finger-pointing about where the problems are and where the fault lies. Most point to the schools and the seemingly one-size-fits-all approach. Others suggest that public schools lack accountability. Still others focus on schools' zero tolerance and readiness to suspend and expel students, simply passing behavioral and disciplinary problems on to someone else rather than dealing with them. Evidence shows that those students who are suspended are twice as likely to drop out as those who are not. No Child Left Behind (NCLB) was also criticized as part of the problem, with a relentless focus on test scores and teaching the test. In the aftermath of NCLB, President Obama signed the Every Student Succeeds Act (ESSA) into law in December 2015, effectively eliminating No Child Left Behind. It is too soon to tell what the impact will be on the administration of public education. Standardized testing is still required under the ESSA; however, local districts have more autonomy and discretion in addressing underperforming schools.

Some suggest that better teachers are better able to pick and choose where they teach, resulting in less qualified teachers being relegated to the worse schools. This is aggravated by the fact that most schools have no control over teacher salaries and raises. These tend to be set at the state or district level and are generally independent of teacher performance. Thus, there is not as much incentive as there could be to motivate improvement.

What would public education look like if we did not have private schools? This is a totally hypothetical question, but the logic is simple: If the folks who send their kids to private schools had to rely on public education, chances are they would put sufficient pressure on school systems, elected officials, and policy makers to turn public education around.

That, however, is not the case. Unfortunately, many urban school systems are constrained by eroding tax bases and competition with things like infrastructure, transportation, and criminal justice for local funding.

It is no coincidence that public schools are failing those segments of the population that tend to populate the justice system. Lack of education has significant implications for employment and one's ability to make money in legitimate ways. Once again, for a variety of reasons, we seem content to let the justice system clean up the mess of a failing public education system. But just as is the case with public substance abuse and mental health treatment, it certainly is neither more effective nor cheaper to let the criminal justice system try to fix these problems. California spends $216,000 annually on each inmate in the juvenile justice system. In contrast, it spends only $8,000 on each child attending the problematic Oakland public school system, where the 2011 dropout rate was 37 percent, compared to 18 percent statewide.[21] In Oklahoma, the average annual spending per pupil in public education is $7,587. Oklahoma spends over $56,500 annually per person just to incarcerate juvenile offenders. Louisiana spends nearly $11,000 per public school student annually but $141,000 per person to incarcerate juvenile offenders. The troubling reality is that both institutions—public education and criminal justice—have unacceptably high failure rates. The failure of public education is measured in terms of dropout rates and proficiency metrics, and the justice system in terms of recidivism.

Employment

Unemployment and underemployment are important crime-related circumstances. Recent research shows that while just over two-thirds of prison inmates had a job at arrest, most of them worked jobs in the construction, maintenance, cleaning, automotive, and food service industries. The median hourly wage (as of 2005) was $9. One-third of inmates also relied on illegal income and family for financial support prior to incarceration.[22]

The evidence supports the conventional wisdom—employment, especially stable employment, reduces initiation of crime and subsequent recidivism. So does participation in correctional employment programming. However, the reality is that upon release from incarceration, there are substantial barriers to offenders obtaining a job. Most inmates (70 percent) included in a post-release survey felt that their criminal record affected their ability to find a job. Two months after release, 43 percent had been employed since leaving prison, but only 31 percent were employed at the time of the survey, and only one-quarter were employed full time.[23] This is important since employment after release from prison reduces recidivism by between ten and twenty percentage points compared to not working.[24]

Homelessness

Homelessness is a significant problem in American society and has worsened as a consequence of the recession that began in 2008 and the wave of real estate foreclosures that accompanied it. It is estimated that the foreclosures of rental properties added over 310,000 individuals and families to the homeless population in the United States.[25] For a variety of reasons, we have collectively been unable to effectively address homelessness and its root causes. Clearly, a lack of affordable housing and economic circumstance play very important roles, as do substance abuse, mental illness, and involvement with the justice system. A 2009 report by the National Law Center on Homelessness and Poverty and the National Coalition for the Homeless details what is called the criminalization of homelessness, whereby, just as is the case with mental illness, the justice system is used to manage the homelessness problem.

Homelessness is a common gateway into the justice system, as well as a primary risk factor for recidivism. The incidence of homelessness among prison inmates in state and federal prisons (meaning homeless one year before their incarceration) is four to six times that of the general population. They are also more likely to have had prior criminal justice involvement, to suffer from mental illness and/or substance abuse, and to have been unemployed or employed with a low income.[26]

Many individuals returning to the free world initially live with family; however, these living arrangements are often only temporary. Offenders released from prison face a variety of challenges, including a shortage of affordable housing and the inability to rent housing because of their criminal record. This is, in one sense, very understandable. It is not hard to see why a landlord would not want to rent to someone with a criminal conviction. However, we also know that being homeless is a significant predictor of returning to prison compared to those with stable housing. And the problem can be substantial; one study of California parolees shows that between 30 percent and 50 percent of individuals paroled to urban areas such as San Francisco and Los Angeles are homeless at any given time.[27] Other primary crime-related conditions, such as substance abuse, mental illness, and poverty, increase the risk of homelessness and the risk of recidivism. It should not be surprising that these conditions tend to co-occur, which exacerbates the situation and the risk for justice involvement. For example, the co-occurrence of mental illness and homelessness or substance abuse and poverty and homelessness serves to aggravate the other conditions that are present.

The American justice system consists of a series of handoffs, where the individual is passed off from one agency or set of individuals to another. No one is in charge of the bigger picture and no one is accountable for the longer-term outcomes. We have had one strategy, and it is clear that it has not worked. It is now time to implement a new approach, one that is focused on changing behavior through scientifically validated methods. It is also time for the key individuals involved in the administration of the justice system to change how they think about crime, criminals, punishment, and human behavior and to accept and share responsibility for the outcomes of this system.

CHANGING CRIMINAL BEHAVIOR

These days it seems that we take notice of the success story of an offender who emerges from the American criminal justice system and not only doesn't go back but also goes on to do something productive with his life. There will be the occasional profile piece in a newspaper or a magazine detailing the circumstances of the individual who overcomes difficult odds to become a conforming and productive member of society. Take, for example, the *Huffington Post* article about Rudy Holder, an African American man from Harlem who served twelve years in prison.[28] Holder was a small kid who stuttered. He was often ridiculed and bullied in his childhood. That led to anger and fighting, which escalated to gun violence. He was incarcerated for shooting several individuals at a party after getting into a fight with them. Nothing remarkable in this story. He was paroled back to the East Harlem neighborhood where he used to get into trouble, back to the circumstances of his youth, back to the friends and enemies he had before he went to prison. What is remarkable is that he did not get into trouble again. We catch up with him ten years after he was released from prison. He is working at a nonprofit called Exodus Transitional Community, which is a local facility that assists released offenders to reintegrate into the community. He arrived there just days after his release and has been there ever since, crime free and helping other released offenders go straight.

So why is Rudy Holder's story newsworthy? Because it is the exception. It is the exception because Rudy Holder's experience is not what the American justice system is designed to produce. It is not what we typically see. Rudy Holder was able to turn his life around despite overwhelming odds, many of which are created by the very system that is supposed to promote public safety. I'm not saying that the Rudy Holders of the world are not responsible for their behavior. There should be consequences for criminal behavior. I'm not saying we should feel sorry for criminal offenders. But the goal here should be to get criminal offenders to stop offending.

How can we forge a system that does not needlessly put us at risk of being crime victims? How can we design a system that actually reduces the likelihood of returning time and time again? What does a justice system that is both effective and cost-efficient look like? There are smart, effective ways to do this. That is what the rest of this book is intended to address. In these pages, we first take a look at what we know about the tools for effective behavior change for criminal offenders. Make no mistake, this is not the silver bullet. There will be many, many failures. There will be individuals for whom these tools are not enough, offenders for whom these do not work. There will be individuals we simply do not want to change because they do things we consider unredeemable or because they are simply evil. Some will be chronic, habitual offenders who are unchangeable or others who clinicians determine cannot be changed. For those offenders who are too dangerous, too far gone, or relentlessly uninterested in change, we have incarceration. For the rest, we have these tools, and as we apply these tools and assess how we do, we will get better. It is time to bring science and reason to the table.

What we are about to discuss is not really new. We have known for about twenty years that punishment is unproductive for lowering crime and recidivism, and we have known equally long how to effectively change offender behavior. Over time, the information has gotten better, and we have greater clarity regarding how to go about reducing recidivism. Here, very briefly, is what we know.

The Evidence for Behavior Change

Roughly twenty-five years ago a group of Canadian researchers began compiling evidence of what they call the principles of effective correctional rehabilitation or intervention. The evidence came from a wide variety of correctional programs and interventions designed to change offender behavior. What the results indicate is that following some rather basic principles can reduce recidivism dramatically, by as much as 40–50 percent.[29] The results vary dramatically depending on a number of factors, but under the right circumstances, the tools we now know to be effective can have a fundamental impact on recidivism.

The basic principles are not revolutionary. They include accurately screening and assessing offenders to determine the overall risk of reoffending as well as identifying the primary crime-related deficits, impairments, and problems. This is essentially triage at a trauma unit—what's wrong and how serious is it. There is a risk principle, which indicates that the best use of intervention resources is for higher-risk offenders (again, like in the emergency room, take the most serious cases first).

So diagnose, triage by risk, and then develop a "treatment plan" by determining which deficits, impairments, circumstances, and problems shall be addressed and in what order. One of the major faults of the efforts at rehabilitation we do undertake is that they tend to focus on just one problem or deficit. It is a relatively rare circumstance that an offender presents with only one crime-related circumstance. The research is clear that addressing all primary issues dramatically reduces recidivism. The treatment plan should also identify the appropriate dosage of treatment. This should be a clinical decision that depends on the needs of the offender. One size does not fit all. Too little or too much is ineffective and wasteful of resources.

Next, assess the treatment readiness (willingness) of the individual, and then motivate the offender to participate in programming as needed. There are well-established techniques for assessing treatment readiness and enhancing treatment motivation. It is a waste of resources to treat someone who is not ready and willing, but we do it frequently today when judges order offenders to treatment, and then we wonder why it failed.

The treatment plan should also consider characteristics of the offender in determining which programs he or she shall be assigned. For example, individuals differ by learning style, language, cognitive ability, gender, temperament, and cultural background. The research shows that by carefully matching individuals to programs we can significantly enhance success. Treatment should also be integrated into the sentence/sanction as one component of several, but treatment/intervention should not be cast as punishment.

Interventions should use cognitive-behavioral therapy (CBT). CBT is the recognized best practice for a wide variety of psychotherapeutic treatments on a wide variety of individuals. It involves focusing on problems with cognitive functioning as well as behavioral problems and aims to alter problematic emotions, cognitions, and behaviors through a goal-oriented therapeutic procedure.

Successful interventions also require incentives, not just sanctions. The optimal mix for offender behavior change is roughly four positive reinforcements (rewards or incentives) for every one negative reinforcement (sanctions or punishments). Rehabilitation efforts should also engage prosocial support for offenders in the community in which they reside. These supports serve to reinforce new behaviors acquired from correctional CBT interventions.

These principles are not particularly new to psychotherapy or the practice of behavioral change. Many of these are long-standing, evidence-based practices in medicine—triage, diagnosis, develop a treatment plan with the correct interventions and therapies for all primary/significant disorders with the proper dosages in an appropriate setting. We engage in the proper treatment for individuals who are sick because of ethical considerations and because of a genuine desire for people to get better. That is, in fact, the mission of medicine. That has not been the mission of the American justice system. We tend to think differently about the individuals who harm others through their criminal acts. We have thought that punishment was both what they deserved and what would correct them. We may still believe that punishment is what they deserve, but the jury is back regarding punishment correcting them. Whether we like it or not, the reality is that with many criminal offenders, heading more in the direction of public health will do substantially more to reduce crime, recidivism, victimization, and cost than punishment only.

And the public seems to agree. There is widespread public support for reform. A national public opinion poll of registered voters conducted eight years ago revealed strong support for rehabilitation.

> By almost an 8 to 1 margin (87% to 11%), the U.S. voting public is in favor of rehabilitative services for prisoners as opposed to a punishment-only system. Of those polled, 70% favored services both during incarceration and after release from prison.[30]

A more recent 2014 Massachusetts poll shows that respondents are very supportive of diversion from prison, rehabilitation, drug treatment, and mental health treatment.

> Nearly two-thirds (64 percent) think the criminal justice system should prioritize crime prevention or rehabilitation. This and other findings from this poll are consistent with national and state polls by the Pew Center for the States, in which majorities favored shifting resources from incarceration towards alternatives.[31]

Many things must change in order to comprehensively implement these principles on a scale that produces noticeable reductions in recidivism. There will need to be changes to statute and procedure, especially prosecution, as well as sentences and the sentencing process. We will need to get substantially better at decision making, which will require much greater use of more extensive information by experts in behavioral and clinical matters. Obviously, funding is a huge issue. In simple terms, this involves, in part, a transfer of funding from incarceration to locally based treatment and intervention programming. As we rethink how we should use incarceration (violent, chronic, untreatable offenders, for example), the incarcerated population will decline, as will the funding requirements for prisons. Some of that saved revenue should be redirected to treatment and rehabilitation programming. As local jurisdictions are able to implement effective probation programming—for example, resulting in recidivism reductions and savings to prison systems—they should receive additional performance-based funding as a result of avoided revocations to prison. The reorientation of the business of American criminal justice will also require significant changes in personnel and resources. These changes are considerably challenging, but equally difficult is the required shift in thinking about crime and punishment and the culture of American criminal justice. These issues will be discussed in subsequent chapters.

4

DIVERSION FROM TRADITIONAL CRIMINAL PROSECUTION AND PUNISHMENT

Traditional criminal prosecution and sentencing is designed and operated primarily for one purpose—criminal conviction and punishment. But envision another path, one that focuses on rehabilitation, intervention, and behavior change. Diversion is based on the idea of going about the business of criminal justice in a different way, by actually removing or diverting selected offenders from traditional criminal prosecution and punishment and placing them in an alternative setting. The concept of diversion is based on a balance of public safety, meaning accountability, supervision, and compliance, on the one hand, and rehabilitation and behavior change, on the other. Diversion programs tend to be problem based, meaning they identify particular crime-related circumstances (substance abuse, mental illness, neurodevelopmental problems, employment, education, etc.) and then divert eligible offenders to services in order to address the problems. Diversion programs typically provide rehabilitative interventions in a community setting rather than in prison or jail. The research is clear that interventions that occur in the community are considerably more effective than attempting to rehabilitate individuals in custody.

Before we begin, it might be helpful to understand the traditional criminal processing of individuals in the justice system. It begins with a crime being committed. Once law enforcement know about a crime, they respond, conduct an investigation, and gather evidence. When there is sufficient evidence (that is, when there is probable cause), the police will make an arrest. If the offense is a felony, it is routine to admit (that is, book) the suspect in jail. This is, in theory, short-term detention. Relatively shortly thereafter, the individual is brought before a judge or magistrate for what is called a *preliminary hearing, initial hearing, first appearance*, or *magistration*. The primary purpose of this hearing is to determine detention status—whether the individual should be detained pending case processing or released. If the decision is release, the court will set the terms of release (typically, a bond amount). The case will be transferred to the prosecutor's office, where it will be screened to determine whether there is sufficient evidence to prosecute. If so, the case will be carried forward for prosecution, where the charges will be determined. At some point, the case will be brought for indictment either by a prosecutor or by a grand jury. The grand jury's role is to evaluate the evidence and determine whether it is sufficient for formal charging and prosecution.[1] Once a case is indicted, it is then set for adjudication (a finding of guilt or innocence). The vast majority of all felony cases that are indicted result in a conviction. And the vast majority of those convictions are achieved by a negotiated plea. Approximately 90 percent to 95 percent of all felony indictments are resolved through a plea deal, where the government typically offers the offender a lesser punishment in exchange for the defendant waiving the right to trial and/or providing evidence to the government about this crime or another. A handful of cases go to trial, where about 75 percent result in a conviction. The final stage of this process is a separate proceeding called a *sentencing hearing*, where the court will hear evidence and then determine the appropriate punishment or sanction. This process is similar in many important respects for misdemeanor cases.

Diversion can occur at multiple points during the typical processing of felony and misdemeanor cases. Regardless of where it occurs, the common elements include removing the individual from traditional criminal prosecution and punishment and balancing supervision and risk management with treatment and rehabilitative strategies intended to address the individual's crime-related problems and, in turn, reduce recidivism. We begin with what is called pre-booking diversion.

PRE-ARREST OR PRE-BOOKING DIVERSION

Pre-arrest or pre-booking diversion is an opportunity for law enforcement to exercise street-level discretion for dealing with incidents involving offenders who are mentally ill. Pre-booking diversion of mentally ill offenders, as the name implies, diverts individuals from jail at the very front end. It typically involves and requires strong, collaborative partnerships with local mental health and substance abuse service providers. The concept of pre-arrest or pre-booking diversion was the result of a perceived revolving door of mentally ill individuals cycling in and out of the justice system. The Memphis, Tennessee, police department (PD) is credited with initiating the idea of training officers to handle situations involving mentally ill individuals. The Memphis PD created special police units called crisis intervention teams (CITs). The CIT model is now in use in over twenty-seven thousand communities in forty states.[2] The point is that rather than arresting mentally ill individuals and putting them into jail, where they likely would further decompensate, the CIT model diverts appropriate cases to local mental health treatment providers. A similar model, called the coresponder model, pairs mental health professionals with police in order to respond together to mental health situations and divert individuals to treatment when appropriate.

The evidence indicates that the CIT and coresponder models are quite effective in reducing officer injuries and avoiding inappropriate arrest and jailing of mentally ill individuals. Pre-arrest diversion is an opportunity to reduce the flow of mentally ill into the justice system and increase the flow to local, community-based mental health treatment. Clearly, the success of these types of efforts depends on a number of factors, including the availability of local treatment capacity for effectively addressing not only a mental health crisis but also longer-term treatment and maintenance. Lack of treatment capacity is a substantial problem. However, the Affordable Care Act (ACA) requires coverage and resources for mental health treatment at parity with medical services. This is a very important step in the direction of true mental health treatment in the United States. The ACA may signal the beginning of alternatives to mental health treatment in the community rather than in the justice system.

PRE-TRIAL DIVERSION

Pre-trial diversion is an alternative to criminal prosecution. This type of diversion typically includes both felony and misdemeanor offenders who have limited prior criminal involvement and have been arrested for generally less serious, nonviolent offenses. The point is to avoid criminal adjudication and punishment in order to address behavioral health problems such as substance abuse and mental illness, as well as a variety of other issues or problems. In essence, the charges against the individual are put on hold when a defendant is referred to pre-trial diversion. Participants who successfully complete pre-trial diversion typically will have the charges dismissed and thus avoid a criminal conviction. In many cases, they can also legally remove (expunge) the arrest from their criminal record. Deferred prosecution and deferred adjudication are types of pre-trial diversion that involve holding off prosecuting the case while the defendant completes some treatment or rehabilitation as well as community service.

The Travis County (Austin), Texas, Felony Pretrial Diversion Program for Offenders is designed to divert those arrested for a variety of third- and fourth-degree felonies (lower-level felonies), including possession of a controlled substance, criminal mischief, theft, forgery, credit card abuse, graffiti, unauthorized use of a motor vehicle, and several other "white-collar" offenses. Pre-trial diversion programs impose a variety of conditions for successful completion, such as attending regular meetings with a supervision officer, completing community service, paying restitution to victims, submitting to drug screening, and attending required substance abuse, mental health, literacy, and GED programs; individual and family counseling; parenting classes; and so forth.

Pre-trial diversion is designed to reduce the burden on the justice system, decrease recidivism by addressing the reasons for criminal involvement, and increase restitution paid to victims and communities. The evidence indicates that these programs have positive benefits for the justice system (reduction in caseloads, lower recidivism, more cost-effective) and participants (better behavioral health outcomes, less time incarcerated, lower reoffending rates, and avoiding a criminal conviction). Limitations of these programs include scale (they tend not to involve large numbers of offenders, so the impacts, while productive, are not large). A 2010 survey found that there were nearly three hundred pre-trial diversion programs operating in the United States.[3] Another 2009 survey reported that the median annual budget for pre-trial diversion programs is $160,000. The average number of diversion placements is 150.[4] Another limitation of pre-trial diversion programs is the fact that they are limited to lower-level, limited-frequency offenders. At the same time, it is important for there to be options for lower-risk offenders so that we have an opportunity to prevent them from becoming high-risk, serious offenders. The success of pre-trial diversion is also largely dependent on the availability of treatment resources. This has been a serious limitation in the past, but again, the ACA can help mitigate that in terms of substance abuse and mental health treatment.

Pre-arrest, pre-booking, and pre-trial diversion all appear to provide important opportunities for intervention while minimizing exposure to detention in jail and the negative consequences that often result from incarceration. These forms of diversion tend to focus on particularly vulnerable segments of the justice population with mental health and substance abuse problems. The good news is that evaluations of these forms of diversion show that they can be effective means for providing important services to offenders, managing offenders' risk while in the community, and reducing recidivism. The bad news is the extremely limited prevalence of such programs and the very limited capacity where they do exist.

PROBATION OR COMMUNITY SUPERVISION

The most common form of diversion is probation, which is a post-conviction criminal sentence. It is defined as conditional release to the community under supervision in lieu of incarceration. Probation applies to both felons and misdemeanants. Both felony and misdemeanor probationers are subject to revocation to prison or jail if they violate the conditions of release. Deferred adjudication and deferred prosecution are also forms of conditional, supervised release to the community but differ from probation in that they occur prior to a conviction. Thus, they are forms of pre-trial diversion.

The idea behind probation is to provide an appropriate setting (the community) for engaging in programs and services to change offender behavior. Unfortunately, the reality is that these forms of community supervision have not effectively accomplished the goal of offender change and recidivism reduction, in part because probation departments are overwhelmed with offenders and underresourced in terms of programs and services and in part because much of the focus of the justice system has been on supervision and control rather than behavior change. We will discuss probation in more detail in chapter 6.

We now turn to an increasingly popular form of diversion—problem-solving diversion courts.

PROBLEM-SOLVING COURTS

Melissa S. started abusing drugs at the age of fourteen when she first tried heroin. She became addicted to pills, marijuana, and heroin and used these on a regular basis for fifteen years. She was eventually admitted to the Clark County (Indiana) Drug Court, where she was able to detoxify and enter treatment. After a period of sobriety, she was reunited with her two sons, who were two years and six months old. Melissa has remained sober, found stable employment, and was able to rent a townhouse for herself and her children.

The Eau Claire (Wisconsin) Drug Court personnel called Rick a "frequent flyer" due to his thirty-three criminal convictions and four years in jail. Most of his criminal activity was directly related to his substance abuse, which began at age thirteen with alcohol; he added marijuana at age fifteen. By the time he entered the drug court after his ninth OWI (operating a vehicle while intoxicated) offense, he had not been sober for over twenty-five years. Rather than the three-year prison sentence he was facing, the judge sentenced him to probation with the condition that he successfully complete drug and alcohol treatment in the drug court. Not only did Rick get sober, but he has not reoffended since his May 2005 sobriety date and has gained custody of his thirteen-year-old daughter. The drug court judge stated, "Rick is a loving father and does a great job with his grandchildren as well. His children trust him to care for the family. Before drug court, that would never have happened."[5]

Drug courts are the original form of diversion-based problem-solving courts in the United States. The first was launched in 1989 in Dade County (Miami), Florida. It was a product of frustration due to the failure of traditional criminal prosecution and punishment to interrupt the cycle of drug offending. The same people kept parading through the Dade County criminal courts on drug charges, and nothing was changing. The idea was simple: create a new way of doing business for the drug-abusing, addicted segment of the offender population. The point was that punishment does nothing to address substance abuse and addiction. There is nothing therapeutic about incarceration. Contrary to much conventional wisdom, abstinence is not the same as treatment. So a handful of individuals in Miami raised the white flag and experimented. The goal was to balance public safety (accountability, supervision, and compliance) with therapeutic intervention. Drug courts are, as the name implies, courts. There are judges and prosecutors, but there are also clinicians, case managers, and social workers. There are defense lawyers as well, but the environment typically is not adversarial.

Drug courts have been immensely popular. There are roughly three thousand in the United States today in nearly 50 percent of the counties in the nation. They come in a variety of forms and sizes. The examples of Melissa and Rick are both success stories, but, obviously, not all of those who enter drug courts have such positive outcomes. There is a fair amount of variation among drug courts. At the end of the day, however, the research indicates that the drug court model is effective. In fact, today researchers can tell us not only that drug courts can reduce drug use by 35 percent, and recidivism by 35 percent and more, but also what particular components of drug courts are more and less important in reducing recidivism. In effect, we have the tools to build drug courts to maximize the reduction in recidivism and relapse. [6]

The good news is that there is a viable alternative to traditional criminal prosecution and punishment for individuals with substance abuse and addiction problems. The additional good news is that participation in drug court is cheaper than traditional punishment alternatives. The bad news is that drug courts are largely symbolic today since the total capacity of these courts is able to meet about 10 percent of the need. On the other hand, we may be on the brink of substantial change in the treatment of substance abuse problems among criminal offenders. As mentioned before, the ACA requires coverage for substance abuse treatment on parity with medical treatment. This should lead to increased treatment capacity and fewer financial barriers to treatment entry as long as the ACA is law.

While drug courts are by far the most common, other problem-solving diversion courts are designed to address a variety of different behaviors, problems, and situations. Community courts address petty offending like public intoxication, aggressive panhandling, and camping in public. Mental health courts are designed to divert mentally ill individuals from the justice system to community-based treatment. Veterans courts provide assistance to veterans who end up in the justice system, focusing primarily on mental health and substance abuse problems. DWI (driving while intoxicated) courts, as the name implies, provide alcohol abuse treatment for DWI offenders. Domestic violence courts are for individuals who engage in violence against significant others and family. Homeless courts are for assisting the chronically homeless; gambling courts are for those who get into trouble because of gambling, Fathering courts are designed to assist males who have problems paying child support. And then there are many juvenile courts that focus on particular problems associated with juvenile crime and delinquency, problems such as drugs, alcohol, mental health, and truancy.

Well-designed and well-operated problem-solving courts share several common elements, including relying on individuals with a range of expertise in behavioral change, partnerships with a variety of local treatment and social service resources, accurate screening and assessment, case management, and a judge who understands the complexity of crime and crime-related circumstances.

A relatively new version of a problem-solving court is called a swift and certain sanction court. The prototype was developed in Hawaii in 2004 and is called the HOPE court (Hawaii's Opportunity Probation with Enforcement). The HOPE court was designed to increase accountability and compliance among probationers who are in drug treatment. The method is really quite simple. Rather than relying on the severity of punishment, this approach maximizes the certainty and swiftness of modest punishment to enhance compliance. The evaluation research indicates that while severe punishment has very limited behavior-altering effects, swift and certain but modest punishment—a night or two in jail—can be quite effective in getting individuals who violate the conditions of probation to follow the rules. The evaluations to date of the HOPE court and HOPE-type courts show rather dramatic reductions in violations and recidivism and significant increases in program compliance. The HOPE court concept has mainly been applied to a variety of offenders on probation. It is quite reasonable to expand this concept to pre-trial diversion offenders as a tool to enhance compliance and manage the risk of reoffending. Today there are at least sixty jurisdictions in over eighteen states that have HOPE court–based swift and certain sanctioning courts for probationers.

DIVERSION GOING FORWARD

The evidence is pretty clear. We have the tools to effectively reduce recidivism and substantially interrupt the cycle of reoffending for many, many criminal offenders. The evidence tells us that the optimal opportunity for changing criminals' behavior is in a noninstitutional setting. Diversion provides such an opportunity where behavioral-change interventions can be implemented. At the same time, public safety, accountability, and compliance can be effectively managed, and the negative collateral impacts of a criminal conviction and punishment can be avoided.

Drug courts have served as a model for the development of a variety of problem-solving diversion courts designed to address other crime-related circumstances. Given what we currently know and what is being discovered on an ongoing basis regarding the role of neurodevelopmental and neurocognitive impairments in criminal offending, it is important that we investigate the role that problem-solving courts can play in mitigating that link to criminality. To my knowledge, there are no problem-solving courts that focus on neurobiological concerns in any systematic, comprehensive way. The evidence clearly suggests that this could be a very effective path to pursue.

The evidence also clearly indicates that swift and certain sanctioning is a very useful tool for enhancing accountability and compliance among offenders in the community. Current and future diversion programs and problem-solving courts should include swift and certain sanctioning components in a form that preserves the evidence-based elements of sanctioning but is compatible with the design and operation of programming. By that, I mean that swift and certain sanctioning need not necessarily operate as a stand-alone court but may effectively function integrated into a problem-solving court as a special docket.

While diversion programs can and do successively reduce recidivism and manage risk and public safety, they do not currently exist on a large-enough scale to significantly impact recidivism and crime. State legislatures and local officials should expand the eligibility criteria to a larger number and a wider variety of relatively low-risk, nonviolent offenders. There is no shortage of lower-risk felony and misdemeanor offenders with substance abuse and mental health problems who could benefit from services provided in the context of pre-conviction diversion as well as post-conviction probation. This will require increasing the capacity of local mental health and substance abuse service providers, as well as providing services for other significant problems and deficits that are related to criminal offending. Ramping up pre-trial diversion will also require adding staff to pre-trial agencies that are responsible for managing offenders under their control, including increases in supervision officers to monitor offenders on pre-trial release. It will also require increasing public funding to support providing these services. Beyond that, there should be a shift in decision making away from punishment being the first choice to more of a public health perspective, where diversion and behavior change are the priority. There should also be a change in thinking and a change in culture, especially among prosecutors, since they tend to make the key decisions and recommendations about diversion.

All of this is premised on appropriately diverting offenders from traditional prosecution and punishment, which in turn requires the ability to make good decisions about who gets diverted and who goes down the traditional path. Going forward, decision making must be more deliberate and better informed. As local jurisdictions expand the number and types of offenders who are eligible for diversion, the decision-making process regarding who will be diverted must involve a variety of experts who can assist and add value to the process. It is important to emphasize that we need to get better at screening and assessing crime-related problems and deficits as well as risk, and we need to determine the level of motivation for treatment and make appropriate adjustments when a diverted offender is not treatment ready. The decision-making process should involve legal expertise as well as clinical expertise (psychological, neurological, psychiatric, medical, etc.). We would not want a hospital administrator diagnosing what is wrong with us when we walk into the emergency department. Why would we want a judge or a prosecutor doing that for a criminal offender?

Offenders more often than not need help overcoming many of the factors that are related to their crimes. Sitting in prison while contemplating their bad deeds as the path to reform may be fine in theory and makes great black-and-white, 1940s redemption movies. However, in practice, it simply does not work. The sooner we accept this, the sooner we can move forward in reducing crime, recidivism, victimization, and cost.

5

CHANGING PROSECUTION AND SENTENCING

In 1996, Timothy Jackson shoplifted a jacket worth $160 from a department store in New Orleans. At the time of his arrest, Jackson was thirty-six, had a sixth-grade education, and worked as a cook in a restaurant. His crime would normally have resulted in a two-year sentence of incarceration. However, because the prosecutor pushed it, the court imposed a mandatory life without parole sentence based on Louisiana's four-strikes law. To justify the mandatory sentence, the prosecutor used prior convictions from when Jackson was a juvenile—two car burglary convictions and an unarmed robbery conviction.[1]

A first-time offender, Robert Booker was convicted of operating a crack house and sentenced to life without parole. At trial, Judge Terence Evans initially sentenced Booker to twenty years. That sentence could have been enhanced if the judge had concurred with the prosecutor's assertion that Booker used a gun during the commission of the crimes. He was acquitted at trial of the gun charge, but the prosecutor tried to persuade the court to aggravate the sentence based on the gun allegation. The prosecutor appealed the sentence, and it was increased to thirty years. Still not satisfied, the prosecutor appealed again, and before a different judge, Booker was resentenced to life without parole. The original judge, Judge Evans, stated:

> The unfairness of a life sentence without parole for Mr. Booker will be
> a grossly unjust result. [T]he prosecutor wants to lock up Booker and

throw the key away forever. Even bad apples should be treated with some semblance of fairness.[2]

A similar case, that of Tony Allen Gregg, elicited the following response from Judge Andre Davis:

I have never met Tony Allen Gregg, a drug abuser and occasional dealer, a 10th-grade dropout and petty criminal. But the details of Mr. Gregg's life—and the life sentence he is now serving—highlight a major problem in our criminal justice system: mandatory minimum sentencing, an offshoot of our misguided "war on drugs." Federal mandatory minimums, created by an overzealous Congress 25 years ago, require harsh sentences for nonviolent offenders. Such laws do a disservice to the people accused of the crimes, to the judges before whom their cases are reviewed, to communities that are largely poor and black or Latino, and to society. These laws have inappropriately shifted sentencing authority to prosecutors through their charging decisions, impeding judges from considering mitigating factors that would help impose fair and just sentences. They essentially strip away the discretion that judges traditionally employ in sentencing drug offenders, particularly low-level offenders.[3]

All three of these examples serve to illustrate one of the prominent features of the American criminal justice system: prosecutors are the key decision makers and exercise the most power, influence, and discretion in America's justice system.

PROSECUTORIAL DISCRETION AND TOUGH ON CRIME

Discretion is widespread in the American justice system. Police exercise discretion on the street in deciding whether a crime has occurred, who to arrest, and what to charge them with. In effect, police control the front door of the justice system, but the amount of discretion regarding who goes in that door is relatively limited. If the evidence is there, the police will usually make the arrest. Judges exercise discretion, for example, in ruling on motions, in probation revocation decisions, in controlling their dockets, in assigning counsel for indigent defendants, and in sentencing, depending on how much latitude the law provides. Corrections agents exercise discretion in many ways, including enforcing supervision conditions and initiating revocation of probation or parole, filing a disciplinary report for someone who violates prison or jail rules, determining custody level and conditions of incarceration, and deciding whether to grant parole release. While these examples illustrate a good bit of discretion on the part of police, judges, and corrections officers, prosecutors, the lawyers who represent the state or federal government in criminal prosecutions, have the greatest amount of discretion.

This has not always been the case. It is largely the product of a variety of changes to criminal sentencing, changes that parallel the evolution and growth of tough on crime. As discussed in chapter 1, sentencing reform was a response to the perceived unfairness and inequity resulting from sentencing laws that provided judges wide latitude in assessing sentences. Prior to 1975, essentially everyone who was sentenced in the United States, whether in state or federal court, was sentenced under what are called indeterminate sentencing laws. Indeterminate sentencing laws provide for broad ranges of punishment (for example, probation, five to ninety-nine years, twenty-five years to life, two to twenty years) from which the judge is to select what he or she believes is appropriate for a particular offender. It is designed in part to allow the court to sentence not only the offense but also the offender—that is, to consider the circumstances of the offense (amount of harm) as well as characteristics of the offender (for example, mental health, employment history, family situation). In so doing, indeterminate sentencing allows the judge to hear a considerable amount of aggravating (negative) and mitigating (positive) evidence about the crime and the offender. The judge is then permitted to weigh and evaluate that evidence and arrive at the sentence with whatever rationale and goals he or she sees fit. While the potential for bias and disparity in sentences was the prime public rationale for changing sentencing laws, there was also the often-articulated concern that when judges have so much latitude, they tend to be too lenient or soft on crime.

Sentencing reform led to a series of rather dramatic changes to state and federal sentencing laws. Some states implemented fixed or determinate sentences, where there is very little latitude. In effect, the sentences are prescribed by state legislatures, which write the sentencing laws and the sentences. Other states kept indeterminate sentences but implemented an extensive list of mandatory sentences, where the court has no discretion. The federal government implemented the federal sentencing guidelines, which are a highly contentious and punitive version of reform.

Regardless of how extensively states and the federal government changed their sentencing laws, the impact overall was profound. In particular, it directly and dramatically altered discretion over sentencing. Discretion does not evaporate. It is an ever-present characteristic of our legal system, where laws and procedures, due process, and constitutional protections form the structure or framework within which people make decisions. In the case of the American justice system, when sentencing laws were changed and, as a consequence, the discretion of judges was substantially limited, the influence and impact of prosecutorial decisions was dramatically magnified. When sentences tend to be fixed, when larger and larger numbers of offenders are sentenced under mandatory sentences, the decisions prosecutors make become that much more important. It is the prosecutor who decides who to prosecute. It is the prosecutor who decides with what to charge a defendant and what evidence to use to support that charge. It is the prosecutor who decides whether to count the current crime as a qualifying crime under a mandatory sentence. It is the prosecutor who determines the elements of a negotiated plea. Prosecutors routinely make sentence recommendations to the court. The discretion that judges used to exercise did not disappear but simply moved upstream to the prosecutor's office. As Paul Cassell, a former federal judge, puts it, "Judges have lost discretion, and that discretion has accumulated in the hands of prosecutors, who now have the ultimate ability to shape the outcome. With mandatory minimums and other sentencing enhancements out there, prosecutors can often dictate the sentence that will be imposed."[4]

The following example illustrates this concept well. A study conducted by the American Civil Liberties Union (ACLU) discovered that defendants in California were sentenced under the state's 1994 three-strikes law to twenty-five years to life for the following crimes: taking a small number of coins from a parked car, stealing a pair of socks, shoplifting nine children's videotapes to give as Christmas gifts, taking a jack from the back of a tow truck, forging a check for $146, stealing a pair of work gloves from a department store, taking a $100 leaf blower, stealing a slice of pizza, attempting to steal a car radio, shoplifting three golf clubs, shoplifting meat from a grocery store, stealing chocolate chip cookies from a restaurant, attempting to break into a soup kitchen for food, and possession of less than $10 worth of cocaine.[5] In each of these cases, the prosecutor had to make an affirmative finding of prior qualifying offenses as well as qualifying the current offense under the California statute.

There are a number of important implications here, but the one that is relevant at the moment is the fundamental role of the American prosecutor in carrying out the tough-on-crime agenda of the past forty years. Without prosecutors' alignment with tough-on-crime prosecution and sentencing, crime control could not have been accomplished.

As of September 2015, large numbers of policy makers and elected officials are at least skeptical about tough-on-crime incarceration policies, the size of our prison population, and mandatory sentences; many are advocates for their change. The public is equally concerned about the wisdom of American criminal justice policy. There is little appetite for remaining on the path of tough punishment and the expansion of incarceration. Unless one is a member of the National Association of Assistant U.S. Attorneys, which consists of federal prosecutors. They have taken the clear position that federal sentencing reform, particularly reducing or eliminating mandatory sentencing, would have dire consequences, including raising the crime rate. Steve Cook, the association's president, stated that it would be a huge mistake to change sentencing laws, predicting that in such a case, crime would increase. Cook went a step further and said that rather than considering changing sentencing, Congress should expand federal prisons: "Do I think it would be a good investment to build more [prisons]? Yeah, no question about it."[6]

Why have prosecutors been tough-on-crime champions over the course of America's punitive crime policies? Punishment is what prosecutors know. That is how they are socialized into their jobs. Moreover, prosecutors are the state's lawyers, litigators who represent the state's position and interests. The state's position and interests for much of the past forty-five years has largely been focused on punishment. Moreover, there have been few alternatives to the one-size-fits-all solution of punishment. As they say, when the only tool you have is a hammer, everything looks like a nail.

Prosecutors' caseloads are excessive, and whatever can move cases is viewed as productive. The current system of case processing based nearly exclusively on plea negotiation and punishment (about 95 percent of felony indictments are plea negotiated) seems to work in achieving case processing. There is probably a substantial amount of resistance to jeopardizing the efficiencies of the current approach to managing caseloads.

Politics has added substantially to the prosecutor's role as tough-on-crime advocate. District attorneys (DAs), the head prosecutors in local jurisdictions, are elected officials. As crime control and punishment became the centerpiece of American criminal justice policy, there was no better position for an individual running for DA than being tough on crime. Clearly, fair is important, but hard-nosed and tough with high conviction rates tends to resonate with the public. If anyone in the justice system can legitimately claim the tough-on-crime mantle, it is the prosecutor. Prosecutors are viewed as the protectors of the community who represent the public's preference and the state's priority—harsher punishment. The public got it and DAs leveraged it.

Occasionally, tough on crime can run riot and lead to or promote prosecutorial misconduct. A recent example illustrates this point well. Michael Morton's wife was murdered in Williamson County, Texas, in 1986. Morton was suspected of killing his wife and was subsequently arrested, indicted, convicted, and sentenced to prison, despite the fact that there were no witnesses to testify against him, no murder weapon, no credible motive, and no forensic evidence. Mr. Morton spent twenty-five years in prison before DNA evidence exonerated him. He was released from prison and was formally acquitted of the charge. Beyond being a wrongful conviction, this was an illegal conviction. The DA at the time, Ken Anderson, withheld exculpatory evidence from the defense—evidence that the prosecution was required to produce to the defendant. Evidence that exonerated Morton. Williamson County, Texas, has for decades had a well-earned reputation for being particularly tough on crime, which is no small feat, since it is already in, arguably, the toughest on crime state in the nation. Anderson eventually left the DA's office and was elected to the district court in Williamson County. When the investigation in the Morton case unfolded, it was clear that Anderson had broken the law. Anderson's protégé, John Bradley, fought DNA testing in the case for six years until it was eventually ordered by a judge. Anderson was subsequently found in criminal contempt of court, fined $500, ordered to perform five hundred hours of community service, and sentenced to ten days in jail. He served five days. He resigned from the bench and surrendered his law license.

There are many examples of prosecutorial error or misconduct that lead to wrongful or questionable convictions. In some cases, these are mistakes. As we discuss below, prosecutors have enormous caseloads. In turn, the pressure to move cases is a major source of prosecutor error. In others, the pressure to convict and be perceived as tough on crime can lead to bending the rules. In a January 4, 2014, editorial, "Rampant Prosecutorial Misconduct," the *New York Times* Editorial Board makes the argument that with plea negotiation rates north of 95 percent, it is important that prosecutors play fair since much of what they do stays behind closed doors and is not vetted before a jury. In 1963, the Warren Court held in *Brady v. Maryland* that prosecutors are required to provide exculpatory evidence to the defense if that evidence could affect the outcome. The *Times* Editorial Board concluded:

> Far too often, state and federal prosecutors fail to fulfill that constitutional duty, and far too rarely do courts hold them accountable. Last month, Alex Kozinski, the chief judge of the United States Court of Appeals for the Ninth Circuit, issued the most stinging indictment of this systemic failure in recent memory. "There is an epidemic of Brady violations abroad in the land," Judge Kozinski wrote.

How often does this happen? How often does the pressure to convict and achieve tough sentencing outcomes lead to misconduct that harms a defendant? All of this is very hard to know. But a recent investigation by the Arizona Supreme Court made a disturbing discovery. Appellate attorneys alleged that nearly half of the capital cases in Arizona since 2002 involved prosecutorial misconduct. The Supreme Court affirmed that nearly 40 percent of those did in fact involve errors or misconduct by prosecutors. This discovery led to two of the death sentences being thrown out, one prosecutor being disbarred, and one being suspended. At the same time, there is evidence that prosecutors also circumvent mandatory sentences, mandatory minimums, and guideline sentences when they perceive that outcomes are unfair or too harsh.

Case Processing

In Harris County (Houston), Texas, some prosecutors handle nearly fifteen hundred felonies per year and five hundred at any given time. Guidelines indicate that a manageable prosecutor caseload is approximately 150 felonies or 400 misdemeanors. Many jurisdictions surveyed in 2006 had caseloads well in excess of these guidelines.[7] However, these survey data underestimate the caseload size because the responses simply take the number of cases and divide by the number of prosecutors. Not all prosecutors prosecute. Not all prosecutors handle trial-related cases. The bottom line is that the workload per line prosecutor is even more burdensome than the statistics indicate. These caseloads have significant implications. When prosecutors do not have adequate time to review cases and evidence, and because in most cases the evidence is not litigated at trial, most of the decisions regarding culpability and guilt or innocence are made informally, behind closed doors in plea negotiation meetings. Prosecutors likely have insufficient time to adequately review the evidence and determine who is more or less deserving of punishment, who is more or less culpable.

Joe DeCecco, the Sheboygan County, Wisconsin, DA, describes his office as operating like a MASH unit, and other Wisconsin DAs use the term *triage* to describe what their prosecutors do. A 2012 study of Wisconsin DA offices shows that staffing is at about 67 percent of what it needs to be based on caseloads. And Wisconsin is not unique.

Surveys conducted by the U.S. Justice Department reveal that prosecutors see their primary roles and responsibilities as case processors and law enforcers. In light of the caseload pressure, it is not at all surprising that the American justice system relies so heavily on plea negotiation to resolve cases. As sentencing reform has reduced the discretion of judges, in turn placing more power in the hands of prosecutors, the plea rate has increased, resulting in moving more cases more quickly. One important mechanism for increasing plea agreements is the leverage prosecutors have as a result of charging decisions. As state legislatures have implemented more mandatory sentences and made punishment harsher, prosecutors have gained greater ammunition to motivate pleas. Simply by overcharging or threatening harsher charges if a case goes to trial, prosecutors can more easily resolve cases by agreement as opposed to trial.

Travis County (Austin), Texas, caseload statistics portray a troubling situation that is not at all unique to that jurisdiction. In 2010, there were ninety-two hundred new felony indictments filed. The criminal felony courts and their prosecutors were able to dispose of seventy-nine hundred cases. The majority (77 percent) were convictions. At the end of 2010, there were 23,300 pending felony cases. This is a phenomenal number of backlogged felony cases that the courts and prosecutors have to manage and process. The situation is worse at the misdemeanor level. The county courts and misdemeanor prosecutors that handle the more serious class A and B misdemeanors had nearly thirty-one thousand new indictments filed in 2010. They disposed of thirty-three thousand, with 41 percent of those being convictions. At the end of 2010, there were 84,200 pending class A and B misdemeanor cases.

Now consider the following: Two-thirds of the 23,300 felony cases that are pending in Travis County district courts involve individuals with a prior conviction. Nearly one-half of the 84,200 class A and B misdemeanor cases pending in the county courts involve offenders with a prior conviction. The failure to reduce recidivism causes substantial problems for the criminal justice system, including overwhelming the criminal courts and flooding prosecutors' caseloads. Moreover, it compromises public safety and places us all at the needless and avoidable risk of being victims of crime.

The primary job of the prosecutor has certainly been strained and burdensome, but fairly straightforward. Direct traffic—process as many cases as efficiently as possible, enforce the law, and convict. Decide which cases to prosecute, negotiate a plea, and ensure that the appropriate sanction is imposed. In the past, the goal has been to steer in the direction of maximizing the punishment with less regard for behavioral change other than a presumed deterrent effect of punishment. Occasionally there would be some attention paid to diversion and rehabilitation, but that was usually incidental to the real business of processing cases, convicting, and punishing.

THE FUTURE OF CRIMINAL PROSECUTION

Prosecutors occupy a unique, pivotal position in the processing of criminal defendants, which makes them the key decision makers in the American justice system. For that reason, it is important to spend some time carefully considering the role of the prosecutor going forward.

In the future, the job of the prosecutor will become a lot tougher, because the decisions that will need to be made will be different and a good bit more complex. They will involve matters that lawyers are not trained to address and, therefore, require the input of a variety of experts in a variety of disciplines.

As suggested earlier, the primary goals as we transition the justice system and adopt smart-on-crime policies are to reduce crime, recidivism, victimization, and cost. What this means is a sea change for the business of the American prosecutor. It involves substantially changing prosecutors' roles and responsibilities. It will involve structural and organizational changes, changes in resources, new and different individuals working with prosecutors and participating in critical decision making, and perhaps most important, a change in how prosecutors think about crime and criminals. In effect, a change in the culture of criminal prosecution.

An ever-increasing number of organizations, from the ACLU on the left to Right on Crime on the right and dozens in between, have been making very strong cases for criminal justice reform. Although these national-level organizations are beginning to make the case for smart-on-crime policies, at the end of the day, crime and its solutions are local. The type of changes proposed here require individual decision makers to do business in a different way.

Problem-Solving Prosecution

Rose Ann Davidson, a forty-four-year-old central Texas woman, has a problem with alcohol. In 2012, in Hays County, Texas, she was convicted of her third felony DWI (driving while intoxicated; DWIs are enhanced to felonies in Texas after two prior misdemeanor DWI convictions). Under the Texas habitual offender law, she was eligible for life in prison for this third felony DWI. That is what she received.[8] She appealed to the Texas Court of Criminal Appeals on an Eighth Amendment argument that the punishment was cruel and unusual. The appellate court upheld the sentence. The court of appeals held that "it is well established that a sentence of life imprisonment or of similar length is not grossly disproportionate to a felony offense that is committed by a habitual offender, even when the felony is not inherently violent in nature."[9]

What is wrong with this story? First, the only solution the state can come up with to address Davidson's alcohol and DWI problem is to isolate her from society. Is this the best we can do? Second, it will cost a minimum of $900,000 to incarcerate her. Third, it does not deter others from engaging in similar offenses. This is a lose-lose situation: Davidson loses, and the community and the taxpayer lose. Now, to be fair, it could be the case that Davidson is a chronic alcoholic for whom there is no chance for recovery. Perhaps, despite the best that psychiatry, psychology, and addiction treatment have to offer, Davidson is just untreatable.

While this may be the case, I would bet that no one made the effort to determine if it was. That type of thinking, that proactive effort, has just not had a primary place in the repertoire of the prosecutor or the justice system more broadly.

The importance of the role of the prosecutor and the impact that prosecutors' decisions have on case outcomes require that if we want a different justice system that effectively reduces crime and recidivism, we have to change criminal prosecution. Problem-solving prosecution as proposed here begins with the recognition that (a) prosecutors are the most important decision makers in the justice system; (b) the decisions they make directly impact criminal sentences, recidivism, crime, victimization, and cost; (c) prosecutors need to accept responsibility and accountability for reducing recidivism; and (d) the only way to effectively reduce recidivism is through behavioral-change interventions for many and incarceration (incapacitation) for others.

Problem-solving prosecution is not new. Also known as community prosecution, a version of it has been around on a limited scale for some time. However, what we are talking about here is a good bit different. Problem-solving prosecution going forward essentially must include every criminal offender, a willingness to look and think more broadly about how to accomplish public safety, and an entire spectrum of remedies or solutions. We know today that a variety of crime-related problems and circumstances play important roles in criminality. We also know that failing to identify and address these is absolutely counterproductive to reducing recidivism.

Prosecutors are lawyers. Their areas of expertise are the law, criminal procedure, and due process. They are not behavioral, neurological, or cognitive experts. They are not psychologists or psychiatrists or social workers. They are not trained to identify or address crime-related circumstances. That requires a separate set of clinical and behavioral experts, individuals who are trained in screening and assessing offenders for a wide variety of circumstances and conditions and developing risk-informed intervention plans to address identified problems.

Decision making in the prosecutor's office needs to be much more collaborative going forward. In order to accomplish the goal of reducing recidivism, we need to get the right people to the table in order to figure out the best way to do so while still managing the risk of reoffending. We know that diversion programs effectively reduce recidivism and that prosecutors serve as the primary channel or gatekeepers to diversion. As we are able to improve the information and expertise that are brought to the decision about who goes to which diversion program, the better the placements and outcomes will be.

Problem-solving prosecution involves a recognition that incarceration can really only accomplish one thing—incapacitation, separation of an offender from society. Thus, incarceration should be the limited solution for violent offenders, habitual offenders, and untreatable offenders. But unlike the Davidson example, we need to make proactive clinical determinations regarding who is habitual and untreatable and not simply rely on criminal patterns. After all, a habitual offender may simply be a failure of the justice system.

Thus, the model proposed here is where the business of prosecution should become the promotion and facilitation of recidivism reduction, one where prosecution moves away from a focus on cases and case processing toward a focus on problems and problem solving. It is where prosecution shifts from a nearly unilateral focus of the "problem" being the crime and the "solution" being punishment to the problem being the crime and the criminal offender and the solution a balance of justice, due process, accountability, risk management, and behavioral change.

There are stark realities regarding the day to day of criminal prosecution. Caseloads are extraordinarily high, and resources are scarce. Public safety comes first. Managing the risk of reoffending is paramount. Thus, supervision, accountability, and compliance will be the first, but not the exclusive, concern. Hand in hand with these are the programs and interventions designed to change the circumstances that bring so many into the justice system time and time again. The research is clear that these elements of risk management, compliance, accountability, and behavioral change can and do coexist in the hundreds of problem-solving courts and other diversion programs on the ground today.

Clearly, other elements will need to come into play. Community resources such as mental health and substance abuse treatment capacity will need to be able to handle increased demand. Workforce training, education, and affordable housing are other important requirements for addressing the underlying factors that cause or are related to criminal offending. Some offenders will not want to engage in diversion/treatment or are simply not ready. It is important to determine who these are so that we do not waste resources. For those who are not ready, there are strategies that can be used to help move individuals to a more treatment-ready state.

The defense bar will also need to be engaged in this transition. Defense lawyers may not always be on board with prosecutorial decisions regarding diversion and treatment. Some defense attorneys may view diversion as more punitive than straight probation or perhaps even a jail term and see the quick discharge of a criminal sanction as the primary goal. Defense lawyers are advocates in an adversarial process; thus they may not always join in the collaborative process that is envisioned. The defense bar will likely need to be informed about what works in offender behavioral change/rehabilitation and may also need to have a bit of a cultural shift in order to embrace the bigger picture of recidivism reduction while still preserving constitutional protections and due process.

Substantial leadership, political courage, and initiative will also be required. The changes we are talking about are local changes. There are roughly three thousand local jurisdictions (counties) in which these changes will need to occur. While state- and national-level initiatives, assistance, and funding can help move this agenda forward, at the end of the day, local DAs will need to muster the initiative, political courage, and leadership skills necessary to implement problem-solving prosecution.

Perhaps one of the more significant barriers is the perceived political risk involved in not voicing tough-on-crime positions. It is simply a long-ingrained aversion for being considered soft on crime that may hinder some from heading down this road of prosecutorial reform. That can be at least partially mitigated by positioning this as smart on crime and cost saving. In addition, it is relevant to point out that there is, and has been for some time, substantial public support for the kinds of outcomes proposed here. Since the early 2000s, at least, a variety of public polling organizations have been asking the American public about the justice system and its priorities and policies. It is pretty clear that the public embraces a much broader agenda than simple mass punishment, and has done so for more than ten years (the conclusion from the Open Society Institute, below, is from 2002). The following two excerpts illustrate the public's big-picture views about justice policy:

> Public opinion on crime and criminal justice has undergone a significant transformation over the past few years. Support for long prison

sentences as the primary tool in the fight against crime is waning, as most people reject a purely punitive approach to criminal justice. Instead, the public now endorses a balanced, multifaceted solution that focuses on prevention and rehabilitation in concert with other remedies. [10]

1. American voters believe too many people are in prison and the nation spends too much on imprisonment.
2. Voters overwhelmingly support a variety of policy changes that shift non-violent offenders from prison to more effective, less expensive alternatives.
3. Support for sentencing and corrections reforms (including reduced prison terms) is strong across political parties, regions, age, gender and racial/ethnic groups. [11]

Why do we need to do all of this? Why do we need to reform prosecution and treat offenders as if they are ill, in need of clinical intervention, rehabilitation, education, workforce training, and so on? If we want to reduce recidivism, crime, victimization, and criminal justice cost, the evidence is clear that the only way to do it is to understand why individuals commit crime and then mitigate the primary crime-related circumstances associated with criminality. The answer is simple; the task is monumental.

JUDGES, SENTENCING, AND JUDICIAL PROBLEM SOLVING

Analyses of judicial election campaign television advertising show that a very common theme is tough on crime. For example, from recent appellate and trial court judicial elections:

Why did the Alabama Fraternal Order of Police endorse Judge Jones over Brown for Alabama Supreme Court? Because she respects law enforcement. Judge Jones. A twenty-year record fighting crime as a prosecutor and judge. A ninety-one percent conviction rate in DUI cases as a district judge. And last year in two tragic cases, Judge Jones sentenced two convicted murderers to the death penalty. (Alabama Supreme Court candidate)

I'm a prosecution-oriented person, which means seeing legal issues from the perspective of the state instead of the perspective of the defense. (Texas Court of Criminal Appeals candidate)

I will stop suspending sentences and stop putting criminals on probation. (Tippecanoe [Indiana] County Court candidate)

Some complain he is too tough on criminals. And he is. . . . We need him now more than ever. (Jefferson County [Alabama] Circuit Court candidate)[12]

Experts are quick to point out that the public is primed to hear and respond favorably to such judicial campaign messaging. The public generally believes crime is high or increasing despite the reality, often as a result of sensationalized media coverage of crime. Moreover, the content of political campaigns, often focusing on tough-on-crime stances and ridiculing those thought soft on crime, plays an important role is shaping the public perception.

So what's the problem with tough-on-crime judges? We tend to think of judges as the neutral arbiters responsible for ensuring that all proceedings are conducted properly under the law. One of the primary responsibilities of judges is ensuring due process. It seems a bit of a contradiction for that person to also hold such strong feelings about crime and punishment.

The big picture of criminal sentencing was very well stated in 2009 by Judge Michael Marcus, a district court judge in Multnomah County (Portland), Oregon:

The single most daunting impediment to meaningful sentencing improvement: our wholesale surrender to undifferentiated just deserts as mainstream sentencing's only responsibility. That surrender is a demonstrably dysfunctional, cruel, and wasteful allocation of the bulk of corrections resources—jail and prison included. Our use of jail and prison under the resulting paradigm frequently does more harm than good. The harm consists of accelerated recidivism by offenders whose criminality would be better addressed with wiser sentencing choices, by victimizations that smarter sentencing would have avoided, the excessive punishments that serve neither society nor the offender, of an enormous waste of public resources, and a continuing erosion of public trust and confidence.[13]

The past forty-plus years of criminal sentencing in the United States has been largely harm based and punishment focused. The sentencing process has been to emphasize the amount of harm done in the commission of the conviction offense and how much harm the offender has done in known prior crimes and then to come up with a punishment that is some reflection of that harm. The goal in most instances has been to level a punishment proportionate in severity to the amount of harm perpetrated. Sometimes the judge has had wide latitude in doing this, and sometimes the law has dictated the sentence. Regardless of the process, the result has been dramatic increases in the number of offenders going to prison, the length of the sentence imposed, and the amount of time served. This, in turn, led to what many may have considered a surprising result—the failure to reduce recidivism.

Evidence-Based Sentencing

Only in very recent years, since 2008 or 2009, have criminal justice experts begun seriously discussing the concept of evidence-based sentencing. The idea is borrowed from a variety of other professions, most notably medicine, where evidence-based practices have systematically guided and informed medical decision making and the delivery of medical care for decades but gained prominence and a label in the early 1990s. The evidence in evidence based is derived from clinical research demonstrating what is and is not effective. It is defined as "the conscientious and judicious use of current best evidence from clinical care research in the management of individual patients."[14]

Evidence-based sentencing (EBS) has come to mean the incorporation of key principles or strategies that have been demonstrated to effectively reduce recidivism. Given the critical importance of the sentencing process and sentencing decisions, this is welcome news. However, where we are in terms of using EBS is not such good news. While researchers have identified several components of EBS, the reality in American courtrooms is that the most common EBS practice in use today is an offender's estimated risk level.

The use of risk scores is gaining considerable currency in sentencing decisions. In one sense, this is good news—judges increasingly use "objective" information as a basis for decisions. The bad news is that risk estimation is fraught with error. That error is generally of two kinds: false positives, where someone who is not high risk is classified as such, and false negatives, where a high-risk offender is classified as medium or low risk. In both situations, reliance on the estimated risk scores will ill inform the sentencing decision. How much error is involved depends on the type of risk assessment used. The most sophisticated assessment to date, the Philadelphia probation risk assessment, which is a considerable improvement over current instruments, has an estimated accuracy of 66 percent. This means that two-thirds of offenders are classified correctly as high, medium, or low risk. Again, this represents a significant increase in accuracy but still leaves one-third of cases incorrectly classified, which in turn can substantially bias sentencing decisions. Despite the concerns, the American Law Institute (ALI), a high-profile association of lawyers, judges, and other criminal justice professionals, recently stated:

> Although the problem of false positives is an enormous concern—almost paralyzing in its human costs—it cannot rule out, on moral or policy grounds, all use of projections of high risk in the sentencing process. If prediction technology shown to be reasonably accurate is not employed, and crime-preventive terms of confinement are not imposed, the justice system knowingly permits victimizations in the community that could have been avoided.[15]

An August 10, 2014, *New York Times* op-ed piece[16] by Sonja Starr, a law professor at the University of Michigan, points out that former U.S. attorney general Eric Holder had recently criticized the use of risk scores in determining a criminal sentence. The point is that risk scores are based on a variety of factors (which factors depend on which risk instrument is used), including prior criminal activity, which is a reasonable measure of prior harm, but also on characteristics like unemployment, family background, the neighborhood where the offender lives, financial status, education, and family members' criminal involvement, among others. The problem is that a criminal sentence is supposed to reflect the harm done in the commission of the conviction offense, not how well educated someone is, whether they were employed in the past six months, where they live, or whether they are married. Holder and Starr's concern (a legitimate one, in my estimation) is that heavy reliance on risk scores in sentencing is discriminatory. It tends to punish disadvantage, which in turn tends to punish race, since race and disadvantage are strongly correlated.

The guidance going forward is that risk prediction should be only one element, one of several factors that, taken together, inform criminal sentencing. But risk alone, or substantial reliance on risk, should not determine the sentence if the goal is to reduce crime and recidivism. EBS is much broader than risk-based sentencing. EBS makes use of a wide variety of evidence, including risk, crime-related conditions and circumstances, and appropriate and effective interventions and treatment/rehabilitation programs. It also makes use of a variety of expertise, which is largely absent from traditional criminal sentencing.

Paramount to the task of effective behavior change is identifying those factors, conditions, deficits, and impairments that may not cause criminal offending per se but are related to it as motivators, facilitators, or catalysts. Understanding criminal offending requires understanding the criminal offender. This often involves the presentation and interaction of a variety of complex circumstances, including

- mental illness (approximately 40 percent to 50 percent or more of criminal offenders);
- substance abuse (70 percent to 80 percent of criminal offenders);
- co-occurring mental illness and substance abuse disorders (approximately 70 percent to 80 percent of those identified with mental illness have a co-occurring substance abuse disorder, and vice versa);
- neurocognitive deficits and impairments (between 20 percent and 40 percent of adults in the justice system have attention deficit hyperactivity disorder, compared to 8 percent of the general population; 60 percent of adults in prison have experienced traumatic brain injury, often leading to significant neurological and neurocognitive impairments; the evidence is also clear that other neurocognitive deficits are implicated in criminal offending, including learning disabilities and executive dysfunction[17]);
- employment problems, educational deficits, family and marital disruption, physical health problems, and homelessness, among others.

These are potentially changeable, treatable conditions, impairments, and deficits. They are factors that, absent significant intervention, will continue to play a substantial role in criminality and recidivism, keeping offenders cycling in and out of the justice system at extraordinary cost to victims, the community, and taxpayers. How smart is that?

EBS must be collaborative. As the justice system migrates away from a nearly exclusive focus on punishment toward a focus on behavioral change, sentencing will require experts in behavioral science. Collaborative sentencing should involve the judge, the prosecution, the defense, clinical experts, intervention programming experts, and community-based behavioral health treatment providers, as well as educational, employment, and vocational training providers, among others. In order to make appropriate, effective decisions about sentencing, the process needs to include information as well as the right experts to interpret that information and make recommendations. We need those experts to help identify who are truly habitual offenders, who cannot realistically be successfully rehabilitated, and those for whom prior rehabilitation efforts have failed. Many of these individuals, along with violent offenders, should constitute the bulk of the incarcerated population if it is determined that they are sufficiently dangerous and/or that their criminal offending is sufficiently serious and unlikely to stop. Thus, for those who are identified for diversion and engagement in rehabilitation, we need experts to engage and guide the behavioral-change process. The judge, the prosecutor, and the defense counsel are all lawyers who have jobs to do, but those jobs have little to do with behavior change.

Effective sentencing requires experts to identify all of the primary criminogenic problems. For example, research shows that while large numbers of criminal offenders in the justice system suffer mental illness, the data also show that comorbidity is quite common. Mental illness is associated with substance abuse and employment and housing problems, among other things. Treating mental illness is a step in the right direction, but it is just one step. If we fail to identify and treat the other primary problems, we may very well fail to reduce recidivism. And the research shows that the odds of reducing recidivism are directly tied to the number of crime-related problems addressed.

Effective sentencing also requires the expertise to prioritize which problems should be addressed and in what order and which programming is most appropriate for the individual circumstances presented. Currently, probation departments and local treatment providers serve as primary sources of expertise for determining risk and needs and any programming that a nonincarcerated offender receives. Judge Roger Warren, a former

California Superior Court judge, president of the National Center for State Courts, and an expert on a variety of criminal justice issues, including EBS, speaks to the problems of relying on current sources of expertise in making EBS decisions:

> The courts should be able to look to probation departments and program providers for expertise on the principles of EBP [evidence-based practices], but the sad fact is that most community-corrections agencies and treatment providers have had neither the incentive nor the resources to reengineer their operations and programs in accord with EBP. . . . Without proactive judicial leadership in securing the cooperation and collaboration of other local criminal justice system partners in addressing those potential constraints, effective judicial implementation of EBP cannot realistically occur. [18]

If we are going to get serious about this, we need to reach outside of the justice system as currently configured in order to find the expertise necessary to effectively engage in behavior change. The criminal justice system is simply not positioned or resourced to have sufficient numbers of individuals with the required experience and expertise. Nor does the justice system have the necessary resources to provide the level and scale of programming envisioned. This will require substantial increases in community-based capacity for mental health, substance abuse, and cognitive rehabilitation, as well as education, employment, and vocational training, among other things.

Sentencing and the Role of the Judge

The discretion that judges have in criminal sentencing depends on the laws that govern sentencing in a particular jurisdiction. Broadly speaking, judges have more latitude in sentencing in jurisdictions that have indeterminate sentencing laws where the statutes provide for ranges of punishment and the judge is required to determine a sentence within that range. Under indeterminate sentencing law, the court may hear a considerable amount of evidence at the sentencing hearing, some intended to aggravate the sentence and some intended to mitigate. The judge is then to determine an appropriate sentence. Today there are twenty-seven states that still afford the court significant sentencing discretion; however, there are many exceptions. The charging decisions made by the prosecutor determine whether mandatory sentences apply, thus further limiting judicial discretion. Mandatory sentencing, in the form of mandatory minimum sentences, mandatory sentences, and habitual offender (three-strikes) sentences, have dramatically limited the discretion of the judge. For example, those states that still have indeterminate sentences also have mandatory sentences for drug law violations, weapons offenses, repeat offenders, violent offenders, and sex and pornography offenses, among others. Moreover, the reach of mandatory sentences has grown extensively over time, subjecting more and more offenders to mandatory provisions. For example, in Arizona in 1990, 57 percent of all felony offenders were subject to a mandatory sentence. In 2010, 40 percent of convicted offenders in the federal system were subject to a mandatory sentence. As is the case with America's reliance on incarceration and punitiveness, we are exceptional in terms of our use of mandatory sentencing compared to our Western counterparts.

The changes recommended for prosecutors earlier in this chapter—collaboration and problem solving—apply to judges as well. Judges, like prosecutors, must embrace the reality that punishment alone does not reduce criminality and that recidivism reduction is the primary goal of sentencing. Essential to success is the acceptance of responsibility for resolving the problems of crime and recidivism, not just passing them on to some other agency or set of individuals. Furthermore, judges need to recognize and appreciate their limitations in making sentencing decisions. Judges, like prosecutors, are not psychologists or psychiatrists or neurologists. They are lawyers, not behavioral scientists. As such, the decision-making process must change in order to accomplish the goal of reducing recidivism. Those changes include collaborative problem solving, involving a variety of individuals with a range of expertise.

Criminal courts, especially since sentencing reform, tend to sentence categories of offenders rather than individuals. There is often little regard for individual differences, except for offense-specific facts. Sentencing becomes a matter of sorting offenders into one of a limited number of categories: incarceration or probation; violent, property, or drug offender; habitual or infrequent offender. After all, that was the goal of sentencing reform—eliminating the consideration of most individual characteristics such that offenders with similar criminal backgrounds who commit similar crimes receive the same sentence.

Going forward, sentencing decisions need to be informed on a case-by-case basis. The overarching strategy should be guided by a problem-solving approach and be an information-rich, collaborative effort involving experts from a variety of disciplines. Problem solving, which is a central component of diversion courts, can and should be applied in traditional criminal court settings. This involves a new way of thinking and making decisions in criminal courts. It requires information, analysis, assessment, and collaboration. It is premised on considering the presence of an offender as a problem that requires a solution, a solution based not on emotion but on expertise and information—evidence-based sentencing, as discussed above. It is critical that judges and others involved in the collaborative decision-making process consider the unique characteristics and circumstances of each offender in order to determine what is most appropriate in that case for accomplishing public safety and reducing recidivism. As is the case with the prosecutor's office, we are faced with changing the culture and decision-making processes in criminal courts, especially at sentencing.

This realignment of criminal sentencing will require significant increases in resources, including expert clinical staff, administrative support, case management, and programming/treatment capacity for diversion of increasing numbers of offenders. State legislatures and Congress need to move away from determinate and mandatory sentencing, those sentencing laws that made tough on crime possible, and return to more indeterminate laws that provide judges with the discretion to collaboratively implement the processes outlined herein. It also involves a substantial change in attitude. Judge Marcus once again nails it:

> We send thieves to theft talk, drunk drivers to alcohol treatment, bullies to anger counseling, addicts to drug treatment, and sex offenders to sex offender treatment. But we do this as a matter of symmetry rather than of science: we do not select offenders based on their amenability to treatment, but on the crime they have committed. We do not select providers on their impact on criminal behavior, but on their ability to provide timely paperwork. We may ask providers if offenders complete "the program" but we do not ask if they reoffend after treatment. Again, the issue is responsible pursuit of crime reduction—not nominal pursuit.[19]

Judge Marcus affirms the idea that in order for real change to occur, including the sentencing process, sentencing outcomes, and recidivism, it is not just a matter of making organizational and structural changes or increasing resources and funding. It also means changing our way of thinking regarding how we go about the business of accomplishing public safety—the *responsible* pursuit of crime reduction.

RETHINKING CRIMINAL RESPONSIBILITY

James Willie Brown raped and murdered Brenda Watson in 1975, for which he was convicted and sentenced to death. For most of his life, Mr. Brown had suffered from paranoid schizophrenia, which had caused him to hear voices—voices he sometimes thought were God and other times demons. These voices command him to do certain things. He had hallucinations and believed that people were trying to kill him. His condition was certain, having been diagnosed by ten different psychiatrists hired by the state. Despite the record of these diagnoses, the jury that convicted him was told little of his background and informed that he was faking his mental illness. The jury was also told that if Brown had any hallucinations, they were a product of his drug abuse. [20]

Demond Chatman has been in prison for fourteen years. His incarceration is in part a function of his committing a crime and in part a result of the justice system's refusal to appreciate his mental health condition. Chatman has been diagnosed with schizophrenia and/or schizoaffective disorder since he was age ten. Despite the diagnoses and Chatman's defense counsel's efforts to show he was mentally incompetent, the DA's office and the chief justice of the trial court refused to believe that he was mentally ill. Their rationale—he didn't seem crazy to them. [21]

Dale Gaines is in prison on a life sentence for receiving stolen property. His unfortunate story involves a three-strikes law as well as mental retardation and mental illness. Mr. Gaines had a particularly horrific childhood. His grandmother, who was his primary caregiver, routinely beat him and forced him to eat his own feces. Later, he was often homeless. While incarcerated for the second crime, he was diagnosed by prison officials as schizophrenic and mentally disabled (his reading ability is that of a five-year-old). He had no history of violence, and while his mental and cognitive conditions could have been viewed as mitigating circumstances at sentencing, they were not discussed. [22]

These three examples serve to illustrate a general hostility to, or at least disinterest in, the mental and emotional capacity of a criminal defendant. They also reflect the hard fact that we routinely prosecute, convict, and punish mentally disabled and cognitively impaired criminal offenders as if they are aware of their actions and in control of their behavior, as if their mental states and cognitive abilities render them as responsible, as culpable for their crimes as anyone else. We punish these offenders because prosecutors prosecute and convict them, judges sentence them, and the law provides little protection from criminal prosecution and punishment for the mentally ill and cognitively impaired. The evidence is clear that it is time to seriously reconsider this.

The Insanity Defense

Despite what is commonly thought, the insanity defense is rarely used and even more rarely successful. It is only raised in about 1 percent of felony cases and is successful in less than 25 percent of those cases. The basis for insanity in the American justice system is what is known as the right-wrong test. The right-wrong test was developed in 1843 in England in the M'Naghten case and was subsequently adopted by the United States. The current use of M'Naghten requires the defendant to prove that he or she suffered from a mental disease or defect that resulted in the defendant not knowing the nature and quality of the act committed or knowing the nature and quality of the act but not knowing that the act was wrong. The burden of proof is on the defendant to prove that "but for" the mental disease or defect, the crime would not have occurred.

One of the major criticisms of the M'Naghten test is that there are no provisions for a mental disease or defect affecting the volition of an individual. A mentally ill offender may know that a crime is wrong but nevertheless may not be able to control his or her actions. This concern was partially addressed by the ALI's Model Penal Code developed in 1962. The code provides that a person is not legally responsible for a crime "if, at the time of such conduct, as a result of mental disease or defect, the individual lacks the substantial capacity to appreciate the criminality of his conduct or to conform his conduct to the requirements of the law."[23] There are two major differences between M'Naghten and the ALI

Model Penal Code's insanity defense: (1) a less stringent test for understanding the wrongfulness of his actions and (2) the provision of the volitional element. The less stringent test for wrongfulness permits juries to consider not just cognitive impairment but also moral, emotional, and legal awareness of the consequences of the behavior. The volitional element allows a defendant to acknowledge that even though they knew that the act in question was wrong, they were unable to abide by the law or control their actions. By 1980, most states had incorporated a volitional or control test into their insanity defense laws.

Then John Hinckley entered the story and tried to assassinate President Reagan in 1981. Hinckley was found not guilty by reason of insanity under the ALI Model Penal Code's insanity defense provisions. The public outrage over the verdict led to major and troubling reforms to the insanity defense. The Insanity Defense Reform Act of 1984 (IDRA) changed federal law governing insanity in important ways, essentially taking it back to M'Naghten. IDRA provides that someone is not criminally responsible if the defendant suffers from a *severe* mental disease or defect that caused the defendant to be unable to appreciate the nature and quality of his or her act or the wrongfulness of his or her act. IDRA effectively limited the psychiatric diagnoses to psychoses and mental retardation and eliminated the volitional element of the Model Penal Code. Further, IDRA made it clear that insanity was an affirmative defense and, as such, placed the burden of proof on the defendant.

The impact of IDRA was substantial. Most states reevaluated their insanity defense laws as a result. The majority (thirty-nine) made insanity an affirmative defense, placing the burden of proof on the defendant. Twenty-seven states use the M'Naghten provisions, nineteen use a version of the ALI Model Penal Code, and four states (Utah, Montana, Idaho, and Kansas) abolished the insanity defense.

Mental Illness and Neurodevelopmental and Cognitive Impairment More Broadly

The insanity defense is only a very small fraction of the bigger problem of mentally disabled, compromised, or incompetent defendants being prosecuted, convicted, and punished just like all other defendants. There is a much larger gray area involving many, many more criminal defendants who may not be legally insane but whose behavior and actions are influenced to varying degrees by mental and/or cognitive impairments. There are few provisions in the law regarding the legal responsibility or culpability of those defendants. We treat them essentially as all other defendants, without inquiring about whether or how their mental or cognitive health played a role in their behavior.

Advances in neuroscience have clearly established the fact that abnormalities of the brain have profound impacts on our decision making and our ability to control our behavior. For example, the frontal lobes of the brain are clearly implicated in impulsivity. Circumstances that can impact impulse control include lesions, brain trauma, reduced volume of grey matter in the prefrontal cortex and hippocampus, and reduced prefrontal activity and increased subcortical activity. All of this can be understood in terms of the balance or imbalance between two components of the impulse control system: the amygdala, which provides immediate information about pain and pleasure, and the prefrontal cortex, which considers the longer-term consequences of our actions and behaviors. In effect, the impulsive individual's behavior is attributed to the inability of the prefrontal cortex, because of trauma or developmental deficits and impairments, to suppress impulsive behavior. Put a different way, the amygdala signals pleasure and the prefrontal cortex is unable to effectively interrupt the pursuit of that pleasure. There is a substantial amount of research documenting impulsivity among criminal offenders, leading to the question of whether we should consider such matters when we convict and punish those with these and other neurodevelopmental disorders. Should we hold such individuals responsible for their crimes and punish them just as we convict and punish others without this behavioral disability?

One possible source of relief for those criminal defendants who are considered legally sane but mentally and cognitively impaired is what is referred to as *diminished capacity*. Diminished capacity is not really a criminal defense, rather it is designed to reduce or mitigate responsibility and, thus, punishment. The doctrine of diminished capacity exists in either statute or case law in about half of the states and is considerably broader than insanity in terms of the evidence that can be used to prove it.

Diminished capacity has been invoked in a number of specific circumstances involving matters such as post-traumatic stress disorder (PTSD), battered woman syndrome, premenstrual syndrome (PMS), media intoxication, and, more recently, affluenza. These and other applications of diminished capacity arguments vary in terms of their success. Those involving recognized mental illnesses fare better than abuse and neglect arguments. Unfortunately, the sensational cases have led to less than complimentary characterizations of such attempts to prove diminished capacity and have likely harmed more legitimate efforts based on established psychiatric research. As one legal expert puts it:

> Even when diminished capacity is not extended into the realm of an abuse excuse, courts still dislike the doctrine. Judicial hostility to diminished capacity evidence may "reflect the traditional judicial distrust of the vagaries, uncertainties, and mysteries of psychiatric explanations, particularly when invoked to assess varying shades of capacity to perform such basic functions as intending and believing."[24]

It appears that the continued narrowing of the insanity defense, the general distaste for diminished capacity arguments, and the impact of recent U.S. Supreme Court decisions regarding diminished capacity evidence will further erode the ability of mentally and cognitively impaired defendants to seek relief based on the impact of such disabilities on their decision-making abilities and volition. What is required is for the law, policy, and practice to catch up with science. While there are challenges, such as how to prove diminished responsibility, this should not prevent us from appreciating the broader implications of mental and cognitive disabilities. As long as the law fails to recognize the impacts of mental and cognitive disabilities on behavior, and as long as prosecutors and judges continue to indict, prosecute, convict, and punish those with significant mental and cognitive disorders, we will continue to use the American criminal justice system as the preferred repository for the mentally ill and cognitively impaired. We will also continue to fail to appropriately intervene and treat the disorders that are associated with their criminal involvement; we will fail to reduce their criminality and recidivism and needlessly spend extraordinary amounts of public money to no productive end.

Whether one is compelled by the moral issues involving blameworthiness, whom we shall hold legally responsible for a criminal act and whom we shall punish to the full extent of the law, or the more pragmatic considerations of the revolving door of the American justice system, the conclusion is the same. We need to reconsider how we go about the business of criminal justice for the many who are mentally and cognitive-

ly disabled. Whether it is a significant expansion of the laws of diminished capacity or some other comparable statutory provision, we need to
facilitate treatment for those whose mental and cognitive impairments
play a fundamental role in their criminal offending. And a component of
this approach is appreciating, when appropriate, that not all criminal offenders are equally culpable. I'm not suggesting that we send serial killers
to group therapy. I have already suggested that violent, habitual, untreatable offenders should probably be incarcerated. However, the law should
promote the treatment of those with mental and cognitive disabilities and
not perpetuate their unproductive and expensive criminalization and punishment.

What is being proposed here is a fairly radical restructuring of criminal prosecution and sentencing. It involves not only changes in policy,
law, and resources but also a dramatic change in thinking about crime and
punishment. In recent decades, the culture of prosecution and sentencing
has been largely harm based and punishment focused. Tough on crime
has guided politics, law, policy, and practice. Now that the dust has
settled, we see a remarkable failure to reduce recidivism, crime, and
criminal victimization and an extraordinary expenditure of public resources.

There was no compelling research in the 1960s indicating that tough
on crime would work. There was no evidence supporting the conclusion
that a policy of harsher punishment deters criminal offending. Rather,
tough on crime was based largely on intuition, common sense, and emotion. We are in a very different position today. The scientific community
has provided clear guidance about where we need to go in order to substantially enhance cost-effective public safety. While all of the components of the American criminal justice system will need to change, and
we will get to this in subsequent chapters, the centerpiece of all this is in
the prosecutor's office and the judge's chambers. Prosecutorial decision
making and criminal sentencing are key, as is changing the processes and
culture of both. We also need to seriously rethink who we make accountable and responsible for his or her actions. The science is increasingly
clear every day that mental illness and cognitive disabilities play important roles in behavior and therefore have important consequences for the
justice system, as well as for our moral authority to punish wrongdoers.
The law needs to change in order to keep up with what we know about
mental and cognitive disabilities and the roles they play in crime.

This may sound like quite an investment. But it pales in comparison to the direct criminal justice costs, especially when we consider that each time someone reoffends and is caught, the criminal justice cash register rings again. There are also victim costs each time someone reoffends. Add to this the extraordinarily high likelihood that as we continue down this path of tough on crime, we are creating an enormous class of individuals who are permanently dependent on public assistance. The economics of this new path away from mass punishment toward behavioral change makes the clear case that it enhances public safety and is financially prudent.

6

RETHINKING PUNISHMENT

The public has been pushing back a bit on punishment for some time, and the evidence from opinion polls is telling. We tend to believe that there are too many people in prison, that too many nonviolent offenders are incarcerated, that we spend too much money incarcerating the wrong people, that mandatory sentences are generally inappropriate, and that changes have to occur that reduce incarceration and spending on incarceration. We tend to believe that the purpose of corrections should be rehabilitation, but we do not think we currently do a very good job of that. We support investing in and expanding programs that divert people from prison and reduce recidivism. A Right on Crime March 2015 poll of attitudes of Texas voters, historically some of the most conservative and tough-on-crime folks around, shows that nearly three-quarters believe that nonviolent drug offenders found guilty of possession should be sent to treatment rather than jail or prison. The majority (61 percent) believe the state should spend more on treatment than prison and should reduce time served so inmates can be released earlier and serve more of their sentence on community supervision (51 percent). Unfortunately, public officials, policy experts, legislators, and others involved in the administration of criminal justice have done little to align policy with public opinion.

Earlier chapters proposed a fairly fundamental shift in criminal justice policies and priorities. I have indicated that the path to greater public safety, reduced crime, recidivism, and victimization, as well as substantial criminal justice cost savings, is found in a much more targeted, judicious use of incarceration and a greatly expanded, proactive, behavioral-change initiative. On top of that is an essential, system-wide change in the culture of criminal justice, a basic shift in how we think about crime and punishment. It also requires each agency, organization, and individual involved in the administration of criminal justice to understand that the overarching purpose is to reduce recidivism and that all are responsible for accomplishing that goal.

Punishment and control, the cornerstones of American justice policy over the past forty-plus years, have a role going forward but a significantly altered role. This chapter lays out what corrections should look like in order to cost-effectively enhance public safety.

THE PURPOSE OF CRIMINAL SANCTIONING

One premise of this discussion of sanctioning is that criminal sentencing can be reengineered to the point that the primary decision makers (prosecutors, judges, and defense counsel, in collaboration with a variety of experts and professionals) are able to make deliberate, informed decisions on a case-by-case basis. The first cut in that decision making is distinguishing between those who should be incarcerated (removed from the community) and everybody else—those who will be under some form of control and supervision but who will receive rehabilitative programming, interventions, and treatment. So, in very simple terms, the options are incarceration or diversion.

There are two questions here: Who do we want in prison, and who should be in prison? This is an important distinction. We may prefer to put a wide swath of the offender population in prison, but decision making from this point forward should be premised more on utility than anger. Those who should be in prison are those we should incapacitate—violent offenders, chronic, habitual offenders, and those for whom, despite our best efforts, rehabilitation does not work.

Rather than relying on some emotional rationale for punishment, we will be better off basing these decisions on evidence of risk and dangerousness, a calculation of likelihood of successful behavior change versus risk to public safety. It should be based on who we are realistically afraid of, not who we are just mad at. If we can bring relevant, diagnostic/assessment information to the table to help inform these important decisions, if we can get more collaborative in the sentencing process, then we will be in a position to be smarter about sentencing and our use of incarceration. After all, incarceration should be considered a failure of sorts, or at least a last resort. There is generally no greater good to come from incarceration other than incapacitation.

Criminal sanctioning should be about accountability, compliance, risk management, supervision and control, behavioral change, and incapacitation. The evidence indicates that sanctioning and corrections need a radical rebalancing. We need prison and jail—just not as much as we currently use them. We need rehabilitation-focused diversion from incarceration much more than we currently use it. What should guide this shift or rebalancing is rational policy making, based more on what we know than what we feel.

THE FUTURE OF PRISONS AND JAILS

The Future of Prisons

Prison admissions reflect who is being sentenced to prison upon conviction of a felony crime. In 2013, violent offenders constituted 29 percent of new prison admissions. An additional 29 percent were property offenders, followed by drug offenders (25 percent) and public order offenders (16 percent).[1] The most common offenses among new prison admissions are drugs, including dealing, burglary, and assault. The statistics indicate that the felony courts are sending substantial numbers of nonviolent offenders to prison. Indeed, 71 percent of prison admissions are nonviolent offenders. What we don't know is the extent to which sentencing this many nonviolent offenders to prison is a good use of incarceration or is needless overreaching. We don't know how often these prison sentences for nonviolent offenders were justified in terms of aggravating circumstances like extensive criminal histories or reflect an effort to be tough on crime or, what is most likely, some of both.

We do know a bit about nonviolent offenders sentenced to prison from a special study conducted by the U.S. Department of Justice. The Justice Department study indicates that the vast majority of nonviolent prisoners have prior criminal involvement in terms of prior arrests and convictions, and nearly one-half had a prior sentence of incarceration. The average number of prior arrests is nine, and the average number of prior convictions is four. This information suggests that a good bit of the incarceration of nonviolent offenders has justification in terms of prior criminal involvement. However, those individuals involved in the criminal justice system in the past forty years or so have grown up in a juvenile and adult system focused primarily on punishment, where little effort has been directed at changing the criminogenic conditions that are related to their criminality. For that reason, it is not at all surprising that the vast majority of nonviolent offenders in prison today have significant criminal histories.

That is not to say that these patterns are inevitable or unavoidable. The point of this book is to lay out a road map for implementing effective behavioral change, which can substantially reduce recidivism. Estimates of recidivism reduction vary considerably depending on the particular intervention(s), the types of offenders, and many other factors. Best-case data show recidivism reductions as high as 40–50 percent. Since the average does not consist exclusively of best cases, it makes sense to adjust expectations downward—say, in the 25–30 percent range for average or typical offenders.

Drug offenders currently constitute 25 percent of new prison admissions and 17 percent of the state inmate population. It is realistic to envision that down the road there will be changes to drug laws and changes to drug treatment interventions that will reduce the presence of drug offenders in prison by a significant percentage. Evaluations of drug diversion courts show reductions in general recidivism and drug-related recidivism of approximately 25 percent.

In addition, some serious, violent offending is avoidable if we are able to intervene early in individuals' criminal careers and change the trajectories of some of those offenders. For example, dozens of evaluations of rehabilitation programs for serious, violent juvenile offenders show reductions in reoffending of approximately 7–13 percent. It is important to point out that those recidivism reductions are achieved with programs and interventions that may or may not be best practices or evidence-based practices. It is reasonable to suspect that implementing programs that are evidence based may very well realize greater returns. So while we may agree that the priority for incarceration should be reserved for serious, violent offenders, it is reasonable to expect that we can reduce the demand for prison space for serious, violent offenders to the extent that we are able to successfully implement those strategies that reduce their reoffending.

How many chronic, habitual offenders we end up incarcerating depends on the definition(s) of chronic and habitual. Research has shown consistently over time that about 6–10 percent of criminal offenders are responsible for the majority of crimes. These offenders also have the highest number of arrests. In terms of setting expectations for the future use of prisons, we are not looking at such sweeping numbers of repeat offenders as encompassed by the popular, metaphorical three-strikes laws and other mandatory sentences for chronic offenders. Rather, assuming a consistent, accurate system for identifying truly chronic, habitual offenders, they should constitute a relatively small portion of the inmate population, probably well under 10 percent.

The point is that as the changes recommended here begin to be rolled out, as we begin to faithfully implement evidence-based diversion programming on a more appropriate (i.e., larger) scale, the incidence of recidivism will decline, resulting in the longer term in the need for fewer prison beds. This reduction in demand for prison beds applies to both nonviolent and violent offenders, although it is likely that most of the reduction in prison populations will be among nonviolent offenders. At the same time, as the prison population declines, it is necessary that we avoid the tendency of the past to fill up vacant prison space with those whose risk does not warrant incapacitation. We should avoid returning to the past of casting wider and wider nets in order to fill prisons.

The Aging Inmate Population

Dale Redding is seventy-seven years old, serving a life sentence for aggravated assault and attempted murder. He has been in and out of prison most of his life and has been locked up this time for twenty-nine years. He is diabetic and arthritic, and he has chronic heart disease, vertigo, and the early stages of dementia. He spends almost as much time in the prison infirmary as in his cell. Redding is unable to walk on his own, so when he is moved, it is in a wheelchair. Unfortunately, there are many, many inmates like Dale Redding in America's prisons.

Today, the U.S. prison system houses nearly 250,000 prison inmates age fifty and over, representing 16 percent of the prison population. In some states, like California and Texas, it is a good bit higher. Twenty-one percent of California inmates are fifty years of age and older, as are 21 percent of Texas inmates. If the current situation persists, it is estimated that in fifteen years there will be over four hundred thousand prison inmates age fifty-five and older. That represents one-third of the entire prison population.[2]

While fifty is considered young in the free world, there is clear consensus among criminologists and correctional officials that it is the beginning point of defining an inmate as elderly. Prison has a variety of negative effects on inmates, including aging individuals beyond their chronological age. Experts observe that, on average, longer-term incarceration adds approximately ten to eleven years to an inmate's actual age.

The growth in the elderly inmate population has far outpaced the growth in the overall inmate population. A 2006 study of sixteen southern states shows that the elderly inmate population grew at a rate two to ten times that of the overall prison population.[3] The statistics indicate that the aging of the inmate population is not due as much to the sentencing of the elderly to prison (like Bernie Madoff and Whitey Bulger, who were imprisoned in their seventies); rather, it is due to the incarceration of younger inmates on such lengthy sentences that they become elderly while in prison. Whether through mandatory sentences such as three strikes or mandatory minimum drug sentences or simply by imposing long sentences served under tough parole restrictions, the end result is what has been labeled the graying of the inmate population.

Despite what one might think, these elderly inmates are not the worst of the worst. For example, Texas houses 27,500 inmates that meet the definition of *elderly*. Two-thirds of them are incarcerated for nonviolent crimes. Forty percent of elderly inmates in the North Carolina prison system are incarcerated for nonviolent crimes. Many of these offenders were caught up in habitual offender laws that require lengthy periods of incarceration even though they did not commit serious, violent crimes.

While many factors lead to desistance from crime, the most important is age. The transition age for many offenders is in the early to mid-twenties, when work, marriage, family, and ties to the community generally steer those involved in crime at younger ages to a crime-free life in adulthood. Obviously, not all individuals reach adulthood the same way. Some persist in criminal activity. However, when offenders begin to reach their forties and fifties, diminishing physical capabilities as well as adjustments in aspirations and expectations, a rethinking of costs and benefits or risks and rewards, all make crime more difficult and less desirable. With a few exceptions, once inmates hit their fifties, the risk of reoffending drops dramatically, essentially to zero.[4] The probability of a fifty-year-old inmate released from prison and then reoffending and being reincarcerated is 5 percent.[5] So we currently incarcerate approximately 250,000 individuals, most of whom have an extremely low risk of reoffending. If the goal is incapacitation, we must ask whether this is a good use of expensive correctional resources. Just how expensive is next.

The price tag for corrections in the United States is approximately $77 billion per year, the vast majority (90 percent) of which is spent on incarceration (compared to probation, parole, and diversion). This works out to over $35,000 per inmate per year for the average offender. However, elderly inmates are not average. It is estimated that the typical elderly inmate, defined as age fifty and over, costs nearly $70,000 per year.[6] This is based on the substantially higher medical costs and special needs of elderly inmates, needs that can range from medical equipment, medication, special beds, special accommodations because of disabilities, and protective custody to keep elderly inmates from predatory younger inmates, among other considerations. And to be clear, the substantially higher costs of incarcerating elderly inmates are not because they receive high-dollar medical care. The higher medical costs, estimated to be between two and five times the cost for younger inmates, are in part due to the frequency of necessary medical attention due to the typically more complex medical situations of elderly inmates. The higher costs are also due to the fact that prisons are not designed to deliver ongoing medical care, especially for a high-needs population with complex medical problems. Moreover, the elderly more frequently require expensive outside medical attention due to the complexity of their medical situations and the lack of appropriate expertise in prisons to deal with those conditions. Such external health care is especially expensive, as it involves transportation and security in addition to the cost of the care itself.

Today we are dealing with one of the unfortunate legacies of tough on crime—a large and growing segment of the inmate population that is extraordinarily low risk of reoffending and exceptionally expensive to incarcerate. What are we accomplishing by keeping elderly individuals incarcerated? Incapacitation is designed to remove criminal opportunity for those who are motivated and able to commit crime. The evidence is clear that these elderly inmates are neither motivated nor able. At the same time, we have to appreciate that many of these inmates committed serious crimes and that the state and some victims may still seek retribution for these crimes. But at what cost? Retribution is expensive with minimal upside. We cannot lose sight of the goal of effective and cost-efficient public policy.

How many elderly inmates can we safely release from prison, and how much could taxpayers potentially save? If the criterion is primarily risk (that is, assuming retribution plays a relatively minor role in the decision making, except for special cases involving particularly horrific crimes), it is realistic to assume that we can release roughly one-third to one-half of elderly inmates, beginning with the lowest risk and nonviolent offenders. This amounts to roughly 80,000 to 125,000 inmates and a gross annual cost savings of between $5.6 billion to $8.8 billion. There would need to be post-release parole supervision costs built into the estimates, but most of the medical-cost burden would be shifted to the federal government (Medicaid and Medicare, as well as mental health treatment covered by the Affordable Care Act parity provision), as would housing expenses (paid for by federal housing vouchers).

There are elderly inmates who have life without parole sentences, and there are elderly inmates whom we just do not want to release because of the nature of their crimes and/or because a sense of retribution prohibits early release. For such inmates who, because of their age and/or physical condition, are lower risk, the justice system or private sector should develop facilities that provide custodial care in a "secure" environment but are much less expensive than prison. Perhaps a step-down type of facility like a secure halfway house, where the environment is controlled and medical care is provided but at a much-reduced cost compared to prison.

So where does all of this leave us in terms of reducing the prison population without compromising public safety? All told, it is reasonable to anticipate that with the right laws, policies, practices, funding, expertise, and culture, we can cut the prison population by a substantial degree. But how much depends on how well we do everything else. The best-case scenario suggests that over time, we can reduce prison admissions by approximately 25 percent with the use of effective intervention strategies. This 25 percent applies to the general inmate population as well as drug and drug-related offenders. Evidence indicates we can also reduce admission for violent crimes by an additional 10 percent. Finally, releasing elderly inmates can reduce the prison population by approximately one hundred thousand offenders. All told, we are looking at an approximate 30–33 percent reduction in incarceration. There are many, many *if*s here, but if we even get close to this—say, a 25 percent reduction in the prison population in 2014 dollars—we can save roughly $17 billion annually in incarceration costs alone. As recidivism rates decline over time, the demand for prison space should decline as well, reducing prison admissions over the long term. How much depends on how well we embrace recidivism reduction.

Parole and Supervised Release

Parole is early release from prison. A paroled inmate is conditionally released under supervision to a halfway house or other step-down facility or to the community. Supervised release is the federal equivalent to monitoring or supervision when someone is released from federal prison. Parole officers supervise released offenders and enforce the conditions of release. If a parolee violates the conditions of release, the parole board can initiate revocation proceedings, whereby the individual can be sent back to prison to finish the original sentence. Eligibility for parole is governed by laws that stipulate what percentage of the sentence must be served before one may be considered for discretionary release. Percentages vary dramatically by state and by offense. For example, truth in sentencing laws often specify that violent offenders serve up to 85 percent of the sentence imposed before they can be considered for release, at which time the decision is up to the discretion of the parole board. However, most felony offenses in Texas require that an inmate serve one-fourth of the sentence imposed, calculated as calendar time plus good-conduct time. Texas law stipulates that for selected aggravated violent crimes (kidnapping, robbery, assault, some sex offenses) an inmate serves one-half of the sentence based just on calendar time before consideration for parole release.

One of the primary failures of American criminal justice policy over the past forty years is not thinking as much as necessary about what happens after someone has been released from prison. We were focused on punishment and doing everything we could to ramp up the severity of that punishment. And we assumed that, once punished, those released would see the light and stop any further criminal involvement. We were very wrong about that.

At age twenty, Leah Gibson was convicted of assault and aiding and abetting robbery. After twelve years of remaining crime free and obtaining a nursing license, she continued to face the stigma associated with a criminal conviction. In spite of her efforts to rehabilitate herself, she continuously encountered substantial problems finding housing and employment. She even was rejected by a dating service. So she tried to use the law to eliminate the barriers that criminal convictions present even to those who have gone straight. She filed a motion arguing that her criminal record from some fifteen years ago was an undue burden, especially since she had obtained a professional degree and had become a responsible, productive member of society. She requested that the Connecticut Superior Court require the state to refrain from releasing her criminal records to the public, including potential landlords and employers. The court held that while the request was reasonable, it had no legal power to impose such an order on the state. [7]

Concern about what has been labeled the reentry issue was first raised in the late 1990s, when the Urban Institute launched the Prisoner Reentry Project. This began focusing attention on the issues of release from prison and reentry to the community. It became evident rather quickly from the research that inmates returning to the community faced a wide variety of challenges, ranging from obtaining health care, mental health care, and substance abuse treatment to housing, employment, education, vocational training, and so on. Not only were local parole offices unprepared for the flood of returning prisoners (some seven hundred thousand per year over the past fifteen years or so), but the culture of parole was not focused on facilitating reintegration and behavior change. The primary purpose of parole was supervision and control. Parole was often viewed as a sorting mechanism—those who can make it do, and those who can't get revoked. Parolees' criminogenic deficits and impairments were not addressed while incarcerated, and parole agencies were ill equipped, not properly resourced, and disinclined to address them once inmates were released. That is a perfect recipe for recidivism. And the statistics bear this out—the vast majority recidivate within three years of release from prison. Parole failures, either by revocation or by a new offense, account for 35 percent of all prison admissions.

It's not hard to understand how this typically plays out. The roadblocks begin almost immediately. The lucky ones have housing, although for many it is temporary. Lack of stable housing has a domino effect in many other areas of life. Transportation is also an issue, which makes other things more difficult. Employment is a substantial problem for those released from prison, as is securing mental health and physical health care. Offenders who went to prison with substance abuse problems, in all likelihood, are released with the same problems. When there are so many barriers, it is just not that surprising that parolees take the path that most do.

The vast majority of prison inmates will be released. Over the next decade or so, we can anticipate between five hundred thousand and eight hundred thousand inmates being released from America's prisons each year. This is both a challenge and an opportunity. Today, there are 850,000 individuals under parole supervision in the United States. The typical parole officer supervises over seventy felons, twice the caseload recommended by parole experts. [8]

We have a choice to make. Either continue down the road of minimal assistance for those released from prison, using parole primarily as an opportunity to catch those who violate the conditions and revoke them back to prison, or begin building the capacity to effectively lower the barriers that offenders face when released from prison and actively address the conditions and circumstances that are related to criminality. What is the value of keeping that revolving door spinning? Every time we release an inmate without the appropriate safety net in place to manage risk, address primary crime-related problems, and lower barriers to successful reentry, we once again expose the public to unnecessary and largely avoidable victimization. We also incur tremendous costs, both financial and social.

Unfortunately, it gets worse. There are many collateral consequences associated with having a criminal record. These affect access to housing, employment and licensing, schooling, public benefits, parental rights, credit and loans, interstate travel, and volunteering, among other concerns. Individuals who undergo background checks or who acknowledge prior arrests and convictions experience difficulties securing housing, employment, state occupational licensing, loans, and so on. To be clear, there is a fine line here. The public has a right to know when someone poses a significant risk to others. There are well over seventy-five to eighty million adults in the United States with criminal records, and, unfortunately, we tend to treat all of them as if they are high risk. It is time that we recognize the longer-term hardships placed on offenders, hardships that make successful reentry and remaining crime free more difficult. It is time that we better identify who is and who is not high risk and treat them accordingly. The National Association of Criminal Defense Lawyers has proposed that

> a broad national initiative to construct the legal infrastructure that will provide individuals with a criminal record with a clear path to equal opportunity. The principle that individuals have paid their debt to society when they have completed their court-imposed sentence should guide this initiative. [9]

Whether motivated by a sense of fairness or prudence, the end result is that this is a smart-on-crime initiative. Why should we continue to impose punishments and constraints that increase the likelihood that someone will return to crime?

If the American justice system goes down the road outlined here, we will see a significantly reduced prison population. We will also see many offenders who are sent to prison for long enough periods of time to incapacitate them beyond their high-risk crime career. This transition in the use of incarceration will take years to accomplish. In the interim, and even after the transition, we will need to accommodate those who are released from prison and jail. By *accommodate*, I mean we will need to address both their public-safety risk and their crime-related circumstances, problems, deficits, and impairments. There must be a dramatic increase in resources in order to reduce caseloads and provide appropriate screening, assessment, and programs and services. There also needs to be extensive training of new officers and retraining of existing officers. In addition, we must change not only the goals and objectives of parole but also the way of thinking about crime and punishment. Parole, like the rest of the justice system, must undergo a substantial culture change. [10]

The Future of Jails

Local jails currently serve a variety of functions, including detention for newly arrested felons and individuals awaiting disposition of their cases, as well as individuals convicted of misdemeanors who have been sentenced to incarceration. The majority of the jail population (nearly two-thirds) is being detained before their trials, awaiting disposition. These are offenders who either were denied release or could not post the bond set by the court. Between 35 and 40 percent are serving a sentence of incarceration in jail, usually a year or less, for a misdemeanor conviction. In 2013, 11.7 million individuals were admitted to local jails, which maintained an average daily population of approximately 731,000 inmates.[11]

The research is compelling regarding the importance of the swiftness and certainty of mild/modest punishment. One of the most important functions of local jails of the future is serving as the primary venue for short-term, swift and certain sanctions for enhancing accountability and compliance of those who have been diverted from incarceration. The HOPE court model, as discussed in chapter 4, is producing some quite remarkable results and should be a central component of diversion programming going forward. Using jails to mete out short terms of confinement should be a powerful tool to use in conjunction with community-based, supervised diversion programs. And as we ramp up the capacity of diversion programs, there will be increasing demand on local jails to perform this function. It is important that administrators of diversion programs (probation departments, problem-solving court staff, etc.) create alignment with jail officials so that there is sufficient capacity to accommodate this increased need. It is also important that local jails continue to serve as detention facilities for dangerous individuals awaiting disposition of their cases. This is an essential public-safety role.

THE FUTURE OF PROBATION AND OTHER DIVERSION PROGRAMS

Probation

Prison is intuitively a much less desirable environment for rehabilitation, and the evidence is quite clear—diversion programs are the preferred venue for efforts at behavioral change. Probation, with approximately four million felony and misdemeanor offenders in 2013, is the largest form of diversion in the United States. Unfortunately, it has been largely a lost opportunity over the past thirty-five to forty years, often serving as the stepping-stone to prison.

Probation, which is a post-conviction criminal sentence, is defined as conditional supervised release to the community. The "conditional" part of *supervised conditional release* refers to the court's stipulated conditions of probation, which include a variety of *do*s and *don't*s, such as don't possess weapons or drugs, don't leave the jurisdiction without permission, don't commit a new crime, don't associate with known criminals, do support your family, do report to your probation officer as ordered, and do pay probation fees. These conditions amount to the justice system's attempt at supervised control. The public-safety net for probation is something known as revocation. If a probationer violates the conditions (one or more), the probation officer can file a motion to revoke probation, which returns the case and the offender to the sentencing court for a hearing, the outcome of which determines whether the offender may remain on probation, perhaps with additional conditions imposed, or be revoked to prison (if a felon) or jail (if a misdemeanant). Only two-thirds of probationers successfully complete the period of supervision. One-third are revoked, abscond, or have some other type of unsuccessful exit from supervision. The unfortunate reality is that despite their success or failure on probation, the majority of probationers recidivate.

In theory, probation was designed to allow offenders to remain in the community, thereby avoiding the negative effects of prison or jail. In turn, they would be able to participate in programs and services to help address their negative circumstances and be supervised in order to manage the risk of reoffending, make sure they are accountable for their crimes and compliant with the conditions of supervision, and ensure that they perform any court-ordered community service and pay any restitution to victims. If only it worked that way. There has been a substantial disconnect between the intent and the reality. The disconnect is largely a product of crime control, with its nearly unilateral focus on punishment and control. Incarceration is exceptionally expensive, and the vast majority of corrections spending over the past few decades has gone to incarceration. The expansion of incarceration requires massive investment in bricks and mortar, as well as the ongoing investment in operations and maintenance. The increase in incarceration took resources away from probation, limiting things like programs and services while expanding caseloads. In fact, from 1990 to today, the probation population increased by 50 percent. However, the share of correctional budgets for community supervision dropped from 25 to 20 percent. At the same time, probation caseloads have risen to unmanageable levels. The end result is that the probation of today is focused primarily on risk management and control;

in other words, largely trying to reduce the likelihood of reoffending by the use of supervision and control rather than efforts at rehabilitation.

The probation report card confirms the inability of probation to reduce recidivism both during and after a period of probation supervision.[12] As Judge Roger Warren, a highly respected jurist and criminal justice policy expert, concludes:

> Recidivism rates among these felony defendants [felony probationers] are at unprecedented levels. Almost 60 percent have been previously convicted and more than 40 percent of those on probation fail to complete probation successfully. The high recidivism rate among felony probation pushes up state crime rates and is one of the principal contributors to our extraordinarily high incarceration rates.[13]

Recidivism rates for offenders after discharge from probation are as high as 60–75 percent. That is not success.

Even when rehabilitation is attempted, recent research indicates a profound lack of available services in combination with a system-wide failure to implement evidence-based practices. A nationwide survey of probation departments found that only 23 percent had any vocational training programs; 19 percent conducted mental health assessments; 17 percent had cognitive skills development; 19 percent had job placement and vocational counseling services; 7 percent offered case management; and 15 percent had educational programming. In terms of use of evidence-based practices, 12 percent reported using evidence-based treatment modalities; 34 percent use a standardized, validated risk assessment; and 22 percent use methods to increase treatment motivation.[14] The picture for modern probation is a bit like going to a hospital emergency department in a very poor country. They lack basic equipment like an X-ray machine, a cardiac monitor, or an EEG; they have only limited medications, no lab for testing blood and other samples, and no cardiologists, orthopedists, or oncologists on staff. They may also lack access to medical research and advances in trauma treatment, so they are using knowledge from many decades ago. Clearly, we would be very concerned about the medical outcomes of patients treated in such facilities. Thus it should come as no surprise that failure while on supervision and recidivism after discharge are as high as they are given the state of probation today.

The evidence clearly indicates that probation needs to be seriously recalibrated. Community supervision should balance risk management, accountability, compliance, control, and supervision, on the one hand, with effective screening and assessment, and the evidence-based treatment and programming that is necessary to address the significant, primary conditions and problems associated with an offender's criminality, on the other. Once again, we do not lack scientifically validated information, strategies, and tools that have been shown to effectively reduce probationer recidivism. We know how to do this. Rather, we lack the appropriate institutional and political support, as well as the proper culture/environment within which to focus on behavioral change. There is also a lack of the expertise and leadership in many probation departments and local jurisdictions that are necessary to implement the types of changes recommended here. So it comes down to a matter of money, politics, leadership, expertise, and culture. Caseloads will need to be cut roughly in half, and funding for appropriate screening and assessment, development of treatment/intervention plans, case management, treatment and intervention programs and services, and aftercare will need to be appropriated. Funding this is a matter involving both local and state government. In California, a funding model referred to as performance incentive or performance-based funding rewards local jurisdictions that reduce revocations through the use of evidence-based practices. The funding comes from incarcerations avoided by the use of evidence-based programs and practices. A portion of the avoided incarceration costs due to the reduction in revocations is given to the local probation department. This appears to be a wise funding approach, taking some of the burden off of local government, which is largely responsible for funding probation. It is also important that states participate in funding the changes I am recommending for probation departments because probation success, meaning reduction in revocations and recidivism after discharge, will save states substantial amounts of money by reducing incarceration, which is a state expense. [15]

Other Diversion Programs

There are many other diversion programs scattered throughout the American justice system. The most common is based on the problem-solving, diversion court model as discussed in chapter 4. In addition, there are all kinds of jail diversion, pre-conviction diversion, post-conviction diversion, boot camps, and so forth. The research on which of these types of programs are effective and, in some cases, what about them is effective is accumulating. We have good evidence that can guide the design, implementation, and operation of effective diversion programs.[16]

What we do not have at this point is the presence of these types of programs on a scale that can result in significant changes to recidivism, crime, victimization, and cost. For example, while drug diversion programs are prevalent, nearly all are small in terms of capacity and funding. As mentioned in chapter 4, while common, these programs accommodate only about 5–10 percent of the actual need.

If we are going to get serious about reducing crime and recidivism, we need to get serious about our path forward. The evidence clearly supports addressing the major underlying crime-related problems and deficits of typical criminal offenders as an effective way to reduce recidivism and crime. Drug and alcohol abuse, dependence and addiction, mental illness, neurocognitive disorders, education deficits, and employment problems commonly accompany criminal offending. Diversion from traditional prosecution and punishment is a much-preferred setting for behavioral change. As such, it should be a priority for the future.

Today we lack the political will and appropriate levels of funding to implement diversion on a scale where it becomes a primary component of American criminal justice policy and practice. Acquiring the will is largely a matter of policy makers and elected officials (1) recognizing that there are effective and cost-efficient alternatives to addressing the crime problem and (2) making it a priority to reduce crime, recidivism, victimization, and public spending.

While much of the burden for funding diversion programs falls on local government, largely because diversion programs tend to be local initiatives, the performance-incentive funding that is driving some probation funding is an appropriate source of state funds for diversion programs at the local level. But it is also important that local jurisdictions recognize that crime is local, as are many of its solutions, requiring local governments to confront the need to appropriately fund diversion.

Restorative Justice

If someone is harmed by another—for example, financially harmed by breach of contract or physically harmed by a mistake made during a medical procedure—the harmed party may seek relief in civil court. That is, the harmed party (the plaintiff) may sue the defendant on whatever cause and theory fit the circumstances. If the plaintiff prevails, then a typical remedy is the awarding of monetary damages in order to make the harmed party whole.

On the criminal side of the docket, we typically have an individual who is harmed either financially or physically. While there typically is a victim, the victim is not the plaintiff in a criminal proceeding. Rather, the state is the plaintiff—the party that "sues" the defendant.

When the defendant is convicted, the state then proceeds to impose the remedy, which is typically some form of punishment. What often gets lost in all of this is the victim. There is little effort to make the victim whole from financial losses or physical harm. There are crime victim compensation funds that states operate to help compensate crime victims, but these are generally to reimburse victims for costs incurred for things such as medical care, mental health care, lost wages, child care, funeral costs, and crime-scene cleanup. They do not cover loss due to property crimes. In Texas, the maximum benefit is $50,000, and there are limits on specific items such as mental health care ($3,000), lost wages ($500 per week), child care ($100 per week), funeral costs ($4,500), and crime-scene cleanup ($750).[17] The point is that this is partial assistance, not an attempt to make one whole. Moreover, it requires a good deal of effort and patience to navigate the bureaucracy in order to even receive these partial benefits. Ironically, the Texas fund reimburses victims for attorney's fees (up to $300) for legal assistance in obtaining these benefits.

The initial intent of restorative justice focuses more on crime victims and the community. As the name implies, the purpose is an attempt to restore the victim and community after a crime has occurred. Crime generally involves some form of harm, including harm perpetrated directly on a victim (the owner of the property stolen, the person assaulted) and the community. The harm to the victim is obvious. The harm to the community may be more subtle but still palpable. Crime can more broadly harm the community in terms of things like perceptions of safety, security, and well-being; quality of life; feelings of fear and mistrust; and property values, among others.

Restorative justice generally involves a diversion from traditional criminal prosecution and punishment:

> Restorative justice focuses on holding the offender accountable in a more meaningful way than simply imposing punishment. The major goals are to repair the harm caused by the crime, reintegrate the offender into the community and achieve a sense of healing for the victim and the greater community. The focal point of restorative justice is a face-to-face meeting between the offender, the victim and the community.[18]

Restorative justice diversion programs have different names (conferences, circles, victim-offender mediation) and differ in some relatively minor ways. Regardless of the name and the particular practice, the goal is to bring together the victim, the offender, and representatives from the community in order to develop a strategy or solution that repairs the harm to the victim and the community. Restorative justice programs are viewed as alternatives to traditional criminal prosecution, conviction, and punishment. But they are not totally independent. Rather, there is a reliance on the justice system for the initial referral to a restorative justice diversion program. Offenders are typically referred to these programs by prosecutors or judges. These programs are an opportunity for the victim to explain the impact of the crime, for the offender to take responsibility, and for the parties involved to agree to a restitution plan, whereby the offender attempts to repair the harm done.

Evaluations of restorative justice programs in the United States, Canada, the United Kingdom, Australia, New Zealand, and other countries have shown clearly that there are significant benefits from such efforts. First, victims and offenders who participate are satisfied with the process and the outcomes. Second, restitution agreements, where the offender provides financial compensation to the victim, performs services for the victim, and/or performs community service, are a very important component of the restorative justice process. They are also an opportunity for the offender to be accountable for the offense and actively take responsibility to repair the harm done. The research indicates that in the vast majority of cases, these restitution agreements are successfully carried out.[19] More recent research affirms the satisfaction that both victims and offenders have with the restorative justice process, as well as the high levels of compliance with restitution agreements. Research likewise shows that these effects are evident across a variety of offender types—property and violent offenders, juvenile and adult. The research also shows significant reductions in recidivism as a result of participation in the process.[20]

While there are a number of important positive outcomes from restorative practices, including victim compensation, repairing harm to the community, overall greater satisfaction of victims and offenders compared to traditional criminal adjudication and punishment, and reduced recidivism, these programs and practices are far from having a significant presence in the big picture of American justice policy. This is understandable, since restorative justice is a rather difficult fit in a policy based largely on punishment. Understandable, but unfortunate. One of the more important aspects of restorative justice is that it brings the community into the process. Up to this point, crime and its solutions have been the responsibility of the government. We have been largely idle bystanders. The advantage here is that community members are involved in decision making and identifying solutions. And in many instances, those solutions are successful both in the short term (the victim is compensated for harm) and in the longer term (reduced recidivism). Restorative justice programs need to have a much-expanded presence in the administration of criminal justice going forward. As is the case with the intervention strategies discussed in earlier chapters, we have the tools to design, implement, and operate highly effective programs. What is required is the development of a balanced, comprehensive approach to crime that allocates a significant role for restorative justice and the community.

THE DEATH PENALTY

There aren't many ways to be tougher on crime than the ultimate punishment of death. The United States is not alone in the use of the death penalty, but we do belong to an ever-shrinking group of nations that have it. Two-thirds of the countries of the world have abolished the death penalty, including all of the nations of the European Union, Canada, Australia, New Zealand, and every other major U.S. trading partner with the exception of Japan. The following nations in the world still have and use the death penalty: Afghanistan, Antigua and Barbuda, Bahamas, Bahrain, Bangladesh, Barbados, Belarus, Belize, Botswana, Chad, China, Comoros, Cuba, the Democratic Republic of the Congo, Dominica, Egypt, Equatorial Guinea, Ethiopia, Gambia, Guatemala, Guinea, Guyana, India,

Indonesia, Iran, Iraq, Jamaica, Japan, Jordan, Kuwait, Lebanon, Lesotho, Libya, Malaysia, Nigeria, North Korea, Oman, Pakistan, the Palestinian Authority, Qatar, Saint Kitts and Nevis, Saint Lucia, Saint Vincent and the Grenadines, Saudi Arabia, Singapore, Somalia, South Sudan, Sudan, Syria, Taiwan, Thailand, Trinidad and Tobago, Uganda, the United Arab Emirates, the United States of America, Vietnam, Yemen, and Zimbabwe. Of these, only nine regularly execute offenders. The top five are China, Iran, Iraq, Saudi Arabia, and the United States. Interesting company we keep.

Today thirty-two U.S. states have the death penalty. Currently (as of April 1, 2015), there are 3,002 convicted inmates on the death rows of those thirty-two states. California leads the way with 742, followed by 410 in Florida, and 278 in Texas. California has such a bulging death row population because they have executed only thirteen individuals since 1992. There have been no executions in California since 2006. Texas led the way in executions in 2013, with sixteen inmates put to death, and Texas has led the way since the death penalty was reinstated by the U.S. Supreme Court in 1976, with a total of 516 executions. The only other states with over 100 executions since 1976 are Oklahoma, with 111, and Virginia, with 110.[21]

Eighteen states have abolished the death penalty, and one-third of those abolished it within the past eight years. There have been between forty and sixty executions per year over the past ten years, which is down considerably from the peak years of the late 1990s and early 2000s. At the same time, the number of death sentences has declined dramatically. In 1995, there were just over three hundred death sentences imposed. Beginning in 2000, the number began declining substantially every year. By 2012, there were eighty-two death sentences in capital cases nationwide. In 2014, it dropped to seventy-two.[22] There is a clear trend away from the imposition of death sentences. This is in part because all thirty-two states with the death penalty now also have life without parole sentences. This gives prosecutors and juries an alternative to death. There is also what appears to be reluctance, or at least substantial delays, in carrying out the death penalty.

Despite a number of serious concerns about the death penalty, the public still seems to support it. Gallup survey results indicate that in 2013, 60 percent of the respondents reported that they are in favor of the death penalty. Nearly one-half believe that the death penalty is not imposed enough, and one-half believe that it is applied fairly (40 percent indicated it was not). Support is related to political party—71 percent of Republicans, 45 percent of Democrats, and 57 percent of independents support the death penalty. Support also seems to rest on the belief by 61 percent of respondents that the death penalty is "morally acceptable." However, when respondents are given options or are asked comparison questions rather than simple "do you support" questions, the picture looks a bit different. In 2007, only 39 percent of those polled had confidence that the justice system sentences to death only those who are truly guilty. Seventy-five percent believe that because mistakes are common and because death is final, there needs to be a higher standard of proof for death penalty cases. Moreover, in 2006 respondents were essentially evenly split in terms of preference for life without parole and the death sentence when given the option of choosing.

The death penalty is expensive. As Sterling Goodspeed, the former district attorney of Warren County, New York, stated, "I think I could prove to you that I could put someone in the Waldorf Astoria Hotel for 60 to 70 years and feed them three meals a day cheaper than we can litigate a single death penalty case."[23] A study by the Urban Institute estimated that in Maryland, a capital case costs about $3 million to prosecute, convict, appeal, and incarcerate until execution.[24] That is $2 million more than a comparable non–death penalty case. In Texas, it is $2.3 million per death penalty case. A study in California estimates that the death penalty costs the state $137 million per year. It would cost $11.5 million if those cases were not death penalty cases. Data from ten states show that the cost of a death penalty case is roughly ten times the cost of a non–death penalty case. In California, it is twenty times the cost of a nondeath case.[25] Another study shows that the cost of death penalty cases ranges between $2 million and $5 million per case, compared to less than $1 million for murder cases where the defendant is sentenced to life without parole.[26] The excess cost to try, convict, sentence, and execute an offender compared to the cost of trying, convicting, sentencing, and incarcerating someone for life in prison without parole is roughly $8.5 billion for the 3,070 inmates currently on death row in the United States. Much of the extra cost is incurred during the prosecution and sentencing phases of a capital case rather than during incarceration and appeal pending execution.

No matter which figures we use, the bottom line is the same—the death penalty is extraordinarily expensive. So what does all of this investment in the death penalty buy? Some believe that the death penalty deters others from committing murder. In fact, one-third of individuals surveyed in a 2011 Gallup poll indicated that they believe the death penalty does deter; two-thirds do not believe that is the case. The evidence is clear— there is little valid, reliable scientific evidence indicating that the death penalty has any utility in terms of being a deterrent. In fact, as recently as 2012, the National Research Council of the National Academies published the definitive work on the death penalty–deterrence debate and concluded that there is no evidence that the death penalty deters.

Absent a deterrent effect, we are left with the question: Is the death penalty worth it? This is real taxpayer money that is being spent. It is the prosecutor's discretion to charge a capital offense, to prosecute it, and to seek the death penalty. Thus, the prosecutor's decision to file a capital indictment and seek the death penalty has significant financial implications.

In addition to cost and the fact that the death penalty does not prevent other crime, there is the issue of error. Analysis of over forty-five hundred capital cases revealed an extraordinary rate of error in the proceedings. In nearly 70 percent of the thousands of cases analyzed, the experts found prejudicial, reversible error. And there are questions about whether the appellate review of cases catches all of the errors. After state courts threw out nearly 50 percent of death sentences, a federal review found serious error in 40 percent of the cases that were not thrown out by state courts.[27]

There have been 317 post-conviction DNA exonerations in the United States; eighteen death row inmates have been exonerated with DNA evidence, and an additional sixteen who were exonerated were capital convictions but were not sentenced to death. An additional 140 death row inmates have been released from death row because of other (non-DNA) evidence of their innocence. Thus, we are aware of 175 cases where evidence exonerated a death row inmate. Those death row inmates who were exonerated with DNA evidence served an average of 13.5 years. Combined, they served over forty-two hundred years in prison.[28] The reasons for wrongful convictions include incorrect eyewitness testimony (an element in 70 percent of the death row exonerations), poor forensic science (an element in 50 percent of the exonerations), and false confessions (62 percent of the homicide cases involved false confessions). Documentaries like *Incendiary: The Willingham Case*, by Joe Bailey Jr. and Steve Mims, or *Frontline*'s "Death by Fire" illustrate many problems with the death penalty and can easily raise very significant questions about wrongful convictions and executions.

Prosecutors charge capital offenses, prosecute them, and obtain the death penalty either with a false belief in deterrence or with some moral entitlement to revenge. But that raises questions as well. For instance, what is the value of revenge? We tend to think of it as getting even, an eye for an eye, motivated by disgust, spite, perhaps hatred for the criminal act and the criminal. Do we feel a sense of relief when someone is executed? The research is relatively clear that the presumed emotional catharsis associated with revenge is not often achieved. [29]

Then there is the question of who benefits from revenge—the victim's friends and relatives, the "community," the prosecutor? Perhaps the victim's family gets some closure, but the research on revenge suggests that while there may be some emotional impact for the victim's friends and relatives, that reaction is not often positive. I would offer that except in high-profile cases, the "community" does not follow such matters, so any benefits to society at large by a particular execution are probably minimal. Undoubtedly, there have been many circumstances where prosecutors have carried the tough-on-crime mantle by charging capital crimes and requesting the death penalty from juries. But is that justice? It's hard to say. Justice per se is not vindictive. Rather, it is an effort to right a wrong by means that are legal, fair, and legitimate. Unfortunately, the errors and inequities in the death penalty raise a question about the extent to which we are really talking about justice.

Some suggest that the right of the government to punish wrongdoers helps reinforce the rule of law. However, such a function of punishment, as the argument goes, is really only necessary where the legal system is dysfunctional or ill defined, not where it is well established and generally considered legitimate. If anything, because of recent discoveries of wrongly convicted death row inmates, public officials in some states are questioning the death penalty.

Jack Harry Smith is a seventy-seven-year-old inmate on death row at the Polunsky Unit in the Texas prison system. Smith was a welder with a sixth-grade education. He was first arrested and convicted for larceny and robbery in 1955 and sentenced to seven years in the Texas Department of

Corrections. He was paroled in 1958. He was convicted again for robbery in 1960 and sentenced to life. He became eligible for parole and was released in 1977. His final conviction was in 1978 for the shooting death of Roy Deputter, who tried to stop Smith and an accomplice during a robbery. Deputter walked in the back door of a convenience store in Pasadena, Texas; pulled a gun on the robbers; and was shot and killed by Smith. Smith and the accomplice fled with an undetermined amount of money. They were apprehended at the accomplice's apartment. Smith was subsequently convicted of capital murder and sentenced to death. He has been on death row for thirty-six years. I saw Mr. Smith at the Polunsky Unit when I was there visiting another death row inmate for whom I was assisting on an appeal. I saw Mr. Smith when they brought him to the visitation area. He was in a wheelchair. I was told that his health is very poor, and he is obviously quite frail. I saw several other older death row inmates and had the same impression. And I thought, "What is the point?"

Nearly 40 percent of Texas's death row inmates have been on death row for fifteen years or more. Ten have been there thirty or more years, twenty-five have been there twenty-five or more years, and fifty-two have been there twenty or more years. By the time we get around to executing death row inmates, many are very different people. There is typically a minimum of fifteen years between conviction and execution (and, in many cases, much more than that). That does not negate what they did to get to death row, nor does it mean we should not be sensitive to the victim's family, but it does raise a question about what we are accomplishing with executing individuals who are substantially different from the person who committed the crime.

7

DRUGS, GUNS, AND GANGS

Perhaps the three greatest crime challenges to the American criminal justice system are drugs, guns, and gangs. In this chapter, we will discuss the nature and scale of each of these problems and what can be done to address and mitigate their impact. The drug problem, both possession and use, as well as manufacture and distribution, seems intractable. After all, we have been fighting a war on drugs for over forty-five years, and whether we are willing to admit it or not, we have profoundly failed. Organized crime, in the form of urban street gangs, plays a primary role in America's dependence on illicit substances. More recently, drug dealing has changed dramatically with the introduction of the Mexican cartels and their liberal use of local gangs to distribute drugs on the street corners of American cities. Moreover, it is an unfortunate fact that weapons are ever present where we find drugs and gangs. Thus, there is a natural intersection of drugs, guns, and gangs that makes the problems that result from that intersection particularly acute and makes remedies at least partially interdependent.

This chapter will discuss a path forward regarding American drug policy, a path that provides for a dramatically enhanced emphasis on demand reduction and harm reduction. We will also discuss effective, evidence-based gun-control strategies, as well as gang interdiction tactics that have been successful in a variety of jurisdictions.

DRUG-CONTROL POLICY PAST AND FUTURE

The United States has a massive drug problem. In 2012, over twenty-two million individuals ages twelve and older were identified as having a substance dependence or abuse problem within the past twelve months. Two-thirds of this is alcohol abuse/dependence. The remainder is drug only or drug and alcohol. This represents 10 percent of the U.S. population twelve and older. The Substance Abuse and Mental Health Services Administration (SAMHSA) estimates that of the over twenty-two million individuals in need of treatment for substance abuse each year, only about two million receive any treatment regardless of type, quality, or length of treatment. That leaves over twenty million annually who go untreated. A primary barrier to treatment for those who want it is cost—individuals do not have sufficient health care coverage or cannot pay out-of-pocket expenses for treatment.

Drug and alcohol abuse have phenomenal public health consequences. SAMHSA estimates that substance abuse results in over 2.3 million hospital emergency room visits per year at an annual cost of nearly $3 billion. There are also approximately thirty thousand drug-related deaths in the United States each year. The U.S. Department of Justice estimates that the total economic impact of substance abuse is $200 billion annually. This includes crime and criminal justice costs, health costs, and lost productivity costs. By way of comparison, the economic impact of cancer is $172 billion and diabetes $132 billion annually. The Columbia University National Center on Addiction and Substance Abuse reported that in 2005, state and federal expenditures for substance abuse amounted to $467 billion. Only 2 percent of that was spent on treating abuse. The vast majority of government spending on substance abuse is on consequences rather than treatment and prevention. At the same time, it is clear that the return on investment of substance abuse treatment is quite favorable. The National Institute on Drug Abuse reports that the return on investment of treatment is twelve to one, meaning that for every dollar invested in substance abuse treatment, governments will save $12 in drug-related health care and criminal justice costs.

It should come as no surprise that U.S. drug policy has been primarily punishment focused and that the criminal justice system has served as the front line in the war on drugs. Take, for example, John Horner, a forty-five-year-old fast-food restaurant worker and father who sold some of his legally prescribed pain medication to an undercover police informant. The informant told Horner he could not afford his prescription pain medication and asked if Horner would sell him some of his. Horner did and was arrested. After his conviction, he received a twenty-five-year mandatory minimum prison sentence. [1]

Consider also the case of Mandy Martinson, who became addicted to meth while living in an abusive relationship. She left her boyfriend and moved in with a drug dealer who had a constant supply of meth. The police raided their house and arrested both Mandy and her new boyfriend. Her boyfriend claimed she assisted him in his drug enterprise and also stated that she possessed a weapon that was found on the premises. Mandy was sentenced to a fifteen-year mandatory minimum prison sentence. Her boyfriend received a twelve-year prison sentence. [2]

Cornel Hood is serving a life sentence for possession of two pounds of marijuana. Hood, a thirty-five-year-old New Orleans resident, had been arrested three times before for possession of marijuana. In all three prior cases, the judge deferred the sentence and placed Hood on probation. Upon conviction in this case, Hood was sentenced to life in prison under Louisiana's three-strikes law. [3]

Background

In 1971, President Richard Nixon declared, "Public enemy number 1 in the United States is drug abuse. In order to fight and defeat this enemy, it is necessary to wage a new, all-out offensive." [4] Thus began the war on drugs, a forty-five-year assault on drug use, possession, manufacture, and distribution. The Reagan administration was largely responsible for ramping up punishment for drug law violations in the federal system and was influential in state-level changes to drug laws. The crack epidemic hit urban areas in the United States in the mid-1980s, adding considerably to the war strategy as the primary focus of drug-control policy. The George H. W. Bush administration was responsible for creating the Office of National Drug Control Policy, an executive-level office presided over by what is known as the drug czar. The Clinton administration further expanded crime-control drug policies, and the George W. Bush administration linked drugs and terrorism—"if you quit drugs, you join the fight against terrorism."

The drug issue has been politically important over the years, and because of that importance, there has been bipartisan support and enthusiasm for the war rhetoric and the policy of tough punishment for users, dealers, and manufacturers. Two of the standard-bearers of tough-on-crime drug laws are New York State, with the Rockefeller Drug Laws, and the federal government's Anti-Drug Abuse Act of 1986, which created mandatory minimum drug sentences in the federal system. The Rockefeller Drug Laws, which were signed into law in 1973 by then Governor Nelson Rockefeller, provided the harshest punishment yet for drug law violations. The penalty for selling 2 ounces (57 grams) or more of heroin, morphine, opium, cocaine, or marijuana, or possessing 4 ounces (113 grams) or more of these substances resulted in a minimum fifteen years to life and a maximum of twenty-five years to life in prison. Michigan quickly followed suit and passed the so-called 650-Lifer Law, which resulted in life without parole for the sale, manufacture, or possession of 650 grams (1.4 pounds) or more of cocaine or opiates.

The 1986 federal Anti-Drug Abuse Act was passed partly in response to the drug-overdose death of basketball star Len Bias, who had just signed with the Boston Celtics. The act was also an effort by congressional Democrats to gain political capital by being tough on drug crime. The Speaker of the House at the time was Tip O'Neill, who was from Boston, the home of the Celtics. He saw the opportunity to position Democrats as tough on drugs and moved the act through the House in time for Democrats to take advantage in the November midterm elections. A primary component of the Anti-Drug Abuse Act was mandatory minimum sentences for drug law violations. Federal mandatory minimum drug sentences apply to nearly all controlled substances. The punishment is tied directly to quantity. For example, the mandatory minimum prison term (without parole) for first-time drug offenders is five years for possession of one gram of LSD, five grams of crack cocaine, one hundred grams of heroin, ten grams of methamphetamine, or ten grams of PCP. Possession of just ten grams of certain drugs when a defendant has one prior felony drug conviction will result in a mandatory minimum of twenty years in prison.

Tough drug laws have had a profound impact on the U.S. justice system. In particular, drug offenders have played an important statistical role in the incarceration explosion. Approximately 25 percent of state prison inmates and two-thirds of federal prison inmates are drug offenders. Absent the drug problem and absent tough drug-control policies, the United States would be incarcerating roughly 500,000 fewer prison inmates (more than 350,000 state and 136,000 federal prisoners).

For a variety of reasons, substance abuse and crime are fundamentally linked. The numbers are particularly staggering—somewhere between 60 percent and 80 percent of U.S. prison inmates meet the standard diagnostic criteria for alcohol and/or drug abuse or dependence. Approximately 70 percent of the entire corrections population (prison, jail, probation, and parole) meet the criteria for alcohol/drug abuse or dependence.[5] Despite huge numbers of drug-abusing offenders, it is remarkable that we have been satisfied to punish them and then release them essentially no better off than when they entered the system. On a good day, only about 15 percent of criminal offenders in need of drug or alcohol treatment receive any kind of treatment while in the justice system.

Supply Control

The primary focus of U.S. drug policy has been on attempting to control supply through a variety of domestic and international interdiction efforts, controlling the flow of drugs over U.S. borders, controlling the movement of drugs domestically, interrupting local drug-distribution networks, and arresting users. The logic, presumably, is that if we can limit the supply of drugs, availability at the local level will become restricted, prices will increase, and economic theory (price elasticity) suggests that users will stop buying. The logic of price elasticity of demand applies to many consumer products. But when factors like dependence or addiction drive decision-making and purchasing behavior, the model loses it predictive utility because demand becomes price inelastic—purchasing is generally insensitive to price.

The other problem with U.S. drug-supply control efforts is that they have not worked. One of the primary measures of supply-control effectiveness is change in the prices of illicit drugs. Assuming demand is constant, as supply declines, prices should increase. The evidence is to the contrary. The Office of National Drug Control Policy tracks the street-level prices of different drugs. Between 1980 and 2012, the prices for cocaine, heroin, crack, and methamphetamine have all declined substantially, especially in the mid-1980s through the 1990s. Marijuana prices actually increased through the early 1990s, then stabilized through the 2000s. That increase has more to do with dramatic increases in quality (potency) than any impact of supply control.

One of the primary reasons for the failure of supply-control efforts is because the U.S. demand for drugs is so strong, and there is so much money to be made in the drug trade. Moreover, the Mexican drug cartels are very well organized, sophisticated, well trained and well equipped, and highly motivated. The reality is that U.S. drug enforcement is not much of a match for the cartels and their extensive network of street-level gangs that distribute drugs locally. Moreover, the cartels are very inventive in terms of getting drugs into the United States. They have their own 747 aircraft, cargo ships, submarines, and fishing vessels. They use trains to ship drugs to U.S. destinations. They also use tunnels under the border, dug with sophisticated horizontal drilling equipment. When the United States built a fence along the Arizona-Mexico border, the cartel made and used a catapult to fling one-hundred-pound bales of marijuana over the border into Arizona. When a Sinaloa tunnel was discovered, the cartel changed course and began putting cocaine in vacuum-sealed cans of jalapeños, which they shipped to local Mexican markets in the United States.

The U.S. Department of Justice estimates that the Mexican cartels gross between $18 billion and $39 billion annually. Other sources such as the RAND Corporation have a much lower estimate of $6.6 billion annually. Regardless of which estimate one uses, the profits are staggering. Consider that one kilo of cocaine from Colombia can be purchased by a cartel for $2,000. In Mexico, that same kilo increases in value to $10,000. Once it crosses the U.S. border, it is worth $30,000. When broken down and sold in grams, it can accrue $100,000. That is a 4,900 percent increase. [6]

It may seem somewhat surprising to conclude that supply control has failed when we consider how much money has been spent on this effort. Since its launch, the war on drugs has cost U.S. taxpayers $1 trillion. One would be hard pressed to find many who would admit that this has been a wise policy. Essentially every major newspaper, television news department, and Internet media outlet has declared the war on drugs a failure. So has the journal *Science*, the Global Commission on Drug Policy, the National Research Council, former presidents Jimmy Carter and Bill Clinton, the United Kingdom's Drug Policy Commission, Right on Crime, and most candid judges and prosecutors, not to mention the U.S.

public. A 2012 survey found that 82 percent of respondents believe that the war on drugs has been a failure.

The Criminal Justice Response

At the same time that the efforts by a variety of federal agencies to keep drugs out of the United States have failed, our criminal justice response has not worked, either. There are two good reasons why. First, punishing users—particularly problem users who are abusing, dependent, or addicted—does nothing to change behavior. There is nothing about being locked up or supervised on probation that addresses the underlying causes of substance abuse. Despite what may be conventional wisdom, drug/alcohol abuse is not simply a matter of just stopping. As well intentioned as it may have been, Nancy Reagan's "Just Say No" campaign was a tremendous disservice to drug and alcohol treatment since it characterized substance abuse as a choice and addiction as something one could just turn off. Alcoholism was recognized as a medical disorder by the American Medical Association in 1956. Similarly, the American Psychiatric Association defined substance abuse as a disorder decades ago. As ridiculous as it is to treat diabetes or cancer by placing someone in custody, it is equally naïve to assume that punishment will treat a substance abuse disorder. Unfortunately, some public opinion is still lagging behind the scientific and medical community. Close to a majority of New Jersey respondents in a recent public opinion survey stated that drug abuse and addiction are a moral failing.

A second problem with the criminal justice response involves the arrest, conviction, and punishment of drug couriers and drug dealers. Much of what has characterized U.S. drug policy is the rather dramatic increase in punishment for drug dealers. This has been accomplished to a considerable extent by the use of mandatory minimums, habitual offender sentences, truth in sentencing laws increasing time served, and determinate sentences that dictate longer terms of incarceration. What aggressive incarceration of dealers fails to appreciate is the fact that they are replaceable. Drug dealers work in environments where there typically is a healthy supply of eager individuals willing to step in and enjoy the benefits of the drug trade, so taking the dealer off the street does not necessarily remove the crime from the street. A drug organization that follows some basic business principles will very likely survive the removal of some street-level dealers or even more senior individuals in the organization. The reason is that demand is so strong and there is so much money to be made.

Nevertheless, we continue down that road. In 2012, there were over 1.5 million individuals in the United States arrested for nonviolent drug offenses. Half of those (750,000) were for marijuana-law violations and the vast majority of those arrests (88 percent) were for possession only.[7] Given what we know about the effectiveness of supply-control efforts and how much that costs and given what we know about the criminal justice response to drug use and how much that costs, it stands to reason that we ask some basic questions. How smart is it to continue wasting billions and billions of dollars in efforts to control the flow of drugs over the border? How smart is it to continue wasting billions and billions of dollars criminalizing and punishing drug possession when it is obvious that punishment does not alter drug use? We should be very concerned that so much money has been wasted when the scientific evidence clearly indicates effective and cost-efficient ways to address the problem of substance abuse. We should also be very concerned that current policies have done little to mitigate the longer-term public health consequences and costs of substance abuse.

Where Do We Go From Here?

Demand Reduction

As logical as supply control sounds, the reality of the situation indicates that a much more balanced approach that includes some supply-control strategies but a much-increased demand and harm reduction focus is warranted. This involves moving much of the drug problem out of the criminal justice arena and into the public health arena.

The Center on Addiction and Substance Abuse at Columbia University reported that of the $467 billion state and federal governments spent on substance abuse and addiction in 2005, only 1.9 percent of that was used for demand reduction—prevention and treatment. The center's 2009 report describes the cost implications of substance abuse in the United States:

A staggering 71.1 percent of total federal and state spending on the burden of addiction is in two areas: health and justice. Almost three-fifths (58.0 percent) of federal and state spending on the burden of substance abuse and addiction (74.1 percent of the federal burden) is in the area of health care where untreated addiction causes or contributes to over 70 other diseases requiring hospitalization. The second largest area of substance-related federal and state burden spending is the justice system (13.1 percent). [8]

In 2012, the Obama administration signaled a change in drug policy. Gil Kerlikowski, the director of the Office of National Drug Control Policy, embraced the medical community's conclusion that substance abuse and addiction are not moral failings or simply bad decisions, but chronic brain diseases that can be treated. As such, Kerlikowski stated that going forward, the national policy will shift the emphasis more toward treatment. In the rollout of the 2012 National Drug Control Policy, Kerlikowski stated:

> Outdated policies like the mass incarceration of nonviolent drug offenders are relics of the past that ignore the need for a balanced public health and safety approach to our drug problem. The policy alternatives contained in our new Strategy support mainstream reforms based on the proven facts that drug addiction is a disease of the brain that can be prevented and treated and that we cannot simply arrest our way out of the drug problem. [9]

The outlook for substance abuse treatment in general has gotten better with the passage of the Affordable Care Act (ACA). The act provides that by 2014, parity for substance abuse treatment will be in effect. This means that coverage for substance abuse treatment shall be on par with coverage for the treatment of other chronic diseases. Moreover, the expansion of Medicaid at the state level provides medical, psychiatric, and substance abuse treatment to large numbers of poor individuals. As of fall 2015, nineteen states have not expanded Medicaid. At the same time that there are effective ways to provide substance abuse treatment for individuals who have no other access, we encounter a troubling irony. Nearly all of the Republican presidential candidates in the 2016 campaign are calling for criminal justice reform, including rethinking the incarceration of nonviolent drug offenders. These are the same candidates who vow to repeal the ACA, and the vast majority of them are from states that have not expanded Medicaid.

The scientific community has clearly substantiated the effectiveness and cost-efficiency of treatment as the primary method for addressing the drug problem. The National Institute on Abuse developed estimates of the return on investment for treating substance abuse. They estimate that for every dollar spent on treatment, there is an expected savings of $12 in criminal justice and health care costs. We know how to effectively treat substance abuse at the same relative level of success as treating other chronic diseases. Treatment failure is, at least in part, a function of using inappropriate treatment modalities; employing untrained, inappropriate, and inadequate treatment staff; providing interventions in less than ideal settings (such as prison); failing to address other physical health and situational problems (for example, other chronic diseases, homelessness, co-occurring mental health disorders, unemployment); and failing to engage in ongoing maintenance, such as twelve-step programs.

The point is that today we have the therapeutic tools to effectively and cost-efficiently treat substance abuse. What is required is using these evidence-based tools in appropriate settings with the appropriate professionals, with ongoing maintenance, and as part of a bigger picture of intervening and addressing the crime-related problems and deficits that are related to an offender's criminality.

Demand reduction through treatment of substance-abusing individuals will reduce the number of individuals entering the justice system, in turn reducing the number of individuals cycling in and out of the justice system. Diversion to drug and alcohol treatment, in the form of either diversion courts or probation programs, is clearly preferable to incarceration.

One of the more promising strategies for identifying individuals with significant substance abuse problems and getting them into treatment uses medical facilities as intercept points. Every year, there are nearly eight million admissions to the nation's emergency rooms (ERs). Data indicate that approximately 60 percent of those admitted to ERs are under the influence of alcohol and/or drugs. SBIRT is a screening and assessment strategy developed by SAMHSA. SBIRT stands for screening, brief intervention, and referral to treatment. It is designed to be used in primary care physicians' offices, ERs, college and university health centers, and community health centers. The goal is universal screening at all medical and dental visits using a standardized screening protocol. The intervention component uses motivating techniques to encourage treatment-seeking behavior. Referral to treatment is intended to be referral to specialty substance abuse treatment, if that is indicated.

One of the primary advantages of SBIRT is that it places substance abuse directly in the public health arena. The success of this approach depends on a number of things, including the availability of appropriate out-patient and in-patient treatment capacity. Again, access to treatment should be facilitated by the substance abuse parity requirement in the ACA. The evidence indicates that SBIRT is effective in detecting and reducing substance abuse, as well as health-related costs associated with abuse and addiction. Financial analyses show that for every dollar invested in SBIRT, there is a $4 saving in health-related costs. SBIRT has been called the future of drug policy in America by the director of the Office of National Drug Control Policy, who also states that it saves lives, saves money, and can reduce the burden that drug abuse puts on the health care and justice systems.[10] The evidence clearly demonstrates that SBIRT needs to become the default approach for the medical community. SBIRT is currently used in only a fraction of the potential sites across the country.

Substance abuse treatment is effective and substantially reduces a variety of collateral consequences. It also saves tremendous amounts of money.[11]

> The National Treatment Improvement Evaluation Study (1997) found that treatment reduces re-arrest by 64%, reduces drug use by 50% and reduces criminal activity by 80%. . . . Research from the National Institutes of Health, Columbia University, University of Pennsylvania, and many other prestigious institutions have demonstrated that drug treatment reduces drug use by 50% to 60%, reduces arrests and therefore criminal justice involvement by 40% or more, increases employment by 60% to 80%, and reduces HIV and provides many other public health benefits. . . . The calculable economic benefits of drug treatment significantly and substantially exceed the costs, whether it is in-prison treatment or treatment provided under community supervision. . . . The annual economic benefit accrued in the domains of avoided crimes, employment, avoided health service utilization, employment income, and money not spent on substances was $42,905 greater than the cost of treatment. The vast majority, $42,151, was due to avoided criminal activity.

Treatment for individuals already in the justice system should be provided primarily in diversion settings like drug courts and probation. However, a number of changes are required in order to make drug and alcohol treatment in noncustodial settings effective. First, there is a considerable gap between what the research indicates are evidence-based practices and what actually occurs in reality. Survey results show that correctional substance abuse treatment is seriously lacking in a number of very important ways. It lacks adequate capacity and expertise, proper screening and assessment protocol, appropriate treatment modalities, appropriate treatment dosage, appropriate use of medication for opiate and alcohol withdrawal, and assurance that those who have completed treatment receive aftercare. Funding is always an issue. Because the courts have not recognized substance abuse as a medical problem, there is no constitutional guarantee to treatment like there is under the Eighth Amendment for health care.

As mentioned earlier, the drug court model is a very good one, and evaluations show considerable success with this approach. However, capacity is seriously constrained—drug courts address about 5–10 percent of the need. If we are going to get serious about effectively addressing the massive drug and alcohol problem in this country, we have to get way beyond the symbolic presence of drug diversion courts and make them a prominent part of the correctional system.

The failure to implement effective substance abuse treatment for the large numbers of offenders in the justice system in need of treatment is extraordinarily shortsighted and expensive. The expense does not accrue just to the justice system. There are massive costs associated with health care, loss of productivity, and social support programs, not to mention the social costs to communities and families. Pretending it is not a problem or assuming that substance abusers will get help elsewhere or trying to punish the addiction out of offenders are strategies with monumentally detrimental consequences. Our failure to effectively reduce demand for drugs has kept the war on drugs alive and well and costing taxpayers hundreds of billions of dollars. It has helped keep America's prisons bulging, and it has kept the cartels and other drug suppliers/traffickers in the driver's seat. How smart is that?

Harm Reduction

Supply control in the United States is nearly impossible to achieve and demand reduction is a massive effort that has just begun. No matter how successful either is, drug use will occur. Harm reduction recognizes that drug use is a fact of life (as is alcohol use and abuse) and focuses on trying to limit the harm.

The Centers for Disease Control (CDC) report that needle-exchange programs can reduce HIV/AIDS transmission by 80 percent among those who inject drugs. One-third of all HIV/AIDS cases (355,000 people) have been caused by sharing infected needles. In 1998, the surgeon general concluded that needle-exchange or clean-needle programs are very effective at reducing needle-borne diseases and do not encourage the use of illicit drugs.

A federal ban on funding needle-exchange programs was implemented in 1988 and survived the first Bush administration, the Clinton administration, and the second Bush administration. The Obama administration lifted the ban in 2009, but Congress reinstated a ban in 2011 that prohibits any federal assistance or financial support for clean-needle programs. In 2013, there were 233 local needle-exchange programs in the United States. Well over one-half of them are in just five states (California, New Mexico, New York, Washington, and Wisconsin). Twenty states do not have any, and the rest have just two to five programs statewide.

Heroin substitution is a safe, effective method for managing heroin use. It also has collateral benefits such as reduced needle use, lower criminality, and enhanced physical health, mental health, cognitive abilities, productivity, and social functioning.

Sobriety centers, also known as restoration centers, are medically supervised places where individuals who are under the influence of alcohol or drugs can go to detoxify and sober up. They are used as a substitute for jail for individuals picked up by the police for public intoxication or being under the influence of drugs. In addition to being a safe place for short-term crisis care and sobering up, they also can provide referral to treatment, as well as harm-reduction services such as heroin substitution, HIV services, physical and mental health referral, and so forth. Sobriety centers are gaining traction, but they are far from being ubiquitous.

172

Decriminalization and Legalization

The drug problem in the United States is substantial and complex. No single strategy is likely to significantly impact drug use and mitigate the collateral consequences. A multipronged, balanced approach should include some supply control, considerable demand and harm reduction, and a serious consideration of decriminalization and legalization. Let's face it, it is time to surrender, whether we like it or not. The war has lost legitimacy, and criminalizing drug possession has accomplished little in terms of reducing use.

In 2000, Portugal introduced a new law that decriminalized the use, possession, and acquisition of a personal amount (defined as a ten-day supply) of all illicit drugs or controlled substances. The intent was not to legalize drugs but to shift the focus from a criminal justice response to substance use to a public health response. The law created commissions or panels, referred to as Commissions for the Dissuasion of Drug Addiction, that consist of social workers, legal experts, and medical professionals. They function to provide advice to drug addicts and encourage them to enter treatment. The goals include use (demand) reduction and harm reduction.

A good deal of attention has been focused on the Portuguese experience, with its across-the-board decriminalization. After fifteen years in place, the evidence indicates relative success. Despite what some critics anticipated, drug use in Portugal has not skyrocketed since decriminalization. There have been off-setting trends—slight increases among adults in use of some drugs and slight declines among teenagers. Importantly, since decriminalization, problematic drug use (intravenous drug use or long-term, regular use of cocaine, heroin, or amphetamines) has declined, a trend that is contrary to what has been happening in other European nations, especially Italy and Spain. Moreover, the evidence shows that drug-related diseases such as HIV and hepatitis have declined, as has drug-related mortality. One of the most important consequences of the Portuguese effort is the substantial increase (62 percent) in drug users entering treatment. There has also been a more than doubling of the number of drug users entering drug-substitution treatment (for example, methadone for heroin use). The Portuguese law also has taken considerable pressure off of the criminal justice system, including large decreases in drug arrests and sentences of incarceration for drug offenses.

As Jordan Woods, one of many astute observers of the Portuguese effort, has noted:

> The Portuguese decriminalization experience illustrates that there are potential benefits to treating the use of all illicit drugs as a matter of public health. Decriminalized regimes have great promise to reduce the harms of problematic drug use (PDU), and especially the intravenous use of heroin, cocaine, and amphetamines. PDU is a serious matter of public concern because of the risks to health and safety that it poses to drug users and to society. By focusing overwhelmingly on cannabis, major players in the U.S. drug decriminalization debate are overlooking some of the most promising aspects of decriminalization. [12]

Of course, Portugal is not the United States. There are many, many important differences that prevent one from simply recommending that we do what they did. But the Portuguese experiment is certainly worth careful examination and consideration. We also have four natural experiments in play in the United States as of spring 2015 in the legalization of marijuana in Colorado, Washington, Alaska, and Oregon. Policy makers should be carefully following how this unfolds in these states, including capturing lessons learned.

Over the past fifteen to twenty years, there have been hundreds of liberal and conservative media declaring the failure of the war on drugs. We have also had many prominent officials on both the right and the left and a variety of well-respected study commissions concluding that U.S. drug policy has been a very expensive failure. It is hard to understand why, in light of such widespread and conclusive evidence, we still continue down this path. Substance abuse is a disease of the central nervous system due to a disorder in the mesolimbic portion of the brain. Unfortunately, there is still a considerable amount of stigma associated with substance abuse, and some may prefer to think of it as a moral failing or a matter of bad choices. These are expensive attitudes. It is time to cut our many losses, admit we were wrong, and develop a comprehensive evidence-based, public health approach to the drug problem, one that apportions an appropriate balance of supply control, demand reduction, and harm reduction. Would we be so entrenched in a failed policy that takes as its primary premise that drug use is criminal if the demographics of drug use in the United States were different?

THE GUN DILEMMA

On September 24, 2014, the Federal Bureau of Investigation (FBI) released a report showing that the frequency of active-shooter incidents has increased in recent years. Active-shooter incidents are those where an individual is actively engaged in killing or attempting to kill people with a firearm in a confined and populated area.[13] The FBI report, motivated by recent shootings at Sandy Hook Elementary School in Connecticut, the movie theater in Aurora, Colorado, and the Navy Yard in Washington, DC, shows that 160 active-shooter incidents occurred between 2000 and 2013. These incidents resulted in 1,043 casualties—486 killed and 557 injured. The statistic that captured the most attention is that an average of 6.4 incidents per year occurred between 2000 and 2007, whereas an average of 16.4 incidents per year occurred between 2007 and 2013. What seemed to be the case, that these types of shootings were increasing, is borne out by the study.

More recently, 3,080 people were killed by guns in America during the three summer months of 2015. An additional nine thousand were wounded. This is 257 more deaths and 1,424 more injuries than the same period in 2014.[14]

There has been a steady increase in recent years in the number of individuals killed or injured in crimes involving the use of firearms. The number of gun-crime victims increased by 26 percent just between 2008 and 2011. Additional FBI data indicate that in 2011, guns were used in 68 percent of murders, 41 percent of robberies, and 21 percent of aggravated assaults in the United States.[15]

The United States has 5 percent of the world's population but approximately 42 percent of the civilian-owned guns. While the image of the United States as a gun-toting society is realistic, it is important to note that the prevalence of gun ownership has declined. In 1970, 50 percent of adults indicated there was at least one gun in their household. In 2000, that had dropped to 35 percent. Today 37 percent of adults state there is at least one gun in their household. While gun ownership is limited to just over one-third of the population, the most recent data indicate that the rate of gun ownership per 100 residents in the United States is between 90 and 101, the highest rate in the world. The reason the rate is so high in the United States is because those who own guns tend to own multiple guns. Other leading civilian gun-owning nations include Yemen (fifty-five per one hundred citizens), Switzerland (forty-six), Finland (forty-five), Cyprus (thirty-six), and Saudi Arabia (thirty-five). [16]

Over the past forty or so years, gun violence has declined and gun ownership has increased. What can we make of this? Is there a relationship between increases in gun ownership and declines in gun-related crime? How about gun ownership and declines in all types of crime, which also has been the case over this time period? The simple, intuitive, sound-bite answer is yes. Just ask the National Rifle Association (NRA). As Wayne LaPierre Jr., the executive vice president and CEO of the NRA, puts it, "The best way to stop a bad guy with a gun is a good guy with a gun." [17] Consider what the Institute for Legislative Action (ILA), the lobbying arm of the NRA, claims:

> Over the last quarter-century, many federal, state and local gun control laws have been eliminated or made less restrictive. The federal "assault weapon" ban, upon which gun control supporters claimed public safety hinged, expired in 2004 and the murder rate has since dropped 10 percent.
>
> As the numbers of "assault weapons" and "large" magazines have soared to all-time highs, violent crime has been cut in half. The nation's total violent crime rate peaked in 1991. Since then, through 2012, it has decreased 49%, to a 42-year low, including a 52% drop in the nation's murder rate, to a 49-year low—perhaps the lowest point in American history. Meanwhile, the number of the most popular firearm that gun control supporters call an "assault weapon"—the AR-15 semi-automatic rifle—has risen by over 4.5 million, the number of all semi-automatic firearms has risen by over 50 million, and the total number of privately-owned firearms has risen by over 130 million. The number of new magazines that hold more than 10 rounds has risen by many tens of millions. [18]

What can we make of such statements? Does the suggestion of a correlation imply causality? If so, then so is the relationship between the divorce rate in Maine and per capita consumption of margarine (correlation is .99) or the number of U.S. political action committees and the number of people who died by falling out of a wheelchair (correlation is .91). Saying so does not make it true. Correlation is not causality.

But that detail seems to escape the NRA. Another statement by the ILA suggests that concealed-carry laws reduce violent crime:

> Except among dyed-in-the-wool anti-gun fanatics, it is a commonly
> accepted fact that Right-to-Carry laws not only do not cause crime to
> increase, they may deter violent crimes. . . . The number of RTC states
> and carry permit holders reached all-time highs as the nation's murder
> rate fell to nearly an all-time low. [19]

The point is pretty clear coming from the NRA and other gun-advo-
cate organizations—an armed society is a safer society, and gun ownership reduces crime. All of this must have had its intended effect on the
Texas legislature, which passed an open-carry law that took effect on
January 1, 2016. And if that is not convincing, the NRA uses fear. La-
Pierre writes in an op-ed piece in February 2013, "Hurricanes. Tornadoes.
Riots. Terrorists. Gangs. Lone criminals. These are perils we are sure to
face—not just maybe. It's not paranoia to buy a gun. It's survival. It's
responsible behavior, and it's time we encourage law-abiding Americans
to do just that."[20]

Then there is the following statement from LaPierre in his address at
the 2014 annual NRA convention:

> We know, in the world that surrounds us, there are terrorists and home
> invaders and drug cartels and carjackers and knockout gamers and
> rapers, haters, campus killers, airport killers, shopping mall killers,
> road-rage killers, and killers who scheme to destroy our country with
> massive storms of violence against our power grids, or vicious waves
> of chemicals or disease that could collapse the society that sustains us
> all. I ask you. Do you trust this government to protect you? We are on
> our own. [21]

While it may be convincing on the surface that the proliferation of
guns deters offenders from committing violent crime, the science does
not support such a conclusion. Does that mean that citizens owning guns
have never stopped a crime or used a gun in self-defense? Of course not.
But the policy question is much more complex, based not on anecdotes
but on larger-scale patterns of behavior. U.S Justice Department statistics
provide some perspective. First, the gun lobby claims that guns are used
for self-defense over 2.5 million times per year. The reality is closer to
sixty-five thousand times, based on crime victimization data. Second,
under 3 percent of homicides are in self-defense or are justifiable, and
less than 1 percent of all violent-crime victims used guns in self-de-

fense. [22] It is much more likely—in fact, 3.5 times more likely—that a gun will be stolen than used for self-defense. Every year, over 230,000 guns are stolen. [23] Moreover, while the gun advocates may like to think that having more guns will help stop mass shootings, the evidence indicates that no mass shootings over the past thirty years have been stopped by armed civilians. Not to mention law enforcement's concern for the simple reasons that civilians are not trained to intervene in mass-shooting situations and that law enforcement will not easily be able to tell the good guy(s) from the bad guy(s) when they encounter such a situation. That logic has not deterred the Texas senate from passing a campus-carry bill in March 2015 that allows students, staff, and faculty at all public colleges and universities in Texas to carry firearms into campus buildings, including dorms and classrooms. The vote was precisely along party lines.

The National Research Council of the National Academies thoroughly investigated the research on the relationship between concealed-carry laws and violent crime and concluded in 2004 that the evidence does not permit drawing any conclusion about concealed-carry laws reducing crime. The National Research Council also has researched the issue about the relationship between gun ownership and violent crime in general. They conclude that the evidence does not permit a conclusion about gun ownership and increases or decreases in violent crime, although they reported that correlation analysis indicates that gun ownership is associated with *higher* crime. Very recent research (November 2014) coming out of Stanford University shows that, in fact, right-to-carry or concealed-carry laws are linked to increases in violent crime. The authors concluded that concealed-carry laws are associated with substantially higher rates of aggravated assault, rape, robbery, and murder. [24]

Recent government data indicate that there are 310 million civilian firearms in the United States (there are four million law enforcement and military firearms). The total U.S. population in 2014 was 316,149,000. So we have essentially one firearm per man, woman, and child, although only 37 percent of adults own at least one firearm. The 310 million firearms consist of 114 million handguns, 86 million shotguns, and 110 million rifles. [25] It is difficult to know how many of the 110 million rifles are assault rifles (typically lightweight and designed to fire fifty rounds or more per minute), but experts estimate that conservatively there are about 4 million. Sales of assault-type weapons have skyrocketed in recent years. For example, sales of the Smith and Wesson M&P15 assault rifle increased over twentyfold between 2006 and 2010, at least in part driven by concerns that the Obama administration would be unfriendly to gun owners.

There are two types of firearms that are of particular concern with regard to crime and criminal justice policy—handguns and assault-type rifles. Handguns were used in the vast majority of gun-related crimes. Approximately 75 percent of homicides and 90 percent of nonfatal gun crimes were committed with a handgun.[26] While assault rifles are much less commonly used, they present a particular concern because of their capacity to harm more individuals more quickly. These tend to be the weapons of choice for active-shooter and mass-killing perpetrators. Assault rifles are also used in about 20 percent of law enforcement murders.

The recent mass shootings at the theater in Aurora, Colorado, Sandy Hook Elementary School in Connecticut, and the Navy Yard in Washington, DC, have raised the issue of mental illness and gun violence. The NRA has been clear on this, stating that the problem is not the availability of guns but mental illness. However, the truth is that the mass shootings engaged in by mentally ill individuals are extremely rare. On the day that the Sandy Hook killer Adam Lanza killed twenty children and six adults, his mother, and himself, eighty-five other individuals in the United States died of gunshot injuries. The day Aaron Alexis killed twelve people and injured three at the Washington Navy Yard, another eighty-five individuals in the United States were killed by guns. It is understandable that the media focus on these horrific events. But they are rare. What we miss by all of the attention on these mass killings is the bigger picture of the daily carnage due to guns that doesn't involve mentally ill, lone gunmen. Yes, we do need to consider the role of mental illness in gun violence, but not to the exclusion of the broader issue of guns and crime and the fact that credible research has linked concealed carry with increases in violent crime.

Gun Policy and Crime

There are many things that can be done to help control and reduce the illegal use of guns. Gun control is important, but simply limiting access to guns is only part of the picture. A balanced strategy is one that adjusts gun policy in important ways and addresses the crime-related circumstances and conditions that compel or facilitate offending. We have already discussed the criminal motivation issue in earlier chapters. Evidence-based gun policy was comprehensively identified in 2013 by the Summit on Reducing Gun Violence in America at the Johns Hopkins Bloomberg School of Public Health. The summit identified the following legislative and regulatory controls as key elements in reducing gun violence.

- Universal background checks, including those who have a license to carry a firearm or a permit to purchase
- Require all sales through a federally licensed gun dealer
- Allow up to ten days for FBI background checks to be completed
- Require all firearm owners to report loss or theft within seventy-two hours of the discovery
- Expand the criminal background exclusions for a firearm purchase, including violent misdemeanors, juvenile violent crimes, drug and alcohol crimes, gang members, and individuals with restraining orders
- Minimum twenty-one-year age limit for handgun purchase
- Focus mental health restrictions on the dangerousness of the individual, not just a psychiatric diagnosis
- Ban the sale of assault weapons and large-capacity magazines (greater than ten rounds)
- Provide greater resources and authority to the Bureau of Alcohol, Tobacco, Firearms and Explosives (ATF) to oversee federally licensed gun dealers, increase frequency of dealer inspections, and enhance sanctions for violations of gun laws, among other things

Other law enforcement interventions that have proven effective include collaboration of local authorities with federal prosecutors to interrupt illicit gun trafficking in urban areas and aggressive federal prosecution of gun crimes (associated with severe consequences under federal law), combined with an extensive media campaign communicating the consequences of gun crime to local gangs. The latter strategy involves face-to-face meetings with gang members, putting them on notice about what happens if there is gun violence, as well as offering community-based services. This is an approach called Ceasefire that was initiated in Boston in the 1990s.

Realistically, there are limits regarding gun-control policy. Despite the fact that the NRA probably has fewer than four million members,[27] it is extremely powerful in keeping Congress and state legislatures from doing much to strengthen U.S. gun-control and gun-safety laws. For example, President Obama's nominee for surgeon general of the United States, Vivek Murthy, was unable to get a confirmation vote in the Senate for thirteen months because he declared that gun violence is a public health issue. He finally received Senate approval in December 2014. At the same time, there is considerable public support for gun reform in the United States. A 2013 survey of nongun owners and gun owners revealed substantial support for the following gun-control strategies:

- Banning the sale of military-style semiautomatic assault weapons (69 percent overall, 77 percent of nongun owners, 46 percent of gun owners)
- Banning the sale of high-capacity (more than ten rounds) magazines (68 percent overall, 75 percent of nongun owners, 48 percent of gun owners)
- Universal background checks (88 percent overall, 90 percent for nongun owners, 84 percent for gun owners)
- Prohibiting individuals from having a gun if they have a prior alcohol/drug conviction, violation of a restraining order, juvenile violent crime conviction, use of a gun in a threatening manner, or domestic violence conviction (83 percent overall and 60 percent of gun owners)
- Allowing the FBI five business days to complete background checks, allowing the ATF to take away a gun dealer's license for record-keeping violations (76 percent overall and 67 percent among gun owners)[28]

It seems policy makers and elected officials have lost sight of the balance between the Second Amendment right as interpreted by the courts and the rights of individuals to be free from gun violence. The Second Amendment is not the Holy Grail, as the NRA seems to think. It is not carte blanche to keep government hands off of every aspect of gun policy and laws. Two-thirds of Americans do not own guns. The vast majority of Americans support what appear to be reasonable changes to gun laws and policies. The failure of Congress and state legislatures to make reasonable changes to gun laws and policies is simply political pandering and another example of needlessly placing individuals in harm's way. Many gun victimizations are avoidable. It seems a matter of generating the political will to make appropriate changes. On top of that, in February 2015, seven medical societies, the American Bar Association, and the American Public Health Association joined together to declare gun-related accidents a public health crisis. Every year, one hundred thousand Americans are injured or killed in gun-related accidents. The coalition of medical and legal professionals has called for the development of solutions free of political influence or restriction.

However, successful gun control, which substantially reduces the availability of guns to criminals, will not be a cure-all for crime. It will reduce the United States' relatively high homicide rate, but beyond that, there is little evidence that gun control will significantly reduce violent crime in the United States. European nations have, in comparison to the United States, quite restrictive gun laws and policies. Yet they have violent (and property) crime rates similar to or greater than those in the United States. For example, the United States and the United Kingdom have essentially the same robbery rate. Belgium, Spain, Portugal, and France have higher rates of robbery than the United States. Eleven European nations have higher assault rates than the United States.

It is important for policy makers to appreciate that guns are but a tool for committing crime, an element of criminal opportunity. Removing guns will not necessarily remove crimes. Criminals may simply substitute other weapons if guns are effectively restricted. Sixty percent of U.S. homicides are committed with a firearm, facilitated by the wide availability of firearms. In European nations, where access to firearms is much more restricted, substantially fewer intentional murders are committed with guns, but knives and other lethal weapons are commonly used to kill people. For example, about 7 percent of homicides in the United Kingdom are committed with a firearm, but 40 percent involve use of a knife or other sharp weapon and just over one-half are committed by using weapons other than knives and guns. The United Nations reports that 41 percent of homicides worldwide are committed with a firearm; one-third involve a blunt object, physical force, poison, and so forth; and just under 25 percent are accomplished with the use of a knife or other sharp object.[29] So even if the United States were able to successfully control the possession of illegal firearms, which would take considerable time to accomplish, it is important to be clear about expectations in terms of crime-related outcomes. Perhaps the greatest impact is that the lethality of some violent crimes will decline as other, less deadly weapons are used to commit those crimes. Beyond that, the evidence is simply unclear.

In addition to implementing changes to gun-control policies and laws, the balanced perspective includes reducing motivation for crimes involving the use of guns by mitigating the crime-related conditions that underlie criminal offending. This is similar to the drug-policy issues discussed above—controlling supply is futile by itself. If we do not address motivation, offenders will, in all likelihood, continue offending and, when necessary, simply find substitutes when particular means like firearms are unavailable.[30]

ORGANIZED CRIME: STREET GANGS AND CARTELS

The FBI estimates that there are 27,000 violent street gangs in the United States with some 850,000 members.[31] Gangs vary in size, organization, and location. Some are national in scope (for example, the Bloods, Crips, Gangster Disciples, ALKQN, and MS-13), and others are specific to particular urban neighborhoods. About 80 percent of gang members are located in larger cities; the remaining 20 percent reside in small cities and rural areas. In addition to street gangs, prison gangs and organized motorcycle gangs engage in criminal enterprises.

Street gangs annually account for nearly 50 percent of violent crime in most jurisdictions in the United States, up to 90 percent in some. These crimes include homicides, robberies, and assaults, and most involve the use of a firearm. In the gang capitals of Los Angeles and Chicago, one-half of homicides are gang related.[32]

The primary criminal enterprise of gangs is drug distribution. However, gangs also have a substantial involvement in prostitution and weapons trafficking. The National Gang Threat Assessment for 2014 indicates that in approximately 40 percent of jurisdictions in the United States, criminal gangs are involved in weapons trafficking. Gang involvement in weapons trafficking is particularly severe in urban areas in New York, Arizona, California, New Jersey, Maryland, Pennsylvania, South Carolina, and Virginia. Gangs are also expanding their criminal activities into sex trafficking, identity theft, and credit card fraud.

In recent years, local street gangs have aligned with the larger-scale Mexican drug cartels, most commonly Los Zetas and the Sinaloa Cartel. Local street gangs distribute the cartels' drugs in communities throughout the United States. Gangs are also aligned with African, Asian, Russian, Italian, and Eurasian crime syndicates. These alliances involve gangs in extortion, debt collection, and money laundering.

There are several risk factors that influence the likelihood of individuals joining gangs. Individual-level factors include drug and alcohol use, engaging in antisocial behavior such as delinquency, aggression, risky sexual behavior, mental health problems, neurocognitive deficits and impairments, abuse and neglect, and negative life events. An unstable family situation (divorce, death, multiple transitions), poor parenting, abuse, and neglect play a significant role. Peer involvement in crime and delinquency is one of the strongest predictors of gang membership. Poor performance in school is also a strong predictor. Potential gang members have a low degree of commitment to school and lack involvement in school and attachment to teachers. There is a considerable amount of research that shows that poorly functioning schools can be a breeding ground for gang members. Schools are also where much of gang recruiting occurs. A report by the Office of Juvenile Justice and Delinquency Prevention notes:

> Poorly functioning schools with high levels of student and teacher victimization, large student-teacher ratios, poor academic quality, poor school climates, and high rates of social sanctions (e.g., suspensions, expulsions, and referrals to juvenile court) hold a greater percentage of students who form and join gangs.[33]

Community-level factors also play a very important role in gang membership. Certain neighborhood conditions, including poverty, high crime, availability of firearms and drugs, existing criminal enterprises, and a large number of youth engaging in criminal behavior, increase gang membership. Some risk factors provide motivation to join gangs, and some provide the opportunity.

Gangs are a substantial and growing problem in the United States. They are generally well organized, resourceful, and effective. Moreover, in many communities in the United States, recruiting for gang membership is relatively easy. Gangs offer many things to recruits and members that they do not get elsewhere—acceptance, support, protection, money, sex, excitement. The alliances of street gangs with other criminal enterprises such as the Mexican drug cartels are especially troubling since these alliances provide substantial incentives and rewards to local gangs.

So what can be done to address the gang problem? By far, the most common approach is the suppression of gang activity through the use of law enforcement and the criminal justice system. Aggressive arrest policies through the use of directed patrols, hot-spot policing, and gang crackdowns have been the most frequent responses. There is some evidence that hot-spot policing focusing on the illegal use of guns has been successful. However, longer-term success of such interventions is problematic due to crime displacement and the widespread availability of guns. The Boston Ceasefire model has been tried in other cities, and the outcomes are generally what were experienced in Boston. For a variety of reasons, approaches like Ceasefire are very difficult to sustain over time.

Targeted prosecution, involving special prosecution teams that deal only with gang cases, typically have reduced caseloads and enhanced investigation resources to prosecute gang activity. Potential federal prosecution of gun possession cases is also a suppression tactic that has been used in recent years for gang suppression. Other jurisdictions have used gang suppression strategies based on civil laws against assembly. The so-called gang injunction provides for criminal sanctions for gathering in groups in public. The intent is to deter a gang's ability to act collectively in public.

The popularity of gang suppression has less to do with its success and more to do with the lack of resources in local communities to engage other strategies. Over the longer term, traditional criminal justice interventions are unlikely to be successful in addressing the gang problem. Arresting gang members typically does not remove the criminal activity from the street. Others quickly take their place. Moreover, punishing gang members does little to mitigate the risk factors that drive individuals to gangs in the first place. It is really the same issue I have discussed throughout this book—what is it about punishment that changes the crime-related factors associated with gang involvement and criminality?

The path forward for reducing gang activity and involvement is a balanced one, involving prevention, intervention, and suppression strategies. This kind of an approach treats gang involvement and gang activity as a public health problem and a criminal justice problem. Targeted suppression tactics by law enforcement focus on the most serious, chronic gang members and involve arrest, prosecution, and incarceration. Prevention and intervention strategies address the individual, family, school, and community risk factors that exist among those at high risk of gang involvement. Intervention and prevention policies are designed to mitigate the risk and motivational factors that lead to gang involvement and enhance the protective factors that reduce the likelihood of joining a gang. One of the more high-profile efforts at addressing risk factors is the Harlem Children's Zone (HCZ). The HCZ is a comprehensive program that targets poverty, poor education, and poor health care at the neighborhood level. The program's primary goal is academic success through creating a continuum of support that follows children from the early ages through college graduation. The strategy of the HCZ is to engage an entire neighborhood at a scale that transforms the culture of the community, as well as the physical and social environment. At the same time, supports are provided to families and the larger community to promote a healthy family life and build community among residents, local institutions, and stakeholders. The HCZ covers nearly one hundred blocks of Harlem and served over 12,000 children and over 12,400 adults in 2013. Evaluations have demonstrated HCZ's success in the remarkable academic achievement of participants. The success of the effort is attributed to providing early, comprehensive, continuous, and concentrated interventions and having dynamic, energetic leadership.

One thing that is obvious from our discussion of drugs, guns, and gangs is that the criminal justice "solution" to these problems is extraordinarily limited. While it is important for law enforcement and the courts to manage some of the drug problem, some of the gun problem, and some of the gang problem, at the end of the day the evidence is clear that treating each of these as a public health matter and, in turn, reducing the demand for drugs, guns, and gangs will provide much better outcomes. Again, crime can be understood in terms of the two key components of motivation and opportunity. We got here by a primary focus on opportunity reduction. If we do not address motivation—the circumstances that drive demand for drugs, guns, and gangs—our efforts will continue to fail to reduce crime, recidivism, victimization, and spending.

8

JUVENILE JUSTICE
The Critical Opportunity

She was fifteen years old but had already lived a lifetime most people would not wish on anyone. In a matter-of-fact tone, she spent thirty minutes telling me about how she had been repeatedly raped by the males in her extended family, including brothers, uncles, and her father. That started when she was eight years old. She told me about her life on the streets as a prostitute after she ran away from home at age eleven. How she had used drugs to numb reality. She also stated that she had mental health problems. As I sat across the table from her at the Brownwood State School, a part of the juvenile prison in Texas, I was shocked by what she had gone through at such a young age. But there was something else that I saw, something more compelling, more profound, which I will never forget. Her eyes were empty, vacant, lifeless. She was fifteen but essentially already dead.

In 2003, I was one of several researchers involved in a nationwide study estimating the frequency of mental illness in the U.S. juvenile justice population. I headed up the Texas segment of this project. That is what took me to the Brownwood State School and this little fifteen-year-old girl. What officially got her to Brownwood were truancy and minor property crimes. What really got her to Brownwood was that there is nowhere else for her to go. She is the product of a variety of failures that has resulted in our dumping hundreds of thousands of kids in a system that is designed simply to keep them away from us.

Predictably, this girl was one of the 65 percent of youth in America's juvenile justice system with at least one diagnosable mental illness.[1] We also know there is a remarkably high incidence of neurocognitive impairment among these youth due to normal developmental processes as well as the impact of genetic and environmental conditions. Take those factors and add to them that kids involved in or at risk of criminal involvement tend to have poor academic achievement; come from troubled households where there is a greater risk of abuse and neglect; grow up in disadvantaged, chaotic, and violent neighborhoods; are exposed to a variety of environmental toxins, such as lead paint; do not have access to community resources that stimulate normal psychosocial development; are often enticed by the excitement of gang life and drugs; and many more risk factors. In effect, we have nearly perfect incubators for creating juvenile offenders, and we have very little in place to turn that around.

BACKGROUND OF THE AMERICAN JUVENILE JUSTICE SYSTEM

The American juvenile justice system was originally designed with the philosophy of *parens patriae*—literally, the state as parent. Its intention was to "save" delinquent youth by creating a system separate from the adult criminal justice system in order to divert them from the negative effects of the criminal justice system, especially the consequences of prison. The juvenile court and juvenile probation were developed to rehabilitate juvenile offenders with a presumption that the factors that brought them into the system could be changed. This is not unlike the rehabilitative ideal of the criminal justice system during the first half of the twentieth century. However, several factors converged that resulted in the juvenile justice system becoming the criminal justice system for younger offenders.

One of the consequences of the Warren Court's concern with due process was the likely inadvertent or unintended transformation of the American juvenile justice system. Between 1962 and 1972, the Warren Court handed down a number of decisions that provided substance to various constitutional protections afforded criminal defendants. While most of the attention of the court was on adult offenders, several decisions targeted the juvenile justice system. In the case *Kent v. United*

States (1966), Justice Abe Fortas wrote that research on the status of the juvenile justice system showed "grounds for concern that the child receives the worst of both worlds; that he gets neither the protection accorded to adults nor the solicitous care and regenerative treatment postulated for children."[2] Prior to this point, juvenile proceedings were relatively informal, facilitating the more benevolent, rehabilitative approach that characterized the juvenile court. One year after *Kent, In re Gault* (1967) challenged the reality of juvenile proceedings and extended a number of due process protections to juvenile defendants, including the right to counsel, the right to confront and cross-examine witnesses, and the privilege against self-incrimination. In 1970, the court in *In re Winship* imposed the reasonable doubt standard of proof in juvenile prosecutions, again rendering juvenile prosecutions much like adult prosecutions.

Many observers have noted that *Kent, Gault,* and *Winship* collectively helped move the juvenile court from the benevolent, rehabilitative model to something much more akin to a criminal court. As one expert stated, they "transformed the juvenile court from a social welfare agency into a wholly owned subsidiary of the criminal justice system."[3] As another put it, the due process changes to the juvenile court had the effect of shifting "the focus on juvenile court proceedings from identifying and eliminating the behavioral causes of delinquency to holding juveniles more directly accountable for the harm caused by their offenses."[4] This began the transition of juvenile justice from *parens patriae* to just deserts, from rehabilitation to punishment. Fueled in part by a significant rise in juvenile crime in the 1980s and early 1990s, especially violent crime, gun crime, and the crack epidemic, states launched the "get tough" era for juvenile crime. Phrases like "adult crime, adult time" and "accountability" guided policy making.

Getting tough in the juvenile system had several components, including harm-based, just deserts punishment, mandatory sentences, and mandatory minimums, as well as more liberal laws for transferring juveniles to adult criminal courts. By the year 2000, it is estimated that nearly two hundred thousand juvenile offenders were being tried in adult criminal courts for a variety of offenses, not all serious or violent. As the juvenile justice system became increasingly harsh, mirroring the punishment-focused criminal justice system, communities became increasingly fearful of youth, fueled in part by the claim by academics that there was an emerging generation of juvenile "superpredators" who presumably roam the streets killing, raping, and maiming. Despite the fact that this was an urban myth, the deed was done. Fear of youthful offenders worked its way into lawmakers' rhetoric and policy.

That fear spilled over into public schools, where zero-tolerance policies, use of metal detectors, drug-sniffing dogs, routine searches of persons and lockers, and the increasing use of sworn police officers serving as school "resource officers" resulted in the arrests of hundreds of thousands of youth for relatively minor infractions like disorderly conduct, truancy, and disturbing the peace, behaviors that may be more a result of immaturity than criminality. For example, in 2013 in Texas, there were 113,000 truant juveniles who had criminal charges filed against them in adult court for failure to attend school.

This massive increase in the removal of youth from mainstream schools to the juvenile justice system substantially widened the net of those who ended up in juvenile courts and corrections. The juvenile justice system became the day-to-day first choice for student misconduct rather than the last resort. Apparently it is easier for school officials to simply call the authorities rather than to try to address the problem when it arises. This appears to be how truancy has been handled in Texas (until September 2015, when the Texas legislature decriminalized truancy). What those school officials who simply call the police fail to appreciate is that once a kid enters the juvenile justice system, there are many direct and collateral consequences that dramatically increase the likelihood of returning to the juvenile justice system and then eventually entering the criminal justice system.

Reliance on incarceration has increased significantly over time in response to changes in punishment policies in the juvenile justice system. Between 1985 and the late 1990s and early 2000s, the number of youth who were incarcerated in juvenile facilities increased by about 65 percent. However, after peaking in the early 2000s, youth incarceration declined. Today about one-quarter of cases adjudicated delinquent (convicted) result in out-of-home placement (incarceration). That is down from 31 percent in 1985. The majority (60 percent) of adjudicated cases are sentenced to probation.

Despite this decline, we lead the world in the use of incarceration for youthful offenders. The juvenile incarceration rate in the United States is roughly six times that of the Netherlands, seven times that of the United Kingdom, twelve times that of Australia and Germany, over sixteen times that of France, twenty-seven times that of Italy, seventy-five times that of Finland and Sweden, and three hundred times that of Japan.[5]

For a variety of reasons, we have turned the American juvenile justice system into the dumping ground for problem children. Juvenile lockups have become the de facto repository for youth for whom we have few other options. Looking through the typically extensive files of the kids we interviewed in the project I referenced earlier confirmed for me the stark reality of how these kids get to juvenile detention. These files were full of neglect, sexual abuse, physical abuse, poverty, violence, bad parenting, cruelty, broken homes, psychiatric comorbidity, and drug use, often starting in the preteens with sniffing glue, paint, and gasoline and then graduating to drugs. Running away from home and truancy were nearly universal. Learning disabilities, attention deficit disorders, and hyperactivity disorders were more likely than not. Male and female prostitution served as a means of making money while on the street. Not to mention crime, where adolescents and teens have adult-sized rap sheets, detailing dozens of arrests, previous detentions and probations, and continued high risk of reoffending.

How have we let these kids get in such bad shape at such a young age? How do these kids get to the point of being locked up? There is plenty of responsibility to go around. Parents and families, schools, communities, public health and mental health, the justice system, just to name a few. Parents provide the genetic tendencies and initial environment that set in motion a trajectory of either success or disaster. What parents provide genetically and what they do in terms of child rearing have profound consequences for the near term and the long term. The extent to which schools are able to socialize, educate, or provide vocational training substantially affects which road a kid goes down. The extent to which communities have the capacity and resources to assist with child rearing and caretaking can mitigate or aggravate a difficult situation. The failure of public health to address a variety of life-changing conditions, physical, mental, and cognitive, is fundamental. Then there is the failure of the juvenile justice system on multiple counts.

How can we have kids that act so badly, so far from what we would consider normal? How can children engage in such shocking behavior when they should be at home reading Harry Potter or helping pick out a Christmas tree? How do we have kids in detention for sex offenses when they are barely old enough to have sex? It's because many of these kids are the throwaways. Many are the ones who perpetually fall through the cracks. And when they enter the justice system, the prognosis simply worsens. "Adult crime, adult time" might get some folks elected, but it is probably the most harmful path we could take.

THE AMERICAN JUVENILE JUSTICE SYSTEM TODAY

There were nearly 1.3 million juvenile arrests in the United States in 2012. Only about 5 percent of those were for serious violent crimes such as murder, rape, robbery, and aggravated assault. About one-quarter of the arrests were for felony property offenses (burglary, theft, and motor vehicle theft). Eighteen percent were drug and alcohol related, and another quarter were for simple assault and disorderly conduct. [6]

Juvenile offenders are responsible for a relatively small share of overall crime, representing 11 percent of all arrests. Juveniles commit a larger share of property crimes (20 percent) and are responsible for nearly one-quarter of arrests for robbery. The typical juvenile offender is male, although females represent just under one-third of all juvenile arrests. Two-thirds of juvenile arrestees are white. [7]

The majority of arrested juvenile offenders were referred to juvenile court. The juvenile justice systems in most states allow some discretion in whether a juvenile arrest is referred to court or handled within law enforcement agencies. Sixty-eight percent of the 1.3 million arrests in 2012 were referred to juvenile court, 22 percent were handled at the law enforcement level, and 7 percent were sent to adult criminal court. [8]

A minority of arrested youth who have been referred to court are detained prior to the disposition of their cases (20 percent). The percentage is a bit higher for cases involving violent crimes and a bit lower for property crimes. In addition to the detention decision, there is the decision about formal or informal processing of the case. Formal disposition involves filing a petition asking a judge to make a formal ruling in a case. Formal disposition will result in a finding of delinquent or not and, if so, imposition of sanctions. Informal disposition bypasses the petition and the formal ruling, presumably providing more flexibility in processing the case. Prior to the get tough era, the majority of cases (54 percent) were handled informally. Today the majority (56 percent) are handled formally, and the majority of those cases (65 percent) result in a finding of delinquency (i.e., a conviction).

Sanctions include out-of-home placement (incarceration), probation, or some other sanction (e.g., restitution, fine, community service, or treatment and counseling). Cases that are not formally petitioned can result in probation as well as other sanctions, as can cases that were petitioned where the juvenile is not found delinquent.

In 2010, there were 112,600 convicted youth sentenced to out-of-home placement. The majority of juveniles incarcerated are male (87 percent) and minority (68 percent). Blacks make up 41 percent of committed youth, followed by whites (32 percent) and Hispanics (22 percent). Another way of looking at this is in terms of incarceration rates, which adjust for population. The white juvenile incarceration rate is 128, meaning there are 128 white kids incarcerated per 100,000 white youth in the United States. The black rate is 606, and the Hispanic rate is 228.[9]

While we might think that juvenile incarceration is reserved for the worst offenders, the reality is often the opposite. The majority of youth who are incarcerated are confined for a nonviolent offense. Only about one-quarter are locked up for a major violent crime such as murder, rape, robbery, or aggravated assault. Forty percent are in prison for technical probation violations (i.e., violating the conditions of their probation and being revoked to incarceration), low-level property crimes and drug possession, and status offenses such as truancy and possession of alcohol.

In 2010, there were 260,300 juveniles sentenced to probation. The likelihood of an adjudicated juvenile being sentenced to probation was higher for white youths. The percentage of cases sentenced to probation has remained stable at roughly 60 percent for the past twenty-five years.[10]

What we do not have are good numbers on who and how many are given alternative sanctions, such as treatment and counseling. We do have outcome measures of recidivism however, and we turn to that next.

WHAT HAVE WE ACCOMPLISHED?

As we look back at the tough-on-crime path taken by the juvenile justice system, we must ask the same question we asked of the adult version of crime control. What has this accomplished?

The news is not good. First, the United States spends about $6 billion annually on juvenile corrections.[11] To make matters worse, various measures of recidivism indicate extraordinary high levels of reoffending for youth released from juvenile correctional custody. Rearrest rates vary from a low of 40–60 percent after one year of release up to 75–90 percent for those released for three years and more. Reconviction rates are equally troubling, ranging from 40 to 60 percent for those released for one year, up to 60–85 percent for those released for three or more years.[12] Subsequent analyses show that the worst outcomes are for youth in secure detention (juvenile prison). Intensive home-based programs had better outcomes than institutional lockups.

To make matters worse, we must remember that recidivism is a measure of official reoffending, meaning the police know about the offense and make an arrest. Again, about 50 percent of crimes are not reported to police, and for those that are reported, many do not result in an arrest. Fewer than 50 percent of reported violent crimes lead to an arrest, and roughly one in five reported property crimes results in an arrest.

The recidivism statistics are troubling for many reasons, not the least of which is that the failure to effectively intervene at the juvenile level has substantial consequences for the criminal justice system. Over 50 percent of all adult offenders have official records of police contact as juveniles. In other words, the majority of adult offenders were juvenile offenders. The failure to interrupt the offending cycle at the juvenile level effectively creates a pipeline into the adult system.

The picture is a bit less bleak if we consider that the majority of juvenile offenders cease offending by age eighteen; approximately 30–40 percent of juvenile offenders reoffend after age eighteen. So a primary concern is with those who do not cease offending and simply graduate from the juvenile justice system to the criminal justice system.

We now turn to a brief discussion of the criminogenic or crime-related factors associated with juvenile offending. When we consider the complexity of factors related to juvenile crime, it should not be surprising that recidivism rates are so high.

WHY KIDS COMMIT CRIME

There are many factors that come into play in understanding crime, and the situation is troubling when we focus on juveniles. We often hear references to kids being immature and therefore making stupid decisions or being easily persuaded by the wrong kinds of friends or even testing boundaries. These simple explanations belie the complexity of behavior, especially when we consider the variety of mental health, developmental, neurocognitive, and environmental influences implicated in juvenile crime.

Mental Illness

Research on mental illness in the juvenile justice system converges with estimates of around 65–70 percent of youth meeting the criteria for at least one mental health diagnosis. Eighty percent of those who met criteria for at least one disorder actually met the criteria for two or more. In fact, 60 percent of those with at least one disorder were diagnosed with three or more mental health disorders. Substance abuse disorders are common comorbid diagnoses. Nearly two-thirds of juveniles with a mental health disorder also met the criteria for a substance abuse disorder. Disruptive disorders such as conduct disorders and substance abuse disorders are the most common (nearly 50 percent), followed by anxiety disorders (one-third) and mood disorders (20 percent). [13]

Post-traumatic stress disorder (PTSD) is an anxiety disorder associated with experiencing one or more traumatic events. Symptoms range from internalizing disorders, such as depression and anxiety, to externalizing disorders like aggression, oppositional defiant disorder, and conduct disorder. In one study, over 90 percent of youth in the juvenile justice system had experienced one traumatic event, 84 percent had experienced more than one, and nearly 60 percent had been exposed to six or more traumatic events. [14] The most common forms of trauma are witnessing someone getting seriously hurt or killed, being threatened with a weapon, and being in a situation where physical harm or death seemed likely to happen. Youth who have experienced significant trauma may develop difficulties self-regulating and engage in impulsive behaviors. PTSD is common among juvenile offenders, occurring at rates three to ten times that in the nonoffending juvenile population. Comorbidity is also very common among youth with PTSD. Over 90 percent of youth with PTSD in the justice system had at least one co-occurring psychiatric diagnosis. Substance abuse is the most common among juvenile offenders with PTSD. Moreover, having a psychiatric disorder increases the odds of acquiring PTSD.

Girls are at a substantially higher risk of a mental disorder. Eighty percent of girls, compared to 67 percent of boys, met the criteria for at least one disorder. Much of that difference is the higher incidence of internalizing disorders among girls, such as anxiety and mood disorders.[15]

Comorbidity of psychiatric disorders is also predictive of enduring criminality. Juvenile offenders who persist into adulthood tend to have more psychopathology and comorbidity as youth than those juvenile offenders who cease offending while still juveniles.

Neurobiological Factors

Recent research and advances in the areas of neurobiology, neuroimaging, neuropsychology, genetics, and endocrinology, among others, is providing a better informed but more complex picture of various developmental and genetic risk factors associated with antisocial behavior and criminal offending. While we may want to keep explanations of why kids go bad simple, the reality is that crime in general, and juvenile crime in particular, is a result of a complex mix of factors. Genetic predisposition; deficits in the frontal, temporal, and cortical regions of the brain; neuropsychological deficits such as verbal, spatial, and executive abilities; hormonal imbalances; and the interaction of many of these conditions with environmental influences all contribute to criminal offending. Neuropsychological impairments characterize antisocial and violent offenders. Research is indicating that such neurocognitive impairments may be how genetic and psychosocial factors lead to antisocial behavior. Very briefly, here is what the current scientific evidence shows.

Research suggests that the magnitude of the genetic influence on antisocial and criminal behavior is in the 40–60 percent range, but it varies considerably. The primary point is that heredity matters, but it seems to matter more in adolescence than childhood and more for aggressive than nonaggressive offending. Moreover, researchers have determined that multiple genes are involved in the risk of antisocial behavior and that interaction of genes with environmental factors is important in understanding juvenile crime.[16]

Neuroimaging research has provided a clear and important link between juvenile crime and brain abnormalities and impairments. Those areas of the brain that are implicated in crime include the amygdala, the temporal lobe, the orbitofrontal/ventromedial and medial prefrontal cortex, as well as the anterior and posterior cingulate. These areas of the brain are involved with development of the capacity for empathy, processing reward and punishment information, moral reasoning, developing inhibitory responses, emotional regulation, and fear conditioning, among others. The behavioral consequences of deficits and abnormalities in these areas of the brain may lead to a reduction in empathy for victims of crime; difficulty inhibiting impulsive behavior, including violent behavior; difficulty regulating emotions, including anger; difficulty understanding cues in the environment; poor reasoning and decision making; and an inability to learn from punishment.

Juvenile offenders and youth with crime-related psychopathology such as conduct disorder tend to also exhibit intellectual deficits, impairments in executive functioning, attention difficulties, and problems with emotional processing. One-third of kids in the justice system have a diagnosed learning disability (compared to 5 percent in the general population). Lower verbal and spatial IQ are characteristic of antisocial youth. Executive functioning refers to cognitive processes that include goal setting, planning, analyzing, goal-directed activity, response inhibition, self-monitoring, and understanding consequences, among others. Executive functioning, which is associated with the prefrontal cortex of the brain, has significant implication for antisocial behavior, especially matters of impulse control and risk assessment. Research has also found attention deficits and problems processing emotions among juveniles with psychopathic traits. Moreover, juvenile offenders with more extensive neurocognitive and psychosocial impairments are substantially more likely to continue offending into adulthood compared to mildly or moderately impaired juveniles, who are more likely to cease offending as children or adolescents. In particular, those young offenders who persist into adulthood are found to have a lower verbal IQ, suffer more abuse and neglect, and have a higher prevalence of attention deficit hyperactivity disorder (ADHD) than those kids who cease offending as adolescents.

Psychophysiology also plays a significant role in criminal offending. Under arousal, such as low resting heart rate and abnormal skin conductance activity, as well as abnormal electrical activity in the brain (measured by an electroencephalogram), are found among youth with conduct disorder and are predictive of antisocial behavior.

Hormonal Imbalances

Intuition tells us that hormones play a role in juvenile antisocial behavior, and science confirms the role of two systems of hormones: cortisol, which is associated with the fear and stress response, and testosterone, which is involved in reward seeking and dominance. An imbalance in cortisol and testosterone, resulting in reduced levels of the former and increased levels of the latter, has been found in antisocial youth. The behavioral implications are low avoidance of harm, low self-control, decreased fear, more aggressive behavior, and reduced sensitivity to punishment and its threat.

This mental health, neurobiological, physiological, and hormonal evidence is relatively new in the juvenile-crime literature. There is much that needs to be done, such as obtaining estimates of the prevalence or frequency of various conditions, disorders, and impairments. We do know that the majority of youth suffer from psychiatric disorders, substance abuse disorders, cognitive disorders, and functional impairment. We know much less about the prevalence of specific conditions, in part because the juvenile justice system has been largely focused on punishing, not treating. Determining or diagnosing such conditions is not all that relevant to punishment.

Family and Parenting

Family structure and parental behaviors have substantial impacts on neurological and neurocognitive development, antisocial behavior, and criminal offending. For a variety of reasons, children raised in a household that consists of both biological parents are at lower risk of antisocial behavior and criminal offending than youth raised in other family structures, such as with a stepparent, cohabiting couple, foster parents, and so forth.

Parental behavior has a substantial effect on the risk of antisocial behavior and criminal involvement of youth. As one noted scientist argues:

> Mistreatment of children in the form of physical abuse, emotional abuse, or neglect is a common societal problem estimated to affect more than 12% of all children. . . . Further, the detrimental effects extend to the cognitive and affective developmental domains. Neurologically, childhood exposure to abuse has produced a variety of deficits including problems in executive functioning that include the ability to synthesize and categorize information, delays in language acquisition leading to learning disabilities, and problems of self-regulation and impulse control. [17]

Harsh and uninvolved parenting, often leading to what is known as attachment disorder, leads to chronic anger, low self-control, and hostile attribution bias, a cognitive bias that causes one to be suspicious of others, presuming they have negative or hostile intentions. Hostile attribution bias has been consistently linked to aggressive behavior.

Neighborhood and Community

Peers are an important environmental risk factor. Juvenile crime is largely social behavior, often involving groups of offenders. Gang membership typically results in more offending, more serious offending, and longer-term offending than similar youth who do not belong to a gang. Gangs are attractive to some youth because they provide things that kids may be lacking in their day-to-day lives, such as social and emotional support, protection, and money.

Schools are associated with the risk for juvenile offending. Poor academic achievement, poor school attendance, detachment from school, and lack of interest in education are characteristic of youth involved in crime. Nearly one-half of kids in the justice system are performing below their age-appropriate grade level. Does this mean that schools are responsible for delinquency? Only partly. Attention deficits, hyperactivity, intellectual deficiency, cognitive problems, and mental health problems are all associated with juvenile crime and academic performance. Thus, many of the risk factors that youth bring to the table do not typically originate in school; however, they can be and often are aggravated there. Schools appear largely unwilling and ill equipped to do much about these risk factors in terms of prevention, identification of problems, or interventions to mitigate their severity and impact. This is unfortunate since school failure substantially exacerbates the risk of criminal involvement.

There are other ways in which schools influence criminality. The demographic composition of students and the location of the school (rural, suburban, and urban) influence the likelihood of juvenile crime. So do the social organization of schools, school culture, discipline management policies, and class size. The location, organization, culture, and policies of some schools actually promote offending. Juvenile offending can be expected to be higher, all else being equal, if a school culture supports deviant behavior; if the social organization inhibits social control of the students; if a school is located in a disadvantaged, urban area; and if discipline policies are viewed by the students as unfair and arbitrary.

Community/neighborhood disadvantage and disorganization contribute significantly to juvenile criminal involvement. The fact that many underprivileged youth lack legitimate opportunities for employment, lack social integration and social control feed into the appeal and prevalence of crime and gang activity. Poverty is linked to a variety of neurodevelopmental problems and deficits, including executive function, memory, cognitive control, and language skills. There is a strong correlation between poverty and poor parenting and child neglect and abuse, as well as prenatal exposure to alcohol and tobacco. The combination of poverty and neglect and abuse is related to an increased prevalence of developmental delay, ADHD, PTSD, conduct disorders, anxiety disorders, and personality disorders, among others. Poverty also exposes kids to noxious elements like lead paint, violence, and trauma. In effect,

> abuse and neglect, combined with prenatal insults to normal brain development, both of which are more common in lower-SES environments, lead to early predisposition to antisocial behavior which, with the right genetic profile, may reach psychopathic/sociopathic proportions. . . . Thus, this study, along with many others that have looked at the neurobiological consequences of abuse and neglect, shows that children who suffer early socioemotional deprivation can indeed develop a number of the neurobiological abnormalities seen in psychopathy. [18]

Knowing what we do know is quite informative in terms of elaborating the complexity of crime. It goes a long way in terms of better understanding how genetic and developmental vulnerabilities interact with and play out in different environments. It also helps us better understand why punishment is ineffective for most youthful offenders. While the research indicates that punishment severity does not deter adult offenders, this is even more the case for juvenile offenders. When the majority of youth in the juvenile justice system have a diagnosable mental illness and a variety of neurodevelopmental deficits and impairments, it seems rather naïve to assume that the threat of punishment or actually experiencing punishment would deter future offending. If kids do not fully comprehend the consequences of their actions, if they lack self-control and self-regulation, if they are desensitized to punishment, how much sense does it make to pretend that punishment should change their behavior? Thus, simple solutions like enhanced punishment or combative strategies like boot camps and Scared Straight encounters are doomed to failure.

What we know today about juvenile crime provides direction to practitioners and policy makers. What we know and what we will continue to discover provides the tools to develop prevention and intervention strategies to effectively reduce juvenile crime and the likelihood that juveniles will simply move from juvenile justice to criminal justice. For example, research shows that juvenile offenders who persist into adulthood tend to have profound neurocognitive and psychosocial impairments. Failure to properly assess/diagnose and intervene early simply postpones what in many cases becomes inevitable.

CULPABILITY

The age of responsibility in the United States is the minimum age at which a youth can be held legally responsible for his or her criminal actions. The age of responsibility varies by state but is most typically age seven, sometimes eight or ten. Age seven is essentially the lowest age of responsibility in the world, and only a handful of predominately English-speaking countries have relatively low ages as well, such as eight (Scotland) and ten (England and Wales, Australia, New Zealand, Ireland). One of the important consequences of such a low age of legal responsibility is that it puts the justice system in the position of being the primary set of individuals and agencies responsible for dealing with juvenile misconduct quite early on in a kid's life. Governments that have higher ages of legal responsibility are motivated to develop and maintain agencies and institutions other than the justice system for addressing juvenile misbehavior. So, in effect, U.S. juvenile justice laws and policies have by default made the juvenile justice system the front line for dealing with the behavioral problems of children and adolescents, as well as teenagers.

The parts of the human brain that are responsible for moral reasoning, decision making, impulse control, empathy, and understanding consequences, among other things, are not fully developed until the early to mid-twenties. Thus, the normal development of the brain has consequences for behavior, sometimes behavior that is criminal. That in combination with mental illness, as well as the variety of influences that contribute to further neurological, intellectual, and psychological deficits and disorders, raises the issue of criminal culpability for at least some juvenile offenders. How can we consider a youth, who by the sheer fact of being young is thus functioning with an underdeveloped frontal lobe, to be as criminally responsible as a fully functioning adult? How can we hold that same kid who also has significant neurological impairment or significant mental illness fully responsible for the crimes he or she commits? And how can we then convict and punish them as if they have behavioral free will?

Criminal responsibility in the law is largely a matter of knowing the difference between right and wrong. One is generally responsible for a criminal act if that person knows that what he or she did is wrong. However, there is an inherent flaw in that logic when it comes to juveniles. As three of the leading experts on the cognitive and psychosocial development of youth conclude:

> Even though adolescents may exhibit intellectual and cognitive abilities comparable to adults, they do not develop the psychosocial maturity, ability to exercise self-control, and competence to make adult quality decisions until their early 20s. The "immaturity gap" represents the cleavage between cognitive maturity—the ability to distinguish right from wrong—which reaches near adult levels by age 16, and adolescents' psychosocial maturity of judgment, risk assessment, and self-control, which may not emerge fully for another decade. [19]

A youth may know that a particular act is wrong but, at the same time, may not be able to control it.

Finding individuals culpable, blameworthy, or responsible for a crime seems necessary on moral grounds in order to extract revenge, in order to punish them. We are on considerably less firm moral ground when we punish someone who is not able to control their behavior or has diminished capacity for doing so. But that is precisely what we have been doing. Tough-on-crime policies for juvenile offenders have sidestepped the issue of moral blameworthiness in favor of an approach that often fails to ask questions about mitigating circumstances like low IQ, neurocognitive impairments, or mental illness. We have taken the approach of lumping kids into categories of more or less dangerous and proceeding with proportional amounts of punishment.

The point is not to excuse bad behavior. Crime is harmful to individual victims as well as to communities. Rather, the point is to appreciate the potential deficiencies and impairments that juvenile offenders may bring into the courtroom, to identify them, and to develop strategies to effectively address them. The U.S. Supreme Court has pierced the veil of this argument by ruling that juveniles are more vulnerable to negative, outside pressures and have an underdeveloped sense of responsibility. For that reason, the court held in *Roper v. Simmons*, 543 U.S. 551 (2005), and *Graham v. Florida*, 560 U.S. (2010), that juveniles may not be sentenced to death or life without parole. Beyond that, the high court essentially has been silent regarding juvenile culpability or criminal responsibility and punishment.

Consider the life of Jacob Ind, who was a subject of a PBS *Frontline* episode.[20] At age fifteen, Jacob killed his mother and stepfather as they slept. His plan was to then commit suicide. The murders were in part a consequence of years of physical, psychological, and sexual abuse by his parents. Apparently, Jacob began thinking about killing them when he was twelve years old, as he saw no other way out of the persistent, long-term abuse. His stepfather sexually abused Jacob and his brother in the bathroom in their home. He would come up behind him, hit him in the face, and throw him into the bathroom. He would then tie him up and sodomize him. Jacob's mother repeatedly emotionally abused him by making it clear that she hated him. Jacob stated that his mother's emotional/psychological abuse was more harmful than his stepfather's sexual and physical abuse.

Jacob seemed to not understand the gravity of what he had done. He stated that he didn't think they'd feel any pain and that he didn't think anyone else would be affected by what he did. "I remember I was sitting in the police station—and this is how out of touch with reality I was. I had a small amount of marijuana, like an eighth of an ounce, in my bedroom. And I'm telling my brother, 'You got to get the marijuana or else I'm in trouble.' I'm arrested for first-degree murder and I don't think I'm in trouble."[21]

Jacob was convicted of two counts of first-degree murder and sentenced to mandatory life without parole. It is clear that he committed a horrific crime. But is it just, moral, right to hold him totally responsible or culpable for this crime?

It is time we confront these questions of culpability. In so doing, we need to weigh or balance the emotional against the pragmatic. Yes, hundreds of thousands of juvenile offenders have entered the juvenile justice system, some for very serious crimes and many more for less serious offenses. If we do not recognize these factors that mitigate culpability, we likely will continue down the road of trying to punish the crime out of juvenile offenders, failing at that effort, unnecessarily placing individuals in harm's way to become victims of crime, keeping the pipeline into the criminal justice system flowing at a healthy rate, and wasting huge sums of money.

JUVENILE JUSTICE REFORM

The bigger picture of understanding why kids commit crime is a complex matter. We are dealing with youth who are in the process of psychosocial development, many of whom suffer from a variety of mental health problems and neurodevelopmental deficits and functional impairments. The path forward requires sophisticated solutions, not Band-Aids. It requires a radical reinvention of how we deal with youth and crime.

Incarceration

For those kids who have committed horrific, violent crimes and for those who are chronic offenders for whom behavior change is unlikely, there is simply separating these offenders from society. These kids are high risk and dangerous, and the priority is public safety. That is not to say that intervention is off the table, just that it probably needs to occur in a secure environment, as undesirable as that is as a therapeutic setting. And we need to adjust our expectations for the longer-term outcomes for the youth we incarcerate. Juvenile incarceration should be the last choice. It should be used very selectively since the evidence is clear that longer-term outcomes for youth who are detained in either jail or juvenile prison are bleak. Recidivism is uniformly higher for these youth, as is continuation of criminal offending as an adult. Moreover, the longer-term educational and employment outcomes for youth who are detained are quite negative.

There has been a substantial reduction in juvenile incarceration in the past ten years or so. As is the case with the criminal justice system, state governments pay for incarceration, thus much of this reduction is due to the 2008/2009 recession as states sought ways to reduce spending. Reductions in juvenile incarceration have also been accomplished by funding formulas in some states that require local jurisdictions to pay the state for youth they send to secure detention. It appears that such funding requirements serve as a disincentive for simply dumping problem kids in state detention facilities.

The evidence indicates that the policy going forward should substantially deemphasize incarceration. Secure detention should be reserved for those who are so dangerous that there is no other reasonable way to manage the risk of harm. The funding formulas in place in states like Ohio, Wisconsin, and Illinois that attach a local financial consequence for sending youth to state-run institutions should help deter dumping kids by simply passing on the problem to the state.

At the same time, secure detention facilities need radical rethinking. The advantages of small, local, treatment-oriented secure detention facilities are compelling. Local facilities allow for engaging families in the process. If the goal of detention is to incapacitate—that is, to separate an offender from potential victims—it is appropriate to aggressively attempt to address the circumstances that brought youth to the system in the first place. The vast majority of these youth will be released, so we need to consider how we can minimize the risk of their reoffending when released. Much of the answer is behavioral change.

Missouri implemented substantial changes to its training-school system in the 1980s. Officials closed the training schools and built regional facilities with a continuum of services, including treatment in nonsecure settings, nonsecure group homes, moderately secure facilities for those who need that level of control, and secure facilities. All of these have a treatment/rehabilitation focus, and none is larger than fifty youth. Each youth is assigned a case manager who stays with that youth from entry through aftercare and reentry to the community. The fact that the facilities are decentralized allows families to be involved in the rehabilitation process and development of reentry plans. They are small, flexible, and tailored to the needs of the youth. Evidence shows that kids coming out of these facilities have some of the lowest recidivism rates in the nation. Reportedly, 8 percent of youth reoffend, and 8 percent reoffend as adults.

Diversion

Research documents that the deeper a youth penetrates the juvenile justice system, the greater the negative effect. In fact, simple involvement with juvenile court proceedings can be crime producing. It appears that the reasonable path is greater informal processing of youth, minimal contact with the juvenile court, and diversion of as many youthful offenders as possible. The evidence supports a policy path designed to effectively intervene and mitigate the criminogenic conditions, situations, impairments, and deficits that bring youth to the juvenile justice system in the first place but to do so in noninstitutional settings. What that looks like will be briefly sketched out here.

First of all, decision makers in the justice system need to dramatically ramp up the process of assessing risk and criminogenic needs. This is particularly complex from a clinical perspective, requiring not only sophisticated, validated risk- and need-screening instruments but also ramping up the expertise of individuals involved in assessing and diagnosing conditions, deficits, and impairments. This cannot just be guesswork or based on brief self-reporting by juvenile offenders. If we are serious about addressing and changing why kids commit crimes, we need to get serious about proper assessment and diagnosis.

Diversion programs for juveniles include a variety of alternative or diversion courts. Teen courts, which number around twelve hundred today, are designed for lower-risk juvenile offenders. Teen courts consist of teens in the roles of judge, prosecutor, defense lawyer, and jury, all acting in mature, responsible ways. The typical outcome of a case referred to teen court is some kind of sanction, perhaps community service or restitution. The unique feature of teen court is peer justice, kids sanctioning kids. The evidence, although not plentiful, suggests that teen courts significantly reduce recidivism and avoid getting youth involved in juvenile court and juvenile corrections. [22]

Juvenile drug courts are also a popular alternative to juvenile court and juvenile corrections. Modeled after the adult version, juvenile drug courts provide a balance of accountability and compliance with substance abuse treatment, mental health services, education, job training, case management, and so on. Compliance is enhanced by swift, certain, and graduated sanctions. Research indicates that drug courts are effective at reducing recidivism and drug use. However, as is the case at the adult level, juvenile drug court capacity is extremely limited, so few juveniles have the opportunity for this type of diversion.

Probation is the most common form of diversion for juvenile offenders, and juveniles who are formally as well as informally processed may be sentenced to probation. Probation is an opportunity to manage the risk of reoffending and provide community-based treatment to address those deficits and impairments that are related to behavioral problems and criminal offending. Probation is supervised, conditional release to the community. If a youth on probation violates one or more of the conditions of probation, he or she is subject to revocation to detention. Revocation is one of the primary ways that kids get incarcerated. In 2012, 50 percent of the youth incarcerated in the Texas Juvenile Justice Department were probation revocations. In 2012, 50 percent of juveniles who received a deferred prosecution disposition (which is a form of probation) were rearrested for a new offense during their period of supervision. Nearly two-thirds of juveniles sentenced to what is called *adjudicated probation*, which is a sentence after conviction, were rearrested for a new offense while on probation. These juvenile probation rearrest statistics are several times the rates for adult probationers, indicating a tougher, higher-risk juvenile probation population, less effective strategies for reducing juvenile offender recidivism, or both.

Research has identified a number of highly effective and cost-efficient intervention programs for juveniles on probation. Those at the top of the list include functional family therapy (FFT), multidimensional treatment foster care (MTFC), multisystemic therapy (MST), and aggression replacement therapy (ART). These interventions tend to focus on the bigger picture of behavioral problems by engaging not only the youth but also their families or foster parents and other social systems with which youth are involved.

The Washington State Institute for Public Policy has compiled an inventory of effective interventions as well as cost-benefit estimates. These include programs and treatment for the juvenile justice population, overall child welfare interventions, pre-K to twelfth-grade education programs, children's mental health, and general prevention programs for children and adolescents. The inventories of effective programming also include things like cognitive-behavioral therapy, case management, social-skills training, academic training, mentoring, and so on. The point is that today there is a wide array of effective and cost-efficient interventions, strategies, and programs that reduce juvenile offending and reduce the risk of youth getting involved in juvenile crime. Where we fail is in implementing these programs. Substantial problems include lack of funding, lack of adequate capacity, improper implementation, inexperienced and ill-trained staff, and failure to monitor and evaluate interventions over time and make appropriate corrections. As is the case with many interventions for adult offenders like drug courts, the programming efforts are largely symbolic.

The justice system also needs to keep up with advances in treating neurocognitive deficits and impairments. Research is continually advancing interventions designed to promote neuroplasticity, the process of changing neural pathways and synapses. These changes involve retraining or rewiring the brain to compensate for impairments as a result of physical and emotional trauma or other genetic and environmental circumstances.

It is critically important that individuals in the juvenile justice system, including probation officers, judges, prosecutors, defense attorneys, case managers, and so forth, all understand and recognize the various ways that the deficits and impairments that many youth bring to the juvenile justice system affect their behavior. Many of the problems we discussed above have important implications for things like compliance with probation conditions or requirements for participation in drug court. What may look like indifference or acting out may in fact be a consequence of an identifiable mental or neurological problem. Those individuals who engage with youth in the justice system need to change how they respond to noncompliance. While swift, certain, and graduated sanctioning for rule violations may work for some, they may not work for all. When sanctioning does not seem to work, when a kid repeatedly violates conditions of probation or drug court rules, it may be that the kid is not simply criminal but lacks the capacity to understand the consequences of his or her behavior or is desensitized to punishment. In that case, continued sanctioning may be ineffective. If that scenario plays out like it has in the past, the kid eventually will be placed in secure detention. That is probably the worst outcome.

One overarching theme is that dealing with youth criminality can be very complex. There can be a variety of situations, conditions, disorders, and deficits that play roles in a youth's criminality. The easy solution is secure detention, but all that does is delay the inevitable. Kids generally do not get better in lockup, and the vast majority will be released. Our decisions in the moment place others at risk down the road. If we do not intervene and at least attempt to address the relevant criminogenic factors, we are simply passing the problem on to someone else. The "someone else" is often future victims and the criminal justice system.

If that is not persuasive, consider the cost: Every time a kid enters the juvenile justice system, the cash register rings. If we fail to address juvenile criminality and a youth graduates to the adult system, the costs keep mounting. It is not difficult to spend hundreds of thousands of dollars on a juvenile who starts engaging in criminal activities early and continues well into adulthood. By the time a career criminal is done, it is not that hard to see an economic impact of that career well into the millions if we consider direct juvenile and criminal justice costs, victim costs, community costs, lost productivity, and other factors.

Decision Making

The front end of the processing of juveniles arrested for criminal offending is particularly important for diversion. The majority of juveniles who have been arrested are referred to the juvenile court by police. The individuals who typically provide the first contact with youth referred from law enforcement serve as the gatekeepers. As it currently stands, the front-end processing of juveniles referred by police falls on probation officers, prosecutors, or both. The intake process consists of several primary activities, including an assessment of legal sufficiency, an assessment of the immediate needs of the offender (e.g., is he or she a danger to themselves or others?), and a decision about formal or informal proceed-ings.[23] There are a number of important issues regarding this intake pro-cess, such as who is primarily responsible for determining whether a case should be carried forward formally or treated informally and diverted; how various assessments are conducted for determining matters such as the presence of mental illness, functional impairments, and neurocogni-tive issues; and what criteria drive the decision to process a case formally in the juvenile court, perhaps eventually transferring it to criminal court. The evidence is pretty clear that the methods for assessing youth who enter the juvenile justice system are haphazard at best. Rarely do intake officers use validated assessment instruments. It seems fair to say that many of those involved in making such decisions are not clinically trained, which is a concern in light of the extraordinarily high incidence of mental and cognitive problems, as well as functional impairments, educational deficits, and so on.

It is important to recognize that these decisions, which are made early on in the process, can and do profoundly impact the overall functioning and outcomes of the juvenile justice system. They shape whether juvenile justice is primarily focused on formal processing and punishment or in-formal processing and the welfare and well-being of the youth. That is why it is necessary to rethink who should be making such decisions, what information those decisions should be based upon, and how we can change the culture of the juvenile justice system to move away from punishment as a first choice.

If the primary focus going forward is on addressing the crime-related circumstances of those juvenile offenders who we determine do not need to be separated from society (incarcerated), then we probably do not currently have the right individuals making those decisions. Probation officers and prosecutors have important roles to occupy and functions to perform in the juvenile justice system, just not that of determining offend-er needs. Rather, as we discussed in the context of the criminal justice system, it is clearly preferable to have a number of individuals with expertise in a variety of clinical areas who can collectively engage on a case-by-case basis and collaborate in the decision-making process. Yes, prosecutors and defense attorneys should be involved, but if treatment is primary, this process also needs professionals who can properly assess and diagnosis, develop a treatment or intervention plan, and then partici-pate in and/or oversee the execution of that plan.

Decisions that come later about incarceration need to be carefully made in a collaborative process where clinical expertise, risk determination, local treatment resources, and legal considerations enter into the calculus. While judges and prosecutors should be involved, these are not decisions best made by lawyers alone. We need to get away from decision making based on who we are mad at and move to decision making based on who we are justifiably afraid of, meaning afraid of with good reason, using valid assessments and clinical determinations. Moreover, the decisions about detention need to appreciate that efforts at behavioral change after detention will be that much more difficult. This is the case for a number of reasons, including typical deterioration while incarcerated for the majority with mental illness, neurodevelopmental problems, and functional impairments. It is also due to the overall negative effects of incarceration.

Changing the procedure is critical. But so is changing how we think about juvenile crime. We need to appreciate that many youth involved in crime come from circumstances that cause, promote, or facilitate offending. We need to recognize the mix of factors that are implicated in juvenile crime and push back from holding juveniles as responsible and culpable as individuals who do not suffer from the variety of mental health, neurocognitive, and developmental problems that seem to characterize large numbers of juvenile offenders. We also need to accept the fact that because of many of these impairments and deficits, punishment is generally ineffective in promoting behavior change.

The fact that states have such a low age of responsibility deters the development and funding of agencies and organizations for addressing crime-related circumstances among youth. We see this routinely with schools' zero-tolerance policies, whereby the juvenile justice system is the first response to even minor misconduct by kids at school. We must end our overreliance on the justice system as the go-to agency for what's wrong with kids.

There is substantial public support for rehabilitation over punishment for juvenile offenders. In fact, survey research shows that the public prefers rehabilitation over incarceration—in fact, they are willing to pay for it through increases in taxes. Moreover, there is support for rehabilitation on both sides of the legislative aisle. Right on Crime has adopted policies that focus much more on rehabilitation and behavior change and changing funding formulas so that local jurisdictions have more state resources for rehabilitative programming. Moreover, Right on Crime endorses the Missouri model discussed above.

BIG-PICTURE ISSUES

What Is the Purpose of the Juvenile Justice System?

Before we are able to effectively reengineer the juvenile justice system, we need to be clear about why we have it and what its purpose is. Is it a first choice or a last resort? Is it the primary problem solver for kids with behavioral problems? Is it the dumping ground for the failures of a variety of other institutions, such as school, public health, family, and community?

In order to answer these questions, we need to shine some light on the issue of how we weigh the relative rights and interests of society, justice, and/or victims, on the one hand, and the child and his or her future life and productivity, on the other. We know that the primary purpose of punishment is the emotional satisfaction that the harm doer has been harmed in return. An eye for an eye, just deserts, retribution. What some call justice. But to what end? And at what cost?

What is clear is that continuing to use the juvenile justice system as the solution for adolescent misconduct is ineffective, wasteful, and costly. Punishment does not work for the majority of kids we punish. It is expensive and a perfect formula for wasting tax dollars. Moreover, current policies compromise the future productivity of the kids we fail to rehabilitate.

Which then brings us to the potentially productive course of rehabilitation. Some individuals who commit particularly bad crimes or who are essentially unable to be rehabilitated should be separated from the community in the interest of public safety, as should the failures of our efforts to rehabilitate. That is a good use for detention. For most other juvenile offenders, there is rehabilitation, the effort to change those circumstances, impairments, and deficits that bring youth to the system in the first place.

If we look at it pragmatically, in terms of what the evidence and cost-benefit analyses tell us, the realistic, practical thing to do is to attempt to rehabilitate the majority of youthful offenders. Again, this is not a get-out-of-jail-free card. It is control and risk management combined with behavioral change. It is a more balanced approach that combines account-ability, supervision, compliance, and public safety, on the one hand, with behavioral, psychiatric, neurocognitive, educational, vocational, and other interventions, on the other. It involves a variety of institutions, agencies, and individuals, including the justice system, schools, public health, nongovernmental organizations, family, and community, among many others.

Age of Legal Responsibility

As long as the age of responsibility for crime is seven or eight, as it is in most states in the United States, the juvenile justice system will continue to serve as a primary destination for child and adolescent misconduct and will lessen the perceived need to develop alternative treatment and intervention capacity. As long as we have such an accepting juvenile justice system, as long as we can put our adolescent failures in institutions that temporarily remove them from society, the juvenile justice system will probably continue to thrive and continue to deter the development of sufficient community-based capacity for addressing the crime-related factors kids have.

Complexity of Treating Underlying Crime-Related Conditions

What we currently know about what kids bring into the justice system is quite troubling. The variety of mental illnesses, functional impairments, neurocognitive problems, emotional disturbances, hormonal imbalances, educational deficiencies, substance abuse, and other issues is breathtak-ing. More often than not, kids present with co-occurring conditions—that is, the presence of multiple deficits, impairments, and disorders that are related in various ways to their criminal offending.

The types and levels of resources and expertise needed to appropriate-ly address these crime-related circumstances are considerable. This involves appropriately screening, assessing, and diagnosing; developing prioritized treatment plans; implementing treatment; case management; monitoring and adjusting treatment; developing maintenance plans; and implementing and supervising ongoing care. Clinically, many of these youth present some of the most difficult diagnostic and treatment challenges that professionals will encounter. What is required is developing a competent treatment infrastructure and populating it with appropriately trained and experienced experts. Our failure to do that outside of the justice system requires that we do it within the justice system if we truly want to turn this thing around.

Funding Considerations

Most of the funding burden for local, community-based intervention and treatment for juvenile offenders has fallen on local jurisdictions. This burden must shift to a more balanced approach where states assume an increased share of paying for the costs of intervention and treatment. An approach like the California performance-incentive model, where local jurisdictions receive state money for reducing the number of prison admissions originating from a particular county and for reducing recidivism for those on community supervision, is very much worth considering. As the reliance on secure detention is reduced, the state will save significant resources, which in turn should be redirected to local communities for supporting treatment capacity.

As of July 2015, there are just over 3,030 inmates on the death rows of this nation. One thing that 2,428 (81 percent) of them have in common is that they had been involved in the juvenile justice system prior to the capital murder that brought them to death row. The subtitle of this chapter refers to the critical opportunity that policy makers have to truly effect change in the lives of those kids who suffer the consequences of the genetic roulette wheel combined with a variety of environmental assaults. Intervening early can pay tremendous dividends in terms of reducing recidivism, averting crime, reducing victimization, reducing the financial and social costs of crime, and enhancing the productivity of those youth who do not continue with a criminal career. In many situations, the longer we wait, the harder it will be to effectively intervene and change behavior, especially after a juvenile has graduated to the criminal justice system.

9

CONCLUSIONS

Some parts of the past forty-five years of American criminal justice policy are understandable. The launch of crime control occurred in the context of unprecedented challenges to law and order. Crime rates were at all-time highs; massive civil unrest swept the nation with hundreds of urban race riots and campus protests over the Vietnam War, and there were the assassinations of Martin Luther King Jr. and Robert Kennedy. Added to the mix was the increase in illegal drug use, largely in poorer, urban areas and on college campuses. All of this disorder and lawlessness caused much concern and created a need for fundamental change. Was crime control or tough on crime the right response? Based on what was known at the time, a punishment-centered policy seemed reasonable. Common sense, logic, intuition, and personal experience all supported a sea change in policy in the direction of punishment. The "experts" were largely silent, except to say that rehabilitation did not work, further justifying the punishment path. Moreover, the politics of crime control made it extremely risky to argue against tough on crime. On balance, it is understandable that we took such a dramatic turn in how we think about crime, criminals, and punishment. Deterrence and incapacitation became the cornerstones of American criminal justice. Retribution gained a legitimate place in our thinking about punishment and promoted anger-based decision making.

We simply went on a binge, a very long, expensive binge, where it seemed we could not get enough, and elected officials and policy makers far and wide were trying to out-tough each other. At the risk of pushing the binge metaphor too far, at some point, one usually wakes from a binge and sees a horrific mess all around. Perhaps that is what we are beginning to see now.

Under civil law, if I harm you by failing to uphold my end of a contract or through medical malpractice, you can sue me to repair the harm done, usually in the form of monetary damages. Under the civil law scenario, you are in control, and you are the one who benefits from any damages awarded by the court. Now shift to criminal justice. You and I get into an argument and I hit you with a baseball bat. You are badly injured. Under criminal law, even though you are the victim, it is the state that is the plaintiff. It is the state that will arrest, prosecute, convict, and punish me. One thing that often gets lost in this story is you, the victim. We cede to the state the authority to represent the interests of crime victims and the collective interests of public safety and justice. Unfortunately, the odds are that whatever happens to offenders in the justice system will do little to reduce the likelihood that they will reoffend, in turn creating new crime victims or revictimizing those who have already been victims. The failures of the criminal justice system place all of us at an unnecessary risk of being crime victims.

WHAT'S AT STAKE?

Plenty. One way to think about it is that in the time it has taken you to read this book, there will have been at least 10 homicides, 60 rapes, 240 robberies, 514 aggravated assaults, 1,542 burglaries, 4,320 felony thefts, and nearly 500 motor vehicle thefts in the United States, not to mention thousands of less serious crimes.[1] The majority of these crimes are committed by recidivists, offenders who have already cycled through the justice system at least once before.

If larger numbers make the point more emphatically, consider the following: In 2014, there were nearly seven million violent crimes and twenty million property crimes in the United States. This means that twenty-seven million individuals and/or households were victimized by crime in 2014 alone (actually, a bit less, given that some are "victimless crimes"). Once again, the majority of these crimes were committed by recidivists. The evidence is clear—substantial numbers of these crimes and victimizations are preventable if the justice system is successful at reducing reoffending.

American criminal justice costs over $260 billion annually. Some might argue that there is a reasonable return on investment since the crime rate has declined over the past twenty-five years. Compelling but flawed logic. True, the crime rate has declined, but most of that has been independent of the administration of criminal justice. At most, 10–15 percent of that decline can be legitimately attributed to justice policies and practices.

Another vantage point on the return on our collective investment is the recidivism rate. Over two-thirds of those we incarcerate are rearrested within three years of their release; over one-half are reincarcerated. And these are the ones we catch. Many more crimes committed by recidivists go unreported and/or do not lead to an arrest.

But the cost of crime is not just what we spend on criminal justice. The tangible and intangible costs of crime are direct criminal justice costs (police, jail, prosecutor, court, corrections); harm and loss suffered by the victim, including pain and suffering; broader social costs, including things like quality of life and property values; lost productivity of offenders; and public assistance for offenders. When these are all added up, the numbers are sobering.

Current criminal justice policies not only fail to reduce recidivism but often increase it. In turn, these policies increase victimization, as well as the direct and indirect costs of crime. Under current law and policy, punishment does not end when an offender is discharged from probation or prison or completes a term on parole. A criminal record will always be there. Today one-quarter of the adult population in the United States has a criminal record. Granted, the extent of criminal involvement varies dramatically among those with a record. But the point is that a criminal record can serve as a formidable barrier to housing, employment, education, credit and loans, and public benefits, to name a few. For example, Texas Occupation Code 53.021 gives licensing agencies broad authority to revoke, suspend, and deny licensure to anyone who has been convicted of a felony or misdemeanor that may somehow be related to or perceived to be related to the duties of the licensed occupation. There are seventy-one occupations covered under 53.021. Clearly, if someone is a significant risk of reoffending, it is prudent to try to minimize criminal opportunity. For example, it is reasonable to prohibit a predatory child sex offender from working at a school or living in a multifamily residence. But, as is often the case, the law is written and enforced in a wholesale manner, taking the baby with the bath water. Consider Kyrone Pinkston, a barber who was convicted of the sexual assault of his wife. He was sentenced to ten years in prison. When he was released, he attempted to renew his barber's license. His ex-wife supported his application, stating that he had become a "remarkable man and father." He had a job lined up at a barbershop, but the licensing agency nonetheless denied the application. An administrative court judge upheld the rejection, stating that the evidence indicated that while Pinkston's risk to the general public was low, it was not zero. Or consider Melinda Diamond, who had a misdemeanor assault charge because she yanked a chain from her boyfriend's neck. She applied for a notary commission. Her application was denied because the state's licensing agents stated that the crime was one of moral turpitude. Or Dimas Pena, who lost his electrician's license because of a misdemeanor theft charge for which he received deferred adjudication (he was not convicted).[2] Granted, there is a fine line here. We do not want to reward criminal behavior, and it is important to manage criminal opportunity. At the same time, it is clearly in our interest to do what can and needs to be done to facilitate the transition from criminal offender to productive, law-abiding citizen. Putting up barriers to gainful employment is not smart, and the critics of such policies may surprise you. Charles and David Koch of Koch Industries are on the record arguing that, among other things, criminal justice policy damages the economy by making it difficult for ex-offenders to obtain employment. A study published in 2010[3] reports that the economic impact on the U.S. economy due to the employment limitations we place on individuals with a felony record is between $57 billion and $65 billion per year. These limitations increase the male unemployment rate in the United States by between 1.5 and 1.7 percentage points. Such restrictions also increase spending on public assistance since those who cannot find work have a much higher likelihood of eventually receiving financial assistance.

Homelessness plagues up to one-third of those released from prison. Not having a residence is a substantial barrier to successful reentry and the transition to a crime-free existence. Other barriers include denying public benefits, mental and physical health care, and education. While the justice system makes successful reentry difficult, it is not alone. A wide variety of agencies and organizations either operate with these barriers or create their own. Housing, employment training, public assistance, public health, and social service organizations often have their own exclusions and restrictions, do not effectively reduce barriers that offenders encounter in trying to access community resources, and/or have insufficient resources to meet the need. For example, in most communities, offenders released from prison or jail who are in need of mental health treatment find it extraordinarily difficult to access local mental health resources. The reason is very limited public mental health capacity.

It is really not a matter of feeling sorry for those who face such difficulties. It is not even a matter of what is fair or just. Placing restrictions on things like employment, housing, medical and mental health care, public assistance, and education is counterproductive in a variety of important ways. First and most important, it increases recidivism, which places us all in harm's way as potential victims. The question we should ask is: What should we expect, not want, but expect, from inmates released from incarceration with nothing different except more barriers to legitimate employment, housing, medical and psychiatric care, and so on?

These policies also increase criminal justice costs, as offenders cycle in and out of the justice system. It contributes to the broader social and economic costs of crime. Such restrictions are also counterproductive in terms of the economic consequences due to offenders' lost productivity. The point is that there are very compelling economic reasons for changing how we deal with many ex-offenders. It is in our public-safety interest and it is in our economic interest to do what it takes to facilitate the transition from offender to productive citizen. We know that not all will be successful. But we have the tools today to substantially improve the longer-term success of offenders transitioning from the criminal justice system to a productive, responsible life.

There are potentially important lessons to be learned from how things are done in other countries. First, incarceration is used relatively sparingly in many European nations. Whereas 70 percent of felony convictions in the United States result in a sentence of incarceration, only 6 percent of convictions in Germany and 10 percent in the Netherlands result in prison. Moreover, mentally ill offenders are not typically sent to prison in these countries. Rather, they are diverted to psychiatric hospitals or mental health clinics, criminal responsibility is generally assessed using a broad-based approach, rather than the all-or-nothing, right-wrong test used in the United States.

When incarceration is the sentence, it is quite different from how we do it here. For example, in Germany and Norway, the purpose of prison is not punishment. Rather, it is separation from society where the primary purpose is resocialization, normalization, and rehabilitation—in effect, preparation for when an offender leaves prison. The goal, upon release, is to live a life of social responsibility free of crime. This goal informs every aspect of incarceration, including the physical design of prison units, the activities in which inmates engage, how inmates are treated by prison staff, the amount of freedom inmates are given, and the training prison staff receive. The prison experience is as similar to life on the outside as possible. Inmates may wear their own clothes, prepare their own meals, and engage in work and educational programming. The staff are trained more like social workers than correctional staff. As one U.S. corrections official touring a German prison noted, "If you treat inmates like humans, they will act like humans."[4]

One very important takeaway from observing German, Dutch, and Norwegian prisons and inmates is that when they are released, they do not face the collateral consequences that U.S. inmates do. They are not stripped of their civil rights; they do not face barriers to housing, employment, social benefits, and so on. This is the case in part because of the way they are treated when incarcerated. They are generally resocialized and rehabilitated when they return to society, so there is less need to impose such restrictions. Moreover, these strategies appear to pay remarkable dividends. The recidivism rates of Dutch, German, and Norwegian inmates released from incarceration range between one-half and one-third of U.S. recidivism rates.

CRIMINAL JUSTICE REFORM SHOULD BE A PRIORITY

Current criminal justice policies and practices have failed in the mission to effectively enhance public safety. There is simply no way to put a good face on abysmal recidivism rates. The fact that many, many criminal victimizations and their associated costs are avoidable should be a serious cause for concern. So should the extraordinary amounts of public revenue the justice system churns through every year with what can only be characterized as a quite poor return on investment. On top of that are the negative impacts that criminal justice policies and practices have on the U.S. economy, cities, neighborhoods, and families.

The criminal justice system is not alone in terms of responsibility. Crime is in part a consequence of the failure of a variety of public institutions, such as education and mental health care, and our inability or unwillingness to effectively combat poverty and its consequences. We have made choices about our public schools, about how much public mental health care and substance abuse treatment we want to provide, and about how much we are willing to do about poverty. The justice system has been placed in the position of cleaning up many of the consequences of these failures. Unfortunately, it is extraordinarily ill equipped to do so with any success.

It is in our interest to set aside most of our moral or emotional needs in order to punish criminal offenders. Retribution comes with a substantial cost. We need to get away from concerns about being too soft on criminals and refocus on being smarter about crime and criminals. We need to move in the direction of accepting that criminals do bad things, but at the same time, many are redeemable and can turn it around when we make a concerted effort to provide the appropriate offenders with the rehabilitative services and human capital necessary to become productive citizens. That is a clear public good in terms of reducing crime, victimization, justice system cost, and the negative social and economic impacts of crime.

I'm not suggesting that we redeem all criminal offenders. There are those we will not want to rehabilitate because of the nature of their crimes and/or the extent of their criminal history. For example, James Holmes, the shooter in the mass murder of twelve individuals at a movie theatre in Colorado, is mentally ill. However, he committed a particularly horrific crime, for which anything other than the life without parole sentence he received would violate a sense of justice. It doesn't require mass murder to have similar beliefs and feelings about other situations. But when we do go down that road, we need to recognize and appreciate that retribution fulfills an emotional need and perhaps a need for justice, whatever that may mean, but has little utility in the bigger picture of crime reduction.

There are those for whom the odds of success at rehabilitation are too low to try, individuals who are too far gone psychiatrically, intellectually, emotionally, or neurocognitively. There are those who will not want to try and those who, despite our best efforts, fail. Many of these offenders are appropriate for separation from society, for incapacitation in prison. That is largely what prison should be reserved for going forward—not as a means to correct or alter behavior but as a means to separate.

WHERE ARE WE TODAY?

In part triggered by the recession that began in 2008, some states have begun looking at crime control more carefully, mainly at the tremendous cost of incarceration. In some instances, that has resulted in modest reductions in prison populations. National statistics on the number of inmates locked up in U.S. prisons and jails indicate that the increase in incarceration has slowed. Is it time to celebrate the beginning of the end of the incarceration explosion? That, unfortunately, would be premature. A 2014 survey conducted by the Pew Charitable Trusts indicates an expected 3 percent increase in the number of state prison inmates over the next three years.[5] Mass incarceration on the scale it has been practiced in the United States is alive and well and appears poised to remain that way into the foreseeable future.

On March 24, 2015, during a congressional hearing, U.S. Supreme Court justices Stephen Breyer and Anthony Kennedy blasted U.S. sentencing and corrections policy, particularly mandatory sentences, long prison sentences, and the use of solitary confinement. Over the past year or so, we have been seeing an expanding national discussion about U.S. justice policy and reform. Driven by organizations like the American Civil Liberties Union (ACLU), the Vera Institute, the Pew Charitable Trusts, the Council on State Governments, the Urban Institute, Right on Crime, the Charles Koch Institute, and initiatives like the former U.S. attorney general's Smart on Crime project, criticism of the criminal justice system is gaining traction and reform is beginning to be mainstream and bipartisan. Charles Koch argues that we are in the midst of an overcriminalization epidemic and is launching a justice reform effort that brings together groups such as the Heritage Foundation, the American Legislative Exchange Council, and the Federalist Society, on the one hand, and Families Against Mandatory Minimums (FAMM), the ACLU, and the National Black Chamber of Commerce, on the other.

In March 2015, Congress held the Bipartisan Summit on Criminal Justice Reform, which brought together liberal and conservative lawmakers, policy experts, and activists. Evidence of the prominence of criminal justice reform is found in the fact that every major candidate for the 2016 presidential nomination, Republican and Democratic, has offered some criminal justice reform measure. So have many high-profile critics of justice policy. Many focus on reducing incarceration and mandatory sentencing. A few mention drug policy, mental health, changing policing, and the death penalty, among other items. The vast majority focus on one or two things. Taken together, it is piecemeal. None of these commentators on criminal justice policy, with perhaps one exception, envision the big picture of reform and what that might mean.

Congress is no exception to reform myopia. On October 1, 2015, the U.S. Senate unveiled the Sentencing Reform and Corrections Act of 2015. On October 8, 2015, the House introduced the Sentencing Reform Act. Both of these bills were hailed by commentators as "landmark," "extensive," and a "game changer." A closer look shows that while they focus on modest reductions in punishment, there is very little in these bills that addresses recidivism reduction. Granted, in some cases the punishment is lessened, but it is still punishment nevertheless. They both seem to be from the same old playbook of a punishment-focused approach to controlling crime with no attention paid to changing the underlying circumstances, deficits, and impairments that are commonly related to criminal offending.

THE FUTURE

Mass incarceration is a prominent part of U.S. criminal justice, but it is far from the whole story. The problems with the criminal justice system run much deeper than prison. The iceberg metaphor works well here— incarceration is the tip (granted, it is a large tip), but there is much more that receives even less attention. This is not just a matter of making changes to a few sentencing laws, such as reducing some mandatory minimum sentences for nonviolent offenders or keeping some low-level drug offenders out of prison.

Fine-tuning the existing justice system will be counterproductive. It will provide the illusion that reform is occurring, when in effect change is piecemeal and largely symbolic—essentially what we are seeing now. Moreover, changes to one segment or component will have consequences for other parts, some anticipated, others not. Ending mass incarceration is a very valuable goal, but it is not as simple as releasing inmates and changing sentencing laws that put low-level, nonviolent offenders in prison. What do we put in place of incarceration for these offenders? What impacts does that have more broadly on other justice agencies, families, communities, and local service providers? There are multiple layers of government fundamentally involved in the administration of criminal justice. Reducing incarceration (a state responsibility and expense) will likely impact local probation departments and diversion programs (local responsibilities and expenses), as well as local social service providers and communities. The justice system is complex, requiring a comprehensive perspective, a big picture of reform.

We need to radically revise the legal structure that has widened the net of the justice system, what many call *overcriminalization*. We need to address issues related to criminal intent or criminal responsibility. Sentencing laws will need to be revised to allow for greater discretion in order to determine the best course on a case-by-case basis, with the guidance that incarceration is reserved for a select set of offenders and is generally considered the exception. We also need to make diversion easier. This will involve changing the laws governing eligibility for probation, problem-solving courts, jail diversion, and deferred adjudication. In turn, a massive expansion of diversion resources will be necessary. Problem-solving courts need to move from being a symbolic gesture to a position of prominence in the justice system. This also includes the expansion of sanction courts to increase accountability and compliance among those who are diverted. We need to reinvent probation so that it functions as the primary venue for providing rehabilitative programs and services for offenders. Diversion should proceed with a clear consideration of public safety, accountability, compliance, and risk management, on the one hand, and behavioral change, on the other. Balance is key.

Both the practice and the culture of prosecution will need to change. Prosecution policies and procedures should be modified to incorporate a more deliberate, information-based, collaborative decision-making process regarding traditional criminal adjudication or diversion. This will also require changing how prosecutors think about crime, punishment, rehabilitation, and prosecution. The end game is to embrace the goal of recidivism reduction and use those strategies that the evidence indicates will accomplish such a goal.

We need a rational drug policy that is premised on the recognition that substance abuse is largely a public health problem. This requires a primary focus on demand reduction and harm reduction. Substantial expansion of substance abuse treatment capacity and access to treatment are necessary. Gun laws also need to change. This should include a ban on assault weapons and large-capacity magazines, implementing universal background checks with sufficient time to properly conduct them, and exclusion for certain prior criminal acts and mental illness (assuming it is an informed determination about someone's mental health). Juvenile justice needs to be reconceptualized by taking a hard look at issues like ending the reliance on the justice system to solve many of the problems that kids experience, rethinking the question of capacity for criminal responsibility, as well as the limitations of punishment and incapacitation. Juvenile justice needs to return to its earlier priority of rehabilitation but making use of contemporary, evidence-based methods.

Our thinking about crime, criminal behavior, punishment, and rehabilitation needs to catch up with the realities of the day. The evidence is simply too compelling to dismiss—punishment has very limited utility, and behavior change can be highly effective. These need to become a part of the culture of the justice system. They need to characterize how we think about crime and its remedies. A very important component of changing the way we think about crime and recidivism is adopting problem-solving strategies that are aimed at accomplishing recidivism reduction.

The processing of criminal defendants amounts to a series of hand-offs—from law enforcement to prosecutors, from prosecutors to judges, and from judges to corrections. Each of these effectively constitutes a silo. That is one of the primary reasons that no one is in charge. No one seems to accept responsibility for the failures of criminal justice. It is imperative that the responsibility for recidivism reduction is shared by all involved in the administration of criminal justice. We need to develop ways to make those involved in the justice system accountable for achieving the goals.

Funding is a very, very big issue. Part of the problem is who pays for and who benefits financially from reform efforts. In most criminal justice systems, prison and parole are state funded; probation is mainly locally funded, but state government provides some resources; and the courts, including prosecution, pre-trial services, and public defense, are paid for locally, as are most law enforcement and jails. Thus, there are some significant questions regarding financial incentives for reform.

The real reform efforts occur at the local level, and much of the expense of reform will be incurred locally as well. To the extent that reform efforts divert larger numbers of offenders from incarceration and over time reduce recidivism, the state will benefit fiscally from lower prison and parole costs. Local jurisdictions will benefit because of enhanced public safety, as well as some (probably modest) cost savings by reducing the burden on the courts, prosecutors, and local jails. However, it is not realistic to think that those cost savings at the local level will be that significant. Rehabilitation will be expensive, and since it is the state that stands to reap the majority of the economic benefits by reduced incarceration, cost and revenue sharing like California's performance-incentive funding should be an important part of the reform effort. State government must contribute substantially to criminal justice reform, and some type of performance-based cost sharing seems like a reasonable way to facilitate innovation and implementation. However, it is naïve to think that tax revenue saved by reducing incarceration will necessarily be redirected to the programs that reduce incarceration. Legislatures must contend with competing interests. At the same time, it is important that legislators and policy makers realize and appreciate the domino effects that reducing crime, recidivism, and victimization have. Benefits accrue to the economy, to the justice system and other government agencies, to the urban tax base, to dependency on public assistance, and to overall quality of life, to name just a few.

In some respects, effectively reducing crime, recidivism, victimization, and cost sounds simple. Change the underlying conditions that are responsible for offenders' crime and, in turn, change their behavior. If it is mental illness that is a primary problem, get a proper diagnosis, prescribe the correct medication, engage in talk therapy, and so forth. If it is a neurocognitive deficit, then cognitive behavioral therapy can retrain the brain to compensate for the deficit and/or medication may be indicated. Substance abuse is quite common, but there are effective treatment methods. Employment and vocational training programs can help prepare offenders to enter the workforce.

But let's be clear: If done properly, comprehensively, on an appropriate scale where there are measurable impacts on recidivism and victimization, this will be a *monumental* effort. This is fundamentally rethinking how we deal with crime and criminal behavior. This is fundamentally reengineering justice systems, including the laws, policies, procedures, and funding priorities of the federal government, fifty state governments, the District of Columbia, and over three thousand counties in the United States. It is also about changing the culture, the way of thinking about crime and punishment, among the 2.5 million individuals employed in the justice system.

As the concept of criminal justice reform is gaining some traction among elected officials, policy makers, the judiciary, prosecutors, and the general public, there is still a very long way to go, and there will likely be plenty of casualties along that path. Politics will claim many of those casualties. For example, on Monday, March 23, 2015, Texas senator Ted Cruz announced that he was running for president. In his announcement speech, he reiterated that one of the first things he would do if elected was dismantle the Affordable Care Act (ACA), also known as Obamacare. It is important to note that Cruz was not alone—most of the other potential Republican presidential contenders were opposed to this law as well, as were most Republicans in Congress. What is important here is the mental health and substance abuse treatment parity provisions in the ACA, which require equivalent treatment coverage for mental health and substance abuse as for general medical and surgical matters. The politics of health care reform place this very important component of the ACA in jeopardy, not only compromising access to treatment but also likely reducing expansion of capacity for treatment. Again, when we consider that the vast majority of those who come into contact with the American criminal justice system have a substance abuse problem and that 40 percent have a diagnosable mental illness, this potential loss of the ACA raises the justice reform stakes dramatically.

Justice reform is not just about changes to the criminal justice system. Crime is, in part, a consequence of other failures, such as health care, education, and mental health treatment. Poverty and disadvantage characterize the vast majority of those who end up in the American criminal justice system. Those of us with resources have quite different alternatives and opportunities. If we get sick, we go to the doctor. We go to private school, or if we go to public school and have difficulties, we hire tutors. If we have emotional or psychological problems, we consult experts. If we get into trouble with drugs or alcohol, we can seek treatment. Policy makers have made a variety of decisions over the years that have placed substantial restrictions on access to medical and psychiatric care for the poor and have underfunded public education, resulting in poor-performing urban schools, high dropout rates, and low graduation rates.

It seems that through their actions, elected officials and policy makers have been reasonably comfortable letting the criminal justice system manage or clean up the consequences of these failures. However, these decisions and policies have important downstream consequences for crime and criminal justice, as well as for the economy, public spending, and quality of life, among other things. Mental health treatment is expensive, but the collective problem of mental health becomes exacerbated by relying on the criminal justice system. The public-safety, economic, and fiscal consequences of failing to provide public mental health treatment either in the free world or in the justice system is phenomenal. There are very similar consequences for substance abuse. However, because it is a much more pervasive crime-related problem, the consequences are considerably greater. Untreated substance abuse is probably the single greatest contributor to the revolving door of American criminal justice. Public education is expensive. In fact, in many jurisdictions, education is the single greatest component of local property taxes. Thus, many may feel that increasing funding for schools is excessive. However, that would look like a bargain compared to the costs of the consequences of underfunded and underperforming public schools.

Calling this a monumental effort is an understatement. However, if over the past forty-plus years we have been able to build the world's largest prison and correctional control systems, wage massive wars on drugs and crime, fundamentally change sentencing laws and procedures, change the way we think about crime and justice, change the culture of the justice system, and radically shift how we spend public revenue, effectively re-creating the U.S. criminal justice system, then, at least in theory, we should be able to once again fundamentally change course and create a sea change in how we deal with crime and punishment.

The political will for true criminal justice reform may be growing, but it is too soon to tell whether it is meaningful. It is reasonable to think that reform should be high on the list. After all, who would not want to reduce crime and recidivism? Who would oppose reducing criminal victimization and the costs associated with crime? And some are beginning to express impatience with the progress to date. Recent headlines proclaim "Why Isn't More Being Done to Reduce America's Bloated Prison Population?" and "The Politics of Mass Incarceration: Latest Stats Show Nano-Scale Reform Remains the Dominant Trend."[6]

There is a compelling story to tell, and the public seems to be behind the basic principles of effective reform. But it is important to be realistic. There are many competing interests that vie for the attention of elected officials and the resources they allocate. However, at the state level, the financial consequences of business as usual are substantial and likely will drive attention for reform. Moreover, since the vast majority of American criminal justice is administered at the state and local levels, targeting state reform is critical in terms of meaningful impacts. At the federal level, where leadership can play an important role in a serious reform effort, it is anybody's guess where the political energy will go. But if the past few years are any indication, it seems naïve to rely heavily on Congress to carry the reform agenda unless the political benefits are substantial. Branding justice reform as smart is important. But it seems that the real traction is not to be found so much in things like less crime, lower recidivism, and lower victimization, although these clearly are public goods. The most political leverage is probably found in the fact that reform can save tremendous amounts of tax dollars.

NOTES

INTRODUCTION

1. Truman and Langton, *Criminal Victimization.*
2. Koch and Holden, "Overcriminalization of America."
3. Koch and Holden, "Overcriminalization of America."
4. Kelly, *Criminal Justice at the Crossroads.*
5. Grassley, "Floor Statement."

1. AMERICAN CRIMINAL JUSTICE

1. These stories are from American Civil Liberties Union, *A Living Death*, and Krey, "Man Sentenced to Seven Years."
2. Data are from Bureau of Justice Statistics, *Census of State and Federal Correctional Facilities*, 1988, 2002, 2012, and 2015.
3. Institute for Criminal Policy Research, World Prison Brief (database).
4. Carson, *Prisoners in 2013.*
5. Bureau of Justice Statistics, *Correctional Populations in the United States.*
6. Bureau of Justice Statistics, *Correctional Populations in the United States.*
7. Leichenger, "How One Milwaukee Zip Code"; Soloman et al., *Understanding the Challenges of Prisoner Reentry.*
8. Federal Bureau of Investigation, *Uniform Crime Reports.*
9. Postrel, "Consequences of the 1960's Race Riots."
10. Alexander, *New Jim Crow*, 40–41.

11. Quoted in Genovese, "Richard M. Nixon and the Politicization of Justice," 76.

12. Hickman, "Courting the Right."

13. Congressional Record, 12800, Senate, May 10, 1968, 309.

14. Congressional Record, 12801, Senate, May 10, 1968, 310.

15. From a speech Reagan made at a Republican platform meeting in 1968, twelve years before he became president (see https://en.wikiquote.org/wiki/Ronald_Reagan).

16. Federal jurisdiction originates in the commerce clause of the Constitution. Because of this, in theory, any drug law violation can invoke federal jurisdiction based on the presumption that a drug crossed state and/or national boundaries.

17. See www.commentarymagazine.com/articles/solving-the-problem-of-too-little-crime/.

18. See http://www.ontheissues.org/celeb/Democratic_Party_Crime.htm.

19. See http://www.ontheissues.org/Archive/Dem_Platform_2004_Crime.htm.

20. Good, "Greatest Campaign Ad Ever?"

21. See http://fairandunbalancedblog.blogspot.com/2014/03/despicable-acts-heroism-of-zealous.html.

22. Beale, "News Media's Influence."

23. Hamilton, *Channeling Violence.*

24. These three examples are from Kittle, "Overcriminalization Costing U.S. Dearly."

25. Walsh and Joslyn, *Without Intent.*

26. Walsh and Joslyn, *Without Intent*, x.

27. Stuntz, *Collapse of American Criminal Justice*, 260.

28. American Law Institute, *Model Penal Code.*

29. Cited in Will, "Plague of Overcriminalization."

30. Kelly, *Criminal Justice at the Crossroads.*

31. Guetzkow and Schoon, "If You Build It."

32. Subramanian et al., *Incarceration's Front Door.*

33. Kelly, *Criminal Justice at the Crossroads.*

34. Corriher, *Criminals and Campaign Cash*, 3.

35. Kelly, *Criminal Justice at the Crossroads.*

36. Pfaff, "Causes of Growth in Prison Admissions."

37. Kelly, *Criminal Justice at the Crossroads*

38. Stuntz, *Collapse of American Criminal Justice.*

39. Stuntz, *Collapse of American Criminal Justice*, 262–64.

40. Kelly, *Criminal Justice at the Crossroads*

41. Carson, *Prisoners in 2013.*

42. Shelton, "Behind the Story."

43. Kessler, "Prison: The New Mental Hospital."

44. *Guardian*, "Rikers Island Jail Criticized"; Sewell and Chang, "L.A. County to Relocate"; National Alliance on Mental Illness, "Spending Money in All the Wrong Places"; Sullivan, "Mentally Ill Are Often"; Geller, "U.S. Jails Struggle"; Torrey et al., *More Mentally Ill Persons*.

45. Torrey et al., *Shortage of Public Hospital Beds*.

46. Aron et al., *State of Public Mental Health*.

47. Lamb and Bachrach, "Some Perspectives on Deinstitutionalization."

48. Bagenstos, "Past and Future of Deinstitutionalization Litigation," 12.

49. James and Glaze, *Mental Health Problems*; Prins and Draper, *Improving Outcomes*.

50. *Frontline*, "The New Asylums."

51. American Civil Liberties Union, *Banking on Bondage*; Justice Policy Institute, *Gaming the System*; In the Public Interest, *Buying Access*.

2. THE HIGH COST OF FAILURE

1. Kristof, "Serving Life for This?"

2. Federal Bureau of Investigation, *Uniform Crime Reports*, various years; Bureau of Justice Statistics, *Census of State and Federal Correctional Facilities*, 1988, 2002, 2012, and 2015.

3. Ironically, in January 2015 McDonnell was sentenced to two years in federal prison for public corruption.

4. National Rifle Association–Institute for Legislative Action, "Right-to-Carry."

5. Tseloni et al., "Exploring the International Decline."

6. Kelly, *Criminal Justice at the Crossroads*.

7. Zimring, *Great American Crime Decline*.

8. Durose, Cooper, and Snyder, *Recidivism of Prisoners*.

9. Pew Center on the States, *State of Recidivism*.

10. CrimeInAmerica.net, "Percent of Released Prisoners."

11. Gallup, "Most Americans Believe Crime."

12. Retribution is a motivation for sentencing as well but one that is emotional rather than instrumental. Retribution is a legitimate rationale for sentencing, but we need to be clear that there should be no expectation of a recidivism-reducing effect.

13. Doob and Webster, "Sentence Severity and Crime," 187, 189.

14. Kelly, *Criminal Justice at the Crossroads*.

15. Doob and Webster, "Sentence Severity and Crime"; Apel and Nagin, "General Deterrence."

16. Cromwell and Birzer, *In Their Own Words*, 37–40, 47, 74.

17. Kelly, *Criminal Justice at the Crossroads*.

18. Marcus, "Archaic Sentencing Liturgy," 78.

19. Abner, "Graying Prisons."

20. Solitary Watch.

21. Marcus, "MPC—the Root of the Problem," 751–52.

22. Law enforcement entails police and sheriffs at the local level, state police at the state level, and several federal law enforcement agencies. The court system includes prosecution, pre-trial services, courts and judges, and all of the administrative staff. Corrections involves the primary components of prison, jail, probation, and parole.

23. McCallister, French, and Fang, "Cost of Crime to Society"; Kelly, *Criminal Justice at the Crossroads*; Chalfin, "Economic Cost of Crime."

24. The offenses include murder, rape/sexual assault, aggravated robbery, motor vehicle theft, arson, burglary, larceny/theft, stolen property, vandalism, forgery/counterfeiting, embezzlement, and fraud.

25. McCallister, French, and Fang, "Cost of Crime to Society."

26. Pennsylvania Department of Corrections, *Recidivism Report 2013*.

27. Truman and Langton, *Criminal Victimization*.

28. Childress, "Todd Clear."

29. Gingrich and Jones, "Prison System."

3. WHY PEOPLE COMMIT CRIME
AND WHAT WE CAN DO ABOUT IT

1. Kristof, "Serving Life for This?"

2. Kleiman, "Smart on Crime."

3. United Nations Office on Drugs and Crime, *World Drug Report 2013*.

4. Substance Abuse and Mental Health Services Administration, *Results from the 2012 National Survey*.

5. Data are from the National Council on Alcoholism and Drug Dependence, "Drugs and Crime"; National Council on Alcoholism and Drug Dependence, "Alcohol, Drugs and Crime"; National Institute on Drug Abuse, *Topics in Brief: Treating Offenders*; Substance Abuse and Mental Health Services Administration, *Results from the 2012 National Survey*.

6. Wright and Decker, *Armed Robbers in Action*, 43.

7. Families Against Mandatory Minimums, "Mandatory Sentencing Was Once."

8. Substance Abuse and Mental Health Services Administration, *Results from the 2012 National Survey*.

9. National Alliance on Mental Illness, *Mental Illness Facts and Numbers*.

10. Cloyes et al., "Time to Prison Return."

11. Ridgeway and Casella, "Criminalizing Mental Illness."

12. recoveringConservative, "My Daughter Sleeps in Jail Tonight."

13. Wright and Decker, *Armed Robbers in Action*, 119.

14. Kelly, *Criminal Justice at the Crossroads*.

15. Harmon, "Brain Injury Rate."

16. Kelly, *Criminal Justice at the Crossroads*, 114.

17. Pascal-Leone et al., "Plastic Human Brain Cortex," 382.

18. Klein, "Failure of American Schools."

19. Smarick, *Urban School System*.

20. Alliance for Excellent Education, *Saving Futures*.

21. Kristof, "Priority Test."

22. Visher, Debus, and Yahner, *Employment after Prison*.

23. Visher, Debus, and Yahner, *Employment after Prison*.

24. Baker et al., *Juvenile Justice Educational Enhancement Program*.

25. National Coalition for the Homeless, "Foreclosure to Homelessness."

26. Greenberg and Rosencheck, "Homelessness in the State."

27. Petersilia, "Prisoner Reentry."

28. Trymaine, "Recidivism Hard to Shake."

29. Kelly, *Criminal Justice at the Crossroads*.

30. Krisberg and Marchionna, "Attitudes of US Voters," 1.

31. Forman, Parr, and Koczela, *Ready for Reform?* 5.

4. DIVERSION FROM TRADITIONAL CRIMINAL PROSECUTION AND PUNISHMENT

1. An *information* is an alternative method of indictment where a prosecutor, rather than a grand jury, reviews the evidence and determines whether it is sufficient.

2. Center for Health and Justice, *No Entry*.

3. Camilletti, *Pretrial Diversion Programs*.

4. Kennedy et al., *Promising Practices*.

5. "Drug Court Success Stories Reduce the Cycle of Addiction, Crime."

6. Rossman, Shelli, Rempel, et al., *Multi-site Adult Drug Court Evaluation*; Rossman, Shelli, Roman, et al., *Multi-site Adult Drug Court Evaluation*.

5. CHANGING PROSECUTION
AND SENTENCING

1. American Civil Liberties Union, *A Living Death*.

2. Cited in American Civil Liberties Union, *A Living Death*, 51.

3. Davis, "Mandatory Minimum Sentences." Andre M. Davis of Baltimore is a judge with the U.S. Court of Appeals for the Fourth Circuit.

4. Oppel, "Sentencing Shift."

5. American Civil Liberties Union, *A Living Death*.

6. Nelson, "Prosecutors Rally."

7. Gershowitz and Killinger, *State (Never) Rests*.

8. *Daily Mail*, "Texas Court Sentences Woman."

9. *Rose Ann Davidson v. the State of Texas*.

10. Peter D. Hart Research Associates, Inc., for the Open Society Institute, *New Politics of Criminal Justice*, 1.

11. Public Opinion Strategies and the Mellman Group, *Public Opinion on Sentencing*, 1.

12. Swisher, "Pro-prosecution Judges," 329.

13. Marcus, "MPC—the Root of the Problem," 751.

14. Claridge and Fabian, "History and Development," 547.

15. Starr, "Evidence-Based Sentencing," 820.

16. Starr, "Sentencing, by the Numbers."

17. Health Resources and Services Administration, *Traumatic Brain Injury*.

18. Warren, "Evidence-Based Sentencing," 156.

19. Marcus, "Smarter Sentencing," 17.

20. Clarkprosecutor.org, "James Willie Brown."

21. Bernstein, "Courts Must Be Crazy."

22. Staples, "California Horror Stories."

23. American Law Institute, *Model Penal Code*, 61.

24. Fradella, "From Insanity," 90.

6. RETHINKING PUNISHMENT

1. Carson, *Prisoners in 2013*.

2. American Civil Liberties Union, *At America's Expense*.

3. Williams, *Aging Inmate Population*.

4. American Civil Liberties Union, *At America's Expense*.

5. Kelly, *Criminal Justice at the Crossroads*.

6. American Civil Liberties Union, *ACLU State Fiscal Impact Analysis*.

7. Norman, "Stymied by the Stigma."

8. Kelly, *Criminal Justice at the Crossroads*.

9. National Association of Criminal Defense Lawyers, *Collateral Damage*, 12.

10. A much more detailed discussion of the path forward for parole is in Kelly, *Criminal Justice at the Crossroads*.

11. Subramanian et al., *Incarceration's Front Door*.

12. Aos, Miller, and Drake, *Evidence-Based Adult Corrections*; Bonta et al., "Exploring the Black Box"; Green and Winik, "Using Random Judge Assignments."

13. Warren, *Arming the Courts with Research*, 1.

14. Taxman et al., "Screening, Assessment, and Referral Practices."

15. A much more detailed discussion of changes to probation is in Kelly, *Criminal Justice at the Crossroads*.

16. For a detailed discussion, see Kelly, *Criminal Justice at the Crossroads*.

17. Attorney General of Texas Ken Paxton website, "Crime Victim's Compensation Fund."

18. Latimer and Kleinknecht, *Effects of Restorative Justice*, 4.

19. Latimer and Kleinknecht, *Effects of Restorative Justice*.

20. Bergseth and Bouffard, "Examining the Effectiveness"; Latimer, Dowden, and Muise, "Effectiveness of Restorative Justice Practices."

21. Death Penalty Information Center, "Facts about the Death Penalty."

22. Death Penalty Information Center, "Facts about the Death Penalty."

23. Equal Justice USA, "Wasteful and Inefficient."

24. Roman et al., *Cost of the Death Penalty*.

25. Alarcon and Mitchell, "Executing the Will of the Voters."

26. Fagan, "Capital Punishment."

27. Liebman, Fagan, and West, "Broken System."

28. Death Penalty Information Center, "Facts about the Death Penalty."

29. Jaffe, "Complicated Psychology of Revenge."

7. DRUGS, GUNS, AND GANGS

1. Friedersdorf, "Heartbreaking Drug Sentence."

2. Families Against Mandatory Minimums, "Mandy Martinson."

3. Vargas, "Fourth Marijuana Conviction."

4. See http://www.presidency.ucsb.edu/ws/index.php?pid=3047#axzz1PCJydjl5.

5. Kelly, *Criminal Justice at the Crossroads*.

6. Figures reported in Keefe, "Cocaine Incorporated."

7. Drug Policy Alliance, "Drug War Statistics."

8. Center on Addiction and Substance Abuse, *Shoveling Up II*, 2.

9. "Obama Administration Releases 21st Century Drug Policy Strategy."

10. "Obama Administration Officials Announce $22 Million Expansion."

11. Kelly, *Criminal Justice at the Crossroads*, 277, 278.

12. Woods, "A Decade after Drug Decriminalization."

13. These exclude domestic violence situations and gang-related and drug-related shootings. As such, active-shooter incidents are a very special, limited case of gun violence.

14. Mascia, Spies, and Yablon, "American Summer."

15. National Institute of Justice, "Gun Violence."

16. Gun statistics are from the Small Arms Survey and Graduate Institute of International Studies, *Small Arms Survey 2007*.

17. See http://washington.cbslocal.com/2012/12/21/nra-only-way-to-stop-a-bad-guy-with-a-gun-is-with-a-good-guy-with-a-gun/.

18. National Rifle Association–Institute for Legislative Action, "Gun Ownership."

19. National Rifle Association–Institute for Legislative Action, "Detroit Police Chief Agrees."

20. See http://www.cbsnews.com/news/nra-ceo-its-not-paranoia-to-buy-a-gun-its-survival/.

21. Lachman, "Wayne LaPierre Warns Fellow Gun Rights Supporters of 'Knockout Gamers,' 'Haters.'"

22. Violence Policy Center, *Firearm Justifiable Homicides*.

23. Crime Report, "230,000 Guns Stolen Annually."

24. Aneja, Donohue, and Zhang, "Impact of Right to Carry Laws."

25. Krouse, *Gun Control Legislation*.

26. Planty and Truman, *Firearm Violence*.

27. Kessker, "Does the NRA?"

28. Webster and Vernick, *Reducing Gun Violence*.

29. United Nations Office of Drugs and Crime, *Global Study on Homicide*.

30. I feel it is necessary to state that I make these recommendations in light of the fact that I am in favor of restrictive gun policies and laws in the United States, especially when it comes to semiautomatic and fully automatic weapons and high-capacity magazines.

31. National Gang Center, *National Youth Gang Survey Analysis*.

32. Federal Bureau of Investigation, *2011 National Gang Threat Assessment*.

33. Howell, "Gang Prevention," 7.

8. JUVENILE JUSTICE

1. Shufelt and Cocozza, *Youth with Mental Health Disorders*.
2. McCord, Widom, and Crowell, eds., *Juvenile Crime, Juvenile Justice*, 159.
3. Feld, *Bad Kids*, 81.
4. Manfredi, *Supreme Court and Juvenile Justice*, 159.
5. Hazel, *Cross-National Comparison*.
6. Puzzanchera, "Juvenile Arrests 2012."
7. Puzzanchera, "Juvenile Arrests 2012."
8. Hockenberry and Puzzanchera, *Juvenile Court Statistics 2013*.
9. Office of Juvenile Justice and Delinquency Prevention, *Juvenile Offenders and Victims*.
10. Office of Juvenile Justice and Delinquency Prevention, *Juvenile Offenders and Victims*.
11. Justice Policy Institute, *Costs of Confinement*.
12. Annie E. Casey Foundation, *No Place for Kids*.
13. Shufelt and Cocozza, *Youth with Mental Health Disorders*.
14. Abram et al., "PTSD."
15. Shufelt and Cocozza, *Youth with Mental Health Disorders*.
16. Feld and Bishop, *Oxford Handbook of Juvenile Crime*.
17. Compton, "Consequences of Neglect in Children," 97.
18. Walsh and Bolen, *Neurobiology of Criminal Behavior*, 163–64.
19. Howell, Feld, and Mears, "Young Offenders," 217.
20. *Frontline*, "When Kids Get Life."
21. *Frontline*, "When Kids Get Life."
22. Butz and Ortiz, "Teen Courts."
23. Mears, "Front End of the Juvenile Court."

9. CONCLUSIONS

1. Federal Bureau of Investigation, "2013 Crime Clock Statistics."
2. These examples are from Dexheimer, "Texas Ex-offenders."
3. Schmitt and Warner, *Ex-offenders and the Labor Market*.
4. Subramanian and Shames, *Sentencing and Prison Practices*, 12.
5. Pew Charitable Trusts, *States Project*.
6. From *Rolling Stone*, June 24, 2015, and *CounterPunch*, September 22, 2015, respectively.

REFERENCES

Abner, Carrie. "Graying Prisons: States Face Challenges of Aging Inmate Population." *State News*, November/December 2006. Retrieved from www.csg.org/knowledgecenter/docs/sn0611GrayingPrisons.pdf.

Abram, Karen M., Linda A. Teplin, Devon C. King, Sandra L. Longworth, Kristin M. Emanuel, Erin G. Romero, Gary M. McClelland, et al. "PTSD, Trauma and Comorbid Psychiatric Disorders in Detained Youth." *Juvenile Justice Bulletin*, June 2013.

Alarcon, Arthur L., and Paula M. Mitchell. "Executing the Will of the Voters: A Roadmap to Mend or End the California Legislature's Multi-Billion-Dollar Death Penalty Debacle." Special issue, *Loyola of Los Angeles Law Review* 44 (2011): S41–S224.

Alexander, Michelle. *The New Jim Crow*. New York: New Press, 2012.

Alliance for Excellent Education. *Saving Futures, Saving Dollars: The Impact of Education on Crime Reduction and Earnings*. Washington, DC: Alliance for Excellent Education, 2013. Retrieved from http://all4ed.org/wp-content/uploads/2013/09/SavingFutures.pdf.

American Civil Liberties Union. *ACLU State Fiscal Impact Analysis*. New York: American Civil Liberties Union, 2012.

———. *At America's Expense: The Mass Incarceration of the Elderly*. New York: American Civil Liberties Union, 2012. Available from https://www.aclu.org/report/americas-expense-mass-incarceration-elderly.

———. *Banking on Bondage: Private Prisons and Mass Incarceration*. New York: American Civil Liberties Union, November 2011. Retrieved from https://www.aclu.org/files/assets/bankingonbondage_20111102.pdf.

———. *A Living Death: Life without Parole for Nonviolent Offenses*. New York: American Civil Liberties Union, 2013. Available from https://www.aclu.org/report/living-death-life-without-parole-nonviolent-offenses.

American Law Institute. *Model Penal Code*. Sec. 4.01(1). Philadelphia: American Law Institute, 1962.

Aneja, Abhay, John Donohue, and Alexandra Zhang. "The Impact of Right to Carry Laws and the NRC Report: The Latest Lessons for the Empirical Evaluation of Law and Policy." Stanford Law and Economics Working Paper 461, Palo Alto, CA, 2014.

Annie E. Casey Foundation. *No Place for Kids: The Case for Reducing Juvenile Incarceration*. Baltimore: Annie E. Casey Foundation, 2011.

Aos, Steven, Marna Geyer Miller, and Elizabeth Drake. *Evidence-Based Adult Corrections Programs: What Works and What Does Not*. Olympia: Washington State Institute for Public Policy, 2006.

Apel, Robert, and Daniel Nagin. 2011. "General Deterrence: A Review of Recent Evidence." In *Crime and Public Policy*, edited by James Q. Wilson and Joan Petersilia. New York: Oxford University Press, 2011.

Aron, Laudan, Ron Honberg, Ken Duckworth, Angela Kimball, Elizabeth Edgar, Bob Carolla, Kimberly Meltzer, et al. "The State of Public Mental Health Services across the Nation." In *Grading the States 2009: A Report on America's Health Care System for Adults with Serious Mental Illness*, by Laudan Aron, Ron Honberg, Ken Duckworth, Angela Kimball, Elizabeth Edgar, Bob Carolla, Kimberly Meltzer, et al., 23–46. Arlington, VA: National Alliance on Mental Illness, 2009. Retrieved from https://www.nami.org/getattachment/About-NAMI/Publications/Reports/NAMI_GTS2009_FullReport.pdf.

Attorney General of Texas Ken Paxton website. "Crime Victim's Compensation." Retrieved from https://www.texasattorneygeneral.gov/cvs/crime-victims-compensation.

Bagenstos, Samuel. "The Past and Future of Deinstitutionalization Litigation." *Cardozo Law Review* 34 (2012): 1–51.

Baker, Suzanne, William D. Bales, Thomas G. Blomberg, Wendy Cavendish, Sabri Çiftçi, Jacquelin Cocke, Carter Hay, et al. *Juvenile Justice Educational Enhancement Program: 2006 Annual Report to the Florida Department of Education.* Tallahassee: Florida State University, College of Criminology and Criminal Justice, Center for Criminology and Public Policy Research, 2006.

Beale, Sara Sun. "The News Media's Influence on Criminal Justice Policy: How Market-Driven News Promotes Punitiveness." *William and Mary Law Review* 48 (2006): 397–481.

Bergseth, Kathleen, and Jeffrey Bouffard. "Examining the Effectiveness of a Restorative Justice Program for Various Types of Juvenile Offenders." *International Journal of Offender Therapy and Comparative Criminology* 57 (2012): 1054–75.

Bernstein, David S. "The Courts Must Be Crazy: Every Doctor Who Has Ever Examined Demond Chatman Has Concluded He Is Mentally Ill. But a DA and Judge Won't Believe It." *Boston Magazine*, April 2004. Retrieved from www.bostonmagazine.com/news/article/2014/03/25/demond-chatman-mental-illness/.

Bonta, James, Tanya Rugge, Terri-Lynne Scott, Guy Bourgon, and Annie Yessine. "Exploring the Black Box of Community Supervision." *Journal of Offender Rehabilitation* 47 (2008): 248–70.

Bureau of Justice Statistics. *Census of State and Federal Correctional Facilities.* Washington, DC: U.S. Department of Justice, 1988.

———. *Census of State and Federal Correctional Facilities.* Washington, DC: U.S. Department of Justice, 2002.

———. *Census of State and Federal Correctional Facilities.* Washington, DC: U.S. Department of Justice, 2012.

———. *Census of State and Federal Correctional Facilities.* Washington, DC: U.S. Department of Justice, 2015.

———. *Correctional Populations in the United States.* Washington, DC: U.S. Department of Justice, 1987–2014.

Butz, Jeffrey, and Jennifer Ortiz. "Teen Courts—Do They Work and Why?" *NYSBA Journal*, January 2011, 18–21. Retrieved from http://johnjayresearch.org/wp-content/uploads/2011/04/buttsortizjrnjan11.pdf.

Camilletti, Catherine. *Pretrial Diversion Programs: Research Summary.* Washington, DC: U.S. Department of Justice, Bureau of Justice Assistance, 2010.

Carson, E. Ann. *Prisoners in 2013.* Bureau of Justice Statistics Bulletin, NCJ 247282. Washington, DC: U.S. Department of Justice, Office of Justice Programs, Bureau of Justice Statistics, September 2014. Revised September 30, 2014.

Center for Health and Justice. *No Entry: A National Survey of Criminal Justice Diversion Programs and Initiatives.* Chicago: Center for Health and Justice at TASC, December 2013. Retrieved from www2.centerforhealthandjustice.org/sites/www2.centerforhealthandjustice.org/files/publications/CHJ%20Diversion%20Report_web.pdf.

Center on Addiction and Substance Abuse. *Shoveling Up II: The Impact of Substance Abuse on Federal, State and Local Budgets.* New York: National Center on Addiction and Substance Abuse at Columbia University, May 2009.

Chalfin, Aaron. "The Economic Cost of Crime." In *The Encyclopedia of Crime and Punishment*, edited by David Levinson. Thousand Oaks, CA: Sage, 2014.

Childress, Sarah. "Todd Clear: Why America's Mass Incarceration Experiment Failed." *Frontline*, April 29, 2014. Retrieved from www.pbs.org/wgbh/frontline/article/todd-clear-why-americas-mass-incarceration-experiment-failed/.

Claridge, Jeffrey A., and Timothy C. Fabian. 2005. "History and Development of Evidence-Based Medicine." *World Journal of Surgery* 29 (2005): 547–53.

Clarkprosecutor.org. "James Willie Brown." Retrieved from www.clarkprosecutor.org/html/death/US/brown879.htm.

Cloyes, Kristin, Bob Wong, Seth Latimer, and Jose Abarca. "Time to Prison Return for Offenders with Serious Mental Illness Released from Prison: A Survival Analysis." *Criminal Justice and Behavior* 37 (2010): 175–87.

Compton, David M. "The Consequences of Neglect in Children: Neurocognitive Comparisons among Conduct Disordered and Non-conduct Disordered Youth Residing in Foster-Care with That of Children from Intact Families." *Psychology and Behavioral Sciences* 2 (2013): 96–105.

Corriher, Bill. *Criminals and Campaign Cash: The Impact of Judicial Campaign Spending on Criminal Defendants*. Legal Progress. Washington, DC: Center for American Progress, 2013.

CrimeInAmerica.net. "Percent of Released Prisoners Returning to Incarceration." September 29, 2010. Updated November 2014. Retrieved from www.crimeinamerica.net/2010/09/29/percent-of-released-prisoners-returning-to-incarceration/.

Crime Report. "230,000 Guns Stolen Annually in Burglaries, Other Property Crimes: BJS." November 8, 2012. Retrieved from www.thecrimereport.org/news/crime-and-justice-news/2012-11-gunburglary-study-for-thursday-bjs.

Cromwell, Paul, and Michael Birzer. *In Their Own Words: Criminals on Crime*. 6th ed. New York: Oxford University Press, 2014.

Daily Mail. "Texas Court Sentences Woman to Life in Prison after Arrest for Sixth DUI Charge Just after Release from Jail over Last Offense." September 19, 2013. Retrieved from www.dailymail.co.uk/news/article-2425340/Texas-court-sentences-woman-life-prison-arrest-sixth-DUI-charge-just-release-jail-offense.html.

Davis, Andre M. "Mandatory Minimum Sentences Impede Justice." *Baltimore Sun*, December 8, 2011. Retrieved from http://articles.baltimoresun.com/2011-12-08/news/bs-ed-sentencing-20111208_1_mandatory-minimums-sentences-mandatory-term.

Death Penalty Information Center. "Facts about the Death Penalty." October 13, 2015. Retrieved from www.deathpenaltyinfo.org/documents/FactSheet.pdf.

Dexheimer, Eric. "Texas Ex-offenders Are Denied Job Licenses." *Austin American-Statesman*, April 11, 2011.

Doob, Anthony, and Cheryl Webster. "Sentence Severity and Crime: Accepting the Null Hypothesis." *Crime and Justice: A Review of Research*, vol. 30, edited by Michael H. Tonry, 143–95. Chicago: University of Chicago Press, 2003.

"Drug Court Success Stories Reduce the Cycle of Addiction, Crime." Hazelden Betty Ford Foundation. Retrieved from http://www.hazelden.org/web/public/ade60626.page?printable=true&showlogo=true&callprint=true.

Drug Policy Alliance. "Drug War Statistics." Accessed July 2015. www.drugpolicy.org/drug-war-statistics.

Durose, Matthew R., Alexia D. Cooper, and Howard N. Snyder. *Recidivism of Prisoners Released in 30 States in 2005: Patterns from 2005 to 2010*. Bureau of Justice Statistics Special Report, NCJ 244205. Washington, DC: U.S. Department of Justice, Office of Justice Programs, Bureau of Justice Statistics, April 2014.

Equal Justice USA. "Wasteful and Inefficient: The Alarming Cost of the Death Penalty." Retrieved from http://ejusa.org/learn/cost.

Fagan, Jeffrey. "Capital Punishment: Deterrent Effects and Capital Costs." Columbia University Law School, 2006.

Families Against Mandatory Minimums. "Mandatory Sentencing Was Once America's Law-and-Order Panacea. Here's Why Its Not Working." *FAMM Primer on Mandatory Sentences.* Retrieved from www.prisonpolicy.org/scans/famm/Primer.pdf.

———. "Mandy Martinson." Retrieved from http://famm.org/mandy-martinson/.

Federal Bureau of Investigation. "2013 Crime Clock Statistics." Retrieved from https://www.fbi.gov/about-us/cjis/ucr/crime-in-the-u.s/2013/crime-in-the-u.s.-2013/offenses-known-to-law-enforcement/crime-clock.

———. *Uniform Crime Reports.* Washington, DC: U.S. Department of Justice, Federal Bureau of Investigation, various years.

Feld, Barry. *Bad Kids: Race and the Transformation of the Juvenile Court.* New York: Oxford University Press, 1999.

Feld, Barry, and Donna Bishop. *The Oxford Handbook of Juvenile Crime and Juvenile Justice.* Oxford and New York: Oxford University Press, 2012.

Forman, Ben, Rich Parr, and Steve Koczela. *Ready for Reform? Public Opinion on Criminal Justice in Massachusetts.* Boston: MassINC, 2014.

Fradella, Henry. "From Insanity to Beyond Diminished Capacity: Mental Illness and Criminal Excuse in the Post-*Clark* Era." *University of Florida Journal of Law and Public Policy* 18 (2007): 7–91.

Friedersdorf, Connor. "A Heartbreaking Drug Sentence of Staggering Idiocy." *Atlantic,* April 3, 2013.

Frontline. "The New Asylums." PBS, May 2005.

———. "When Kids Get Life." PBS, May 2007.

Gallup. "Most Americans Believe Crime in U.S. Is Worsening." October 2011. Retrieved from www.gallup.com/poll/150464/americans-believe-crime-worsening.aspx.

Geller, Adam. "U.S. Jails Struggle with Role as Makeshift Asylums." *Huffington Post,* July 7, 2014.

Genovese, Michael A. "Richard M. Nixon and the Politicization of Justice." In *Watergate and Afterward: The Legacy of Richard M. Nixon,* edited by Leon Friedman and William F. Levantrosser. Westport, CT: Greenwood Press, 1992.

Gershowitz, Adam, and Laura Killinger. "The State (Never) Rests: How Excessive Prosecutorial Caseloads Harm Criminal Defendants." *Northwestern University Law Review* 105 (2011): 261–302.

Gingrich, Newt, and Van Jones. "Prison System Is Failing America." CNN, May 22, 2014. Retrieved from www.cnn.com/2014/05/21/opinion/gingrich-jones-prison-system-fails-america/.

Good, Chris. "Greatest Campaign Ad Ever?" *Atlantic,* May 17, 2010. Retrieved from www.theatlantic.com/politics/archive/2010/05/greatest-campaign-ad-ever/56824/.

Grassley, Chuck. "Floor Statement: Mandatory Minimum Sentencing." Prepared statement by Senator Chuck Grassley of Iowa, March 10, 2015.

Green, Donald P., and Daniel Winik. "Using Random Judge Assignments to Estimate the Effects of Incarceration and Probation on Recidivism among Drug Offenders." *Federal Probation* 48 (2010): 357–87.

Greenberg, Greg A., and Robert A. Rosencheck. "Homelessness in the State and Federal Prison Population." *Criminal Behavior and Mental Health* 18 (2008): 88–103.

Guardian. "Rikers Island Jail Criticized for Keeping Mentally Ill Inmates in Solitary." November 6, 2013. Retrieved from www.theguardian.com/world/2013/nov/06/rikers-island-jail-mentally-ill-solitary-confinement.

Guetzkow, Joshua, and Eric Schoon. "If You Build It They Will Fill It: The Unintended Consequences of Prison Overcrowding Litigation." Unpublished manuscript, Department of Sociology, University of Arizona, Tucson, 2012.

Hamilton, James T. *Channeling Violence: The Economic Market for Violent Television Programming.* Princeton, NJ: Princeton University Press, 1998.

Harmon, Katherine. "Brain Injury Rate 7 Times Greater among U.S. Prisoners." *Scientific American,* February 4, 2012. Retrieved from www.scientificamerican.com/article/traumatic-brain-injury-prison/.

Hazel, Neal. *Cross-National Comparison of Youth Justice.* London: Youth Justice Board, 2008. Retrieved from http://dera.ioe.ac.uk/7996/1/Cross_national_final.pdf.

Health Resources and Services Administration. *Traumatic Brain Injury and the U.S. Criminal Justice System.* Washington, DC: U.S. Department of Health and Human Services, 2011.

Hickman, Chris. "Courting the Right: Richard Nixon's 1968 Campaign against the Warren Court." *Journal of Supreme Court History* 36 (2011): 287–303.

Hockenberry, Sarah, and Charles Puzzanchera. *Juvenile Court Statistics 2013.* NCJ 249164. Washington, DC: U.S. Department of Justice, Office of Juvenile Justice and Delinquency Prevention, July 2015.

Howell, James. "Gang Prevention: An Overview of Research and Programs." *Juvenile Justice Bulletin,* December 2010.

Howell, James, Barry Feld, and Daniel Mears. "Young Offenders and an Effective Justice System Response: What Happens, What Should Happen, and What We Need to Know." In *From Juvenile Delinquency to Adult Crime,* edited by Rolf Loeber and David P. Farrington, 200–244. New York: Oxford University Press, 2012.

Institute for Criminal Policy Research. World Prison Brief (database). Retrieved from www.prisonstudies.org/.

In the Public Interest (ITPI). *Buying Access: How Corporations Influence Decision Makers at Corrections Conferences, Trainings, and Meetings.* Washington, DC: In the Public Interest, August 2015. Retrieved from www.inthepublicinterest.org/wp-content/uploads/Buying-Access-In-the-Public-Interest-PDF.pdf.

Jaffe, Eric. "The Complicated Psychology of Revenge." *Observer* 24 (2011): 1–3.

James, Doris J., and Lauren E. Glaze. *Mental Health Problems of Prison and Jail Inmates.* Bureau of Justice Statistics Special Report, NCJ 213600. Washington, DC: U.S. Department of Justice, Office of Justice Programs, Bureau of Justice Statistics, September 2006. Revised December 14, 2006.

Justice Policy Institute. *The Costs of Confinement: Why Good Juvenile Justice Policies Make Good Fiscal Sense.* Washington, DC: Justice Policy Institute, May 2009. Retrieved from www.justicepolicy.org/images/upload/09_05_rep_costsofconfinement_jj_ps.pdf.

———. *Gaming the System: How the Political Strategies of Private Prison Companies Promote Ineffective Incarceration Policies.* Washington, DC: Justice Policy Institute, June 2011. Retrieved from www.justicepolicy.org/uploads/justicepolicy/documents/gaming_the_system.pdf.

Keefe, Patrick Radden. "Cocaine Incorporated." *New York Times,* June 15, 2012.

Kelly, William R. *Criminal Justice at the Crossroads: Transforming Crime and Punishment.* New York: Columbia University Press, 2015.

Kennedy, Spurgeon, James Brown, Barbara Darbey, Anne Gatti, Tara Klute, Mary Pat Maher, and Daniel Peterca. *Promising Practices in Pretrial Diversion.* Washington, DC: National Association of Pretrial Services Agencies, 2009. Retrieved from www.shopliftingprevention.org/promising-practices-in-pretrial-diversion/.

Kessker, Glenn. "Does the NRA Really Have More than 4.5 Million Members?" *Washington Post,* February 8, 2013.

Kessler, Mike. "Prison: The New Mental Hospital: A California Measure to Reduce Prison Overcrowding Reveals How America Is, Once Again, Failing Some of Its Most Vulnerable." *TakePart,* January 22, 2014. Retrieved from www.takepart.com/feature/2014/01/22/prison-new-mental-hospital.

Kittle, M. D. "Overcriminalization Costing U.S Dearly in Treasure and Liberty, Experts Say." Watchdog.org, May 17, 2013. Retrieved from http://watchdog.org/85303/overcriminalization-costing-u-s-dearly-in-treasure-and-liberty-experts-say/.

Kleiman, Mark. "Smart on Crime." *Democracy, a Journal of Ideas* 28 (Spring 2013). Available from http://democracyjournal.org/magazine/28/smart-on-crime/?page=all.

Klein, Joel. "The Failure of American Schools." *Atlantic,* June 2011.

Koch, Charles G., and Mark V. Holden. "The Overcriminalization of America: How to Reduce Poverty and Improve Race Relations by Rethinking Our Justice System." *Politico,* January 7, 2015. Retrieved from www.politico.com/magazine/story/2015/01/overcriminalization-of-america-113991_Page2.html#ixzz3O9wb2649.

Krey, Patrick. "Man Sentenced to Seven Years in Prison for Lawfully Owned Guns." *New American*, January 31, 2011. Retrieved from www.thenewamerican.com/usnews/crime/item/7409-man-sentenced-to-seven-years-in-prison-for-lawfully-owned-guns.

Krisberg, Barry, and Susan Marchionna. "Attitudes of US Voters toward Prisoner Rehabilitation and Reentry Policies." *Focus: Views from the National Council on Crime and Delinquency*, April 2006.

Kristof, Nicholas. "Inside a Mental Hospital Called Jail." *New York Times*, February 8, 2014.

———. "Priority Test: Health Care or Prisons?" *New York Times*, August 19, 2009.

———. "Serving Life for This?" *New York Times*, November 13, 2013.

Krouse, William. *Gun Control Legislation*. Washington, DC: Congressional Research Service, November 14, 2012.

Lachman, Samantha. "Wayne LaPierre Warns Fellow Gun Rights Supporters of 'Knockout Gamers,' 'Haters.'" *Huffington Post*, April 25, 2014. Retrieved from http://www.huffingtonpost.com/2014/04/25/wayne-lapierre-nra-_n_5214959.html.

Lamb, H., and L. Bachrach. "Some Perspectives on Deinstitutionalization." *Psychiatric Services* 52 (2001): 1039–45.

Latimer, Jeff, Craig Dowden, and Danielle Muise. "The Effectiveness of Restorative Justice Practices: A Meta-Analysis." *Prison Journal* 85 (2005): 127–44.

Latimer, Jeff, and Steven Kleinknecht. *The Effects of Restorative Justice Programming: A Review of the Empirical Research*. Ottawa: Department of Justice Canada, 2000.

Lee, Trymaine. "Recidivism Hard to Shake for Ex-offenders Returning Home to Dim Prospects." *Huffington Post*, June 10, 2012.

Leichenger, Alex. "How One Milwaukee Zip Code Explains America's Mass Incarceration Problem." *Think Progress*, March 20, 2014. Retrieved from http://thinkprogress.org/justice/2014/03/20/3401141/how-one-milwaukee-zip-code-explains-americas-mass-incarceration-problem/.

Liebman, James, Jeffrey Fagan, and Valerie West. "A Broken System: Error Rates in Capital Cases, 1973–1995." Columbia University Law School, 2000.

Manfredi, Christopher. *The Supreme Court and Juvenile Justice*. Lawrence: University Press of Kansas, 1998.

Marcus, Michael. "Archaic Sentencing Liturgy Sacrifices Public Safety: What's Wrong and How We Can Fix It." *Federal Sentencing Reporter* 16 (2003): 76–86.

———. "MPC—the Root of the Problem: Just Deserts and Risk Assessment." *Florida Law Review* 61 (2009): 751–76.

———. "Smarter Sentencing: On the Need to Consider Crime Reduction as a Goal." *Court Review* 40 (2004): 16–25.

Mascia, Jennifer, Mike Spies, and Alexa Yablon. "An American Summer." *Trace*, October 14, 2015. Retrieved from www.thetrace.org/2015/09/summer-gun-violence-america/.

McCallister, Kathryn, Michel French, and Hai Fang. "The Cost of Crime to Society: New Crime-Specific Estimates for Policy and Program Evaluation." *Drug and Alcohol Dependence* 108 (2010): 98–109.

McCord, Joan, Cathy Spatz Widom, and Nancy A. Crowell, eds. *Juvenile Crime, Juvenile Justice*. Washington, DC: National Academy Press, 2001.

Mears, Daniel. "The Front End of the Juvenile Court: Intake and Informal Versus Formal Processing." In *The Oxford Handbook of Juvenile Crime and Juvenile Justice*, edited by Barry Feld and Donna Bishop, 573–605. Oxford and New York: Oxford University Press, 2012.

National Alliance on Mental Illness (NAMI). *Mental Illness Facts and Numbers*. Arlington, VA: National Alliance on Mental Illness, 2013. Retrieved from www2.nami.org/factsheets/mentalillness_factsheet.pdf.

———. "Spending Money in All the Wrong Places: Jails and Prisons." Retrieved from http://pbs.bento.storage.s3.amazonaws.com/hostedbento-prod/filer_public/MPB%20Media/Programs/Southern%20Remedy/Growing%20Pains/306/306-Spending_Money_in_all_the_Wrong_Places_Jails.pdf.

National Association of Criminal Defense Lawyers. *Collateral Damage: America's Failure to Forgive or Forget in the War on Crime: A Roadmap to Restore Rights and Status after*

Arrest and Conviction. Washington, DC: National Association of Criminal Defense Lawyers, May 2014.

National Coalition for the Homeless. "Foreclosure to Homelessness: The Forgotten Victims of the Subprime Crisis." June 2009. Retrieved from www.nationalhomeless.org/factsheets/foreclosure.html.

National Council on Alcoholism and Drug Dependence (NCADD). "Alcohol, Drugs and Crime." Retrieved from https://ncadd.org/about-addiction/alcohol-drugs-and-crime.

———. "Drugs and Crime." Last modified June 27, 2015. Retrieved from https://ncadd.org/learn-about-drugs/drugs-and-crime.

National Gang Center. *National Youth Gang Survey Analysis*. Washington, DC: U.S. Department of Justice, Bureau of Justice Assistance, Office of Juvenile Justice and Delinquency Prevention. Retrieved from https://www.nationalgangcenter.gov/survey-analysis/measuring-the-extent-of-gang-problems.

National Gang Intelligence Center. *2011 National Gang Threat Assessment: Emerging Trends*. Washington, DC: Federal Bureau of Investigation, National Gang Intelligence Center, 2011. Retrieved from https://www.fbi.gov/stats-services/publications/2011-national-gang-threat-assessment.

National Institute of Justice. "Gun Violence." NIJ.gov. Last modified April 4, 2013. Retrieved from www.nij.gov/topics/crime/gun-violence/Pages/welcome.aspx.

National Institute on Drug Abuse (NIDA). *Topics in Brief: Treating Offenders with Drug Problems: Integrating Public Health and Public Safety*. Washington, DC: National Institute on Drug Abuse, 2011.

National Rifle Association–Institute for Legislative Action. "Detroit Police Chief Agrees: More Guns, Less Crime." January 10, 2014.

———. "Gun Ownership at All-Time High, Nation's Murder Rate at Nearly All-Time Low." February 15, 2013.

———. "Right-to-Carry." Retrieved from https://www.nraila.org/issues/right-to-carry/.

Nelson, Steven. "Prosecutors Rally against Sentencing Reform." *U.S. News and World Report*, July 17, 2015.

Norman, David. "Stymied by the Stigma of a Criminal Conviction: Connecticut and the Struggle to Relieve Collateral Consequences." *Quinnipiac Law Review* 31 (2013): 985–1041.

"Obama Administration Officials Announce $22 Million Expansion of Innovative Health Program Aimed at Detecting and Intervening in Drug Addiction Early." White House, Office of National Drug Control Policy (news release), July 25, 2012. www.whitehouse.gov/ondcp/news-releases-remarks/22-million-dollar-grant-medicalizing-drug-prevention.

"Obama Administration Releases 21st Century Drug Policy Strategy." White House, Office of National Drug Control Policy (news release), April 17, 2012. Retrieved from https://www.whitehouse.gov/ondcp/news-releases-remarks/obama-administration-releases-21st-century-drug-policy-strategy.

Office of Juvenile Justice and Delinquency Prevention. *Juvenile Offenders and Victims: 2014 National Report*. Washington, DC: National Center for Juvenile Justice, Office of Juvenile Justice and Delinquency Prevention, 2014.

Oppel, Richard A., Jr. "Sentencing Shift Gives New Leverage to Prosecutors." *New York Times*, September 25, 2011.

Pascal-Leone, Alvaro, Amir Amedi, Felipe Fregni, and Lotfi Merabet. "The Plastic Human Brain Cortex." *Annual Review of Neuroscience* 28 (2005): 377–401.

Pennsylvania Department of Corrections. *Recidivism Report 2013*. Mechanicsburg, PA: Bureau of Planning, Research and Statistics, Office of the Secretary, 2013.

Peter D. Hart Research Associates, Inc. *The New Politics of Criminal Justice: A Research and Messaging Report for the Open Society Institute*. Washington, DC: Peter D. Hart Research Associates, Inc., 2002.

Petersilia, Joan. "Prisoner Reentry: Public Safety and Reintegration Challenges." *Prison Journal* 81 (2001): 360–75.

Pew Center on the States. *State of Recidivism: The Revolving Door of America's Prisons*. Public Safety Performance Project. Washington, DC: Pew Charitable Trusts, April 2011.

Pew Charitable Trusts. *States Project 3 Percent Increase in Prisoners by 2018*. Public Safety Performance Project. Washington, DC: Pew Charitable Trusts, November 2014. Retrieved from www.pewtrusts.org/en/multimedia/data-visualizations/2014/states-project-3-percent-increase-in-prisoners-by-2018.

Pfaff, John F. "The Causes of Growth in Prison Admissions and Populations." Fordham University School of Law, Bronx, NY, July 12, 2011. SSRN, http://ssrn.com/abstract=1884674. http://dx.doi.org/10.2139/ssrn.1884674.

Planty, Michael, and Jennifer L. Truman. *Firearm Violence, 1993–2011*. Bureau of Justice Statistics Special Report, NCJ 241730. Washington, DC: U.S. Department of Justice, Office of Justice Programs, Bureau of Justice Statistics, May 2013.

Postrel, Virginia. "The Consequences of the 1960's Race Riots Come into View." *New York Times*, December 30, 2004.

Prins, Seth Jacob, and Laura Draper. *Improving Outcomes for People with Mental Illnesses under Community Corrections Supervision: A Guide to Research-Informed Policy and Practice*. New York: Council of State Governments Justice Center, 2008.

Public Opinion Strategies and the Mellman Group. *Public Opinion on Sentencing and Corrections Policy in America*. NCJ 238953. Washington, DC: Pew Center on the States, March 2012. Retrieved from www.pewtrusts.org/~/media/assets/2012/03/30/pew_nationalsurvey researchpaper_final.pdf.

Puzzanchera, Charles. "Juvenile Arrests 2012." *Juvenile Offenders and Victims: National Report Series*, December 2014.

recoveringConservative. "My Daughter Sleeps in Jail Tonight: How Mental Health Treatment Fails American Youth, Part I." *Daily Kos*, February 19, 2014. Retrieved from www. dailykos.com/story/2014/02/19/1277498/-My-Daughter-Sleeps-in-Jail-Tonight-How-Mental-Health-Treatment-Fails-America-s-Youth-Part-I.

Ridgeway, James, and Jean Casella. "Criminalizing Mental Illness: The Story of Adam Hall." Solitary Watch, May 14, 2012. Retrieved from http://solitarywatch.com/2012/05/14/criminalizing-mental-illness-the-story-of-adam-hall/.

Robinson, Paul, and Michael Cahill. "Can a Model Penal Code Second Save the States from Themselves?" *Ohio State Journal of Criminal Law* 1 (2003): 169–77.

Rodriguez, Sal. *Solitary Confinement FAQ*. Solitary Watch, 2015. Retrieved from http://solitarywatch.com/facts/faq/.

Roman, John, Aaron Chalfin, Aaron Sundquist, Carly Knight, and Askar Darmenov. *The Cost of the Death Penalty in Maryland*. Washington, DC: Urban Institute, 2008.

Rose Ann Davidson v. the State of Texas. Texas Court of Appeals, Third District at Austin, No. 03-13-00708-Cr, page 2.

Rossman, Shelli, Michael Rempel, John Roman, Janine Zweig, Mia Green, P. Mitchell Downey, Jennifer Yahner, et al. *The Multi-site Adult Drug Court Evaluation: The Impact of Drug Courts*. Vol. 4. Washington, DC: Justice Policy Center/Urban Institute, 2011.

Rossman, Shelli, John Roman, Janine Zweig, Michael Rempel, and Christine Lindquist. *The Multi-site Adult Drug Court Evaluation*. Washington, DC: Justice Policy Center/Urban Institute, 2011.

Schmitt, John, and Kris Warner. *Ex-offenders and the Labor Market*. Washington, DC: Center for Economic and Policy Research, 2010.

Sewell, Abby, and Cindy Chang. "L.A. County to Relocate Some Inmates, Build Jail to Treat the Mentally Ill." *Los Angeles Times*, August 11, 2015.

Shelton, Deborah. "Behind the Story of a Mentally Ill Woman in Jail." *Chicago Tribune*, September 14, 2011.

Shufelt, Jennie, and Joseph Cocozza. *Youth with Mental Health Disorders in the Juvenile Justice System: Results from a Multi-State Prevalence Study*. Delmar, NY: National Center for Mental Health and Juvenile Justice, 2006.

Small Arms Survey and Graduate Institute of International Studies, Geneva, Switzerland. *Small Arms Survey 2007: Guns and the City*. Cambridge and New York: Cambridge University Press, 2007. Retrieved from www.smallarmssurvey.org/publications/by-type/yearbook/small-arms-survey-2007.html.

Smarick, Andy. *The Urban School System of the Future: Applying the Principles and Lessons of Chartering.* Lanham, MD: Rowman & Littlefield Education, 2012.

Solomon, Amy L., Christy Visher, Nancy G. La Vigne, and Jenny Osborne. *Understanding the Challenges of Prisoner Reentry: Research Findings from the Urban Institute's Prisoner Reentry Portfolio.* Washington, DC: Urban Institute, 2006.

Staples, Brent. "California Horror Stories and the Three Strikes Law." *New York Times*, November 24, 2012.

Starr, Sonja. "Evidence-Based Sentencing and the Scientific Rationalization of Discrimination." Michigan Law Paper 13-014, September 2013.

———. "Sentencing, by the Numbers." *New York Times*, August 10, 2014.

Stuntz, William. *The Collapse of American Criminal Justice.* Cambridge, MA: Harvard University Press, 2011.

Subramanian, Ram, Ruth Delaney, Stephen Roberts, Nancy Fishman, and Peggy McGarry. *Incarceration's Front Door: The Misuse of Jails in America.* New York: Vera Institute of Justice, Center on Sentencing and Corrections, 2015.

Subramanian, Ram, and Alison Shames. *Sentencing and Prison Practices in Germany and the Netherlands: Implication for the United States.* New York: Vera Institute of Justice, 2013.

Substance Abuse and Mental Health Services Administration (SAMHSA). *Results from the 2012 National Survey on Drug Use and Health: Summary of National Findings.* NSDUH Series H-46, HHS Publication (SMA) 13-4795. Rockville, MD: Substance Abuse and Mental Health Services Administration, 2013.

Sullivan, Laura. "Mentally Ill Are Often Locked Up in Jails that Can't Help." National Public Radio, January 20, 2014. Updated January 21, 2014. Retrieved from www.npr.org/2014/01/20/263461940/mentally-ill-inmates-often-locked-up-in-jails-that-cant-help.

Swisher, Keith. "Pro-prosecution Judges: 'Tough on Crime,' Soft on Strategy, Ripe for Disqualification." *Arizona Law Review* 52 (2010): 317–93.

Taxman, Faye, Karen Cropsey, Douglas Young, and Harry Wexler. "Screening, Assessment, and Referral Practices in Adult Correctional Settings: A National Perspective." *Criminal Justice and Behavior* 34 (2007): 1216–34.

Texas Legislative Budget Board. *Statewide Criminal Justice Recidivism and Revocation Rates, January 2013.* Austin, TX: Legislative Budget Board, 2013. Retrieved from www.lbb.state.tx.us/Public_Safety_Criminal_Justice/RecRev_Rates/Statewide%20Criminal%20Justice%20Recidivism%20and%20Revocation%20Rates2012.pdf.

Torrey, E. Fuller, Kurt Entsminger, Jeffrey Geller, Jonathan Stanley, and D. J. Jaffe. *The Shortage of Public Hospital Beds for Mentally Ill Persons.* Arlington, VA: Treatment Advocacy Center, n.d. Retrieved from www.treatmentadvocacycenter.org/storage/documents/the_shortage_of_publichospital_beds.pdf.

Torrey, E. Fuller, Aaron D. Kennard, Don Eslinger, Richard Lamb, and James Pavle. *More Mentally Ill Persons Are in Jail and Prisons than Hospitals: A Survey of the States.* Arlington, VA: Treatment Advocacy Center, 2010. Retrieved from www.treatmentadvocacycenter.org/storage/documents/final_jails_v_hospitals_study.pdf.

Truman, Jennifer L., and Lynn Langton. *Criminal Victimization, 2014.* Criminal Victimization Series, Bureau of Justice Statistics Bulletin, NCJ 248973. Washington, DC: U.S. Department of Justice, Office of Justice Programs, Bureau of Justice Statistics, August 2015. Revised September 29, 2015.

Tseloni, Andromachi, Jen Mailley, Graham Farrell, and Nick Tilley. "Exploring the International Decline in Crime Rates." *European Journal of Criminology* 7 (2010): 375–94.

United Nations Office on Drugs and Crime. *Global Study on Homicide 2013: Trends, Contexts, Data.* Vienna, Austria: United Nations, 2013.

———. *World Drug Report 2013.* New York: United Nations, 2013.

Vargas, Ramon. "Fourth Marijuana Conviction Gets Slidell Man Life in Prison." *Times-Picayune* (New Orleans), May 5, 2011.

Violence Policy Center. *Firearm Justifiable Homicides and Non-fatal Self-Defense Gun Use.* Washington, DC: Violence Policy Center, June 2015. Retrieved from www.vpc.org/studies/justifiable15.pdf.

Visher, Christy, Sara Debus, and Jennifer Yahner. *Employment after Prison: A Longitudinal Study of Releases in Three States*. Washington, DC: Urban Institute, 2008.

Walsh, Anthony, and Jonathan Bolen. *The Neurobiology of Criminal Behavior: Gene-Brain-Culture Interaction*. Burlington, VT: Ashgate, 2012.

Walsh, Brian, and Tiffany Joslyn. *Without Intent: How Congress Is Eroding the Criminal Intent Requirement in Federal Law*. Washington, DC: Heritage Foundation, 2010. Retrieved from www.heritage.org/research/reports/2010/05/without-intent.

Warren, Roger K. *Arming the Courts with Research: 10 Evidence-Based Sentencing Initiatives to Control Crime and Reduce Costs*. Public Safety Policy Brief 8. Washington, DC: Pew Center on the States, May 2009. Retrieved from www.pewpublicsafety.org.

———. "Evidence-Based Sentencing: The Application of Principles of Evidence-Based Practice to State Sentencing Practice and Policy." *University of San Francisco Law Review* 43 (2009): 585–634.

Webster, Daniel, and Jon Vernick. *Reducing Gun Violence in America*. Baltimore: Johns Hopkins University Press, 2013.

Will, George. "The Plague of Overcriminalization." *National Review*, December 10, 2014.

Williams, Jeremy L. *The Aging Inmate Population: Southern States Outlook*. Atlanta, GA: Southern Legislative Conference of the Council on State Governments, December 2006.

Woods, Jordan Blair. "A Decade after Drug Decriminalization: What Can the United States Learn from the Portuguese Model?" *District of Columbia Law Review* 15 (2011): 1–32.

Wright, Richard, and Scott Decker. *Armed Robbers in Action: Stickups and Street Culture*. Boston: Northeastern University Press, 1997.

Zimring, Franklin E. *The Great American Crime Decline*. Studies in Crime and Public Policy. Oxford and New York: Oxford University Press, 2006.

INDEX

abuse, and juvenile justice, 199, 200, 203
accountability, lack of, 63
active-shooter incidents, 174
adjudicated probation, 207
administrative segregation (ad seg): effects of, 59–60; and mental illness, 41–42, 73
Affordable Care Act, 93, 167, 227
African Americans: and education, 80–81; incarceration rates for, 12; and juvenile justice, 193
age: and juvenile offenses, 194; and reduction in offending, 58, 138–139; of responsibility, 201–202, 213
aggravating evidence, 31
aggression replacement therapy, 207
aging of inmate population, 58, 137–141, 157
Aitken, Brian, 9
alcohol. See substance abuse
Alexander, Michelle, 15–16
American Civil Liberties Union, 106
American Law Institute (ALI), 119; and insanity defense, 126–127
American Medical Association, 165
American Psychological Association, 165
amygdala, 128
Anderson, Ken, 108
Anti-Drug Abuse Act, 162
assessment, 86; of treatment readiness, 86–87
attachment disorder, 76–77, 199

attention deficit/hyperactivity disorder, 76, 197
autism spectrum disorder, 76

behavior change, 84–88; evidence for, 86–88; punishment and, 56–57; sentencing and, 120
Bias, Len, 162
bipolar disorder, 76
blacks. See African Americans
Blankenship, Don, 32
Bloomberg, Michael, 25
Booker, Robert, 103–104
Bourda, Travis, 9
Bradley, John, 108
Brady v. Maryland, 109
brain studies. See neurocognitive issues
Bratton, William, 25
Breyer, Stephen, 222
Brown, James Willie, 125
Bryant, Phil, 24
Bush, George H. W., 20, 161
Bush, George W., 21, 161

capital punishment, 152–157
Capo, Skylar, 27
cartels, 164, 182–185
Carter, Jimmy, 164
caseloads: parole, 30; probation, 30, 146, 148; of prosecutors, 107, 109–111
Cassell, Paul, 106